Building Europe's Parliament

Building Europe's Parliament

Democratic Representation beyond the Nation-State

Berthold Rittberger

OXFORD
UNIVERSITY PRESS

OXFORD
UNIVERSITY PRESS

Great Clarendon Street, Oxford OX2 6DP

Oxford University Press is a department of the University of Oxford.
It furthers the University's objective of excellence in research,
scholarship, and education by publishing worldwide in

Oxford New York

Auckland Cape Town Dar es Salaam Hong Kong Karachi Kuala Lumpur
Madrid Melbourne Mexico City Nairobi New Delhi Shanghai Taipei Toronto
With offices in

Argentina Austria Brazil Chile Czech Republic France Greece
Guatemala Hungary Italy Japan South Korea Poland Portugal
Singapore Switzerland Thailand Turkey Ukraine Vietnam

Published in the United States
by Oxford University Press Inc., New York

British Library Cataloguing in Publication Data
Data available

Library of Congress Cataloging in Publication Data
Data available

ISBN 0-19-927342-1

3 5 7 9 10 8 6 4 2

Typeset by Kolam Information Services Pvt. Ltd, Pondicherry, India
Printed in Great Britain
on acid-free paper by
Biddles Ltd., King's Lynn, Norfolk

To my parents

Preface

I remember well when I started to think about the questions that this book seeks to answer: Why is there a European Parliament? Why did national governments bestow the European Parliament gradually with new competencies and powers? As a graduate student at the London School of Economics, I attended a seminar on 'Institutional Politics in the EU' taught by Simon Hix. From studying legislative decision-making models I learnt to analyse the European Parliament's powers as a legislator, and recall puzzling over the controversial claim by Garrett and Tsebelis that the introduction of the co-decision procedure at Maastricht actually implied that, compared to the cooperation procedure, the European Parliament's influence in the legislative decision-making game would be reduced. At the time, it seemed tempting to learn the art of formal modelling and to engage in the vibrant debate on EU legislative politics. Accepting my intellectual limitations, I quickly dropped this idea. Nevertheless, I was firmly convinced that the European Parliament was a key player in the Brussels decision-making complex. However, when I found—upon first reading Mark Pollack's article on 'Delegation, agency, and agenda setting in the European Community' (*International Organization* 51, 1: 99–134)—that scholars did not have an answer to the question why there actually is a European Parliament in the first place, I was flabbergasted. And with all these powers! I was genuinely surprised that there was no literature that offered a systematic and comprehensive explanation for why the governments of the Europe of the 'Six' created the Common Assembly in the early 1950s—the European Parliament's forerunner—and why it was that the European Parliament successively acquired its power *trias* of supervisory/control, budgetary, and legislative powers making it, today, one of the most influential parliaments in the world of international organizations (see De Vree (1974) for an exception).

I started work on this project in the spring of 2000, not imagining what a long, sometimes arduous, but also exciting and rewarding journey was ahead of me. Walking past the beautiful premises of the OUP on Walton Street almost weekly, seeing this book published with the Press is the realisation of a dream. Without the help and support of many friends and colleagues, I would not be in the position to write these lines today. Jeremy Richardson, my principal Ph.D. supervisor, has been an abundant source of academic guidance and personal counsel. He made me believe in my project and continues to take his role as supervisor very seriously, and I will be eternally grateful for his support, encouragement, and warm words. Alec Stone Sweet, my College adviser, was the main inspiration behind my spending valuable research time at the European University Institute in Fiesole. In our informal doctoral seminars, I learnt to admire Alec's non-dogmatic, pluralistic approach to the study of political science, which, hopefully, left its mark on this book. My work also benefited from the interaction with numerous colleagues and friends who kindly discussed and commented on parts or the whole of my work. Thanks go to Pablo Beramendi Alvarez, Katrin Auel, Alex Bürgin, Richard Corbett, Anne Deighton, Sander Dekker, Antoaneta Dimitrova, Matt Gabel, Simon Hix, Elisabeth Ivarsflaten, Markus Jachtenfuchs, Jeffrey Lewis, David Levi-Faur, Christine Lipsmeyer, Christian List, Willem Maas, Christine Mahoney, Tanja Malek, Peter Mayer, Margaret McCown, Iain McLean, Anand Menon, Andrew Moravcsik, Chavi Nana, Jürgen Neyer, Tim Noetzel, Mark Pollack, Lothar Rieth, Volker Rittberger, Lorena Ruano, Frank Schimmelfennig, Bruno Scholl, Guido Schwellnus, Roger Scully, Jeff Stacey, Zosia Stemplowska, Ed Turner, Endre Tvinnereim, Amy Verdun, and Antje Wiener. Of all my friends and colleagues at Nuffield, I owe special gratitude to Johannes Lindner, who read and commented on probably every single sentence I wrote, and also for being the staunchest critic of my work, apart from being a best friend. During my year in Mannheim, Martin, Rolf, and Stefan bear responsibility for reintroducing me into the art of 'life' after years of living in Ph.D. mode (and I am quite grateful to them for *not* having been around while I actually had to write the whole thing).

Audiences at the Oxford Graduate Seminar in Political Science, the Nuffield College Political Science Seminar, the Nuffield Social Science Post-doctoral Seminar Series (NSSPSS), at the University of Leiden, the University of Mannheim, and the University of Kentucky provided challenging and hospitable environments in which I was able to present my work-in-progress. I also presented parts of my work at the 7th ECSA biennial conference in Madison (2001), the 4th Pan-European International Relations Conference of the ECPR in Canterbury (2001), the workshop 'Der Beitrag der Integrationsforschung zur Institutionentheorie' in Mannheim (2002), the conference 'The European Parliament at Fifty' in Aberystwyth (2002), the annual convention of the ISA in Portland (2003), the 8th EUSA biennial conference in Nashville (2003), the workshop 'Forschungslogik und Methoden der IB und der Europaforschung' in Hofgeismar (2003), and the CES conference in Chicago (2004).

During my time as a Robert Schuman Scholar in the European Parliament's Secretariat in Luxembourg in the summer of 2000, I gained an insider's view of the institution I studied over the past years. In Luxembourg, Gordon Lake was an exceptional supervisor and colleague; in Brussels, Francis Jacobs, and Michael Shackleton have instilled my periodically recurring wish to become a 'fonctionnaire'.

While conducting my research, I benefited from the generous financial support provided by various funding bodies and other institutions. The ESRC (Grant No. R00429934375) and the DAAD (Doktorandenstipendium im Rahmen des gemeinsamen Hochschulprogramms III) funded my doctoral research. A grant from EUSSIRF (part of the 'The European Commission's Access to Research Infrastructures' section within the Fifth Framework Programme 'Improving Human Research Potential') enabled me to spend the summer of 2001 at the EUI in Fiesole to consult the library and the Historical Archive of the European Communities. I am very grateful to Tom Bourke and the staff at the EUI library and archives for their outstanding help in tracing files and documents. During my year at the University of Mannheim and the MZES, I benefited from a stimulating working environment in which I could continue my work on this book. In this context, I wish to thank Beate Kohler-Koch and Frank Schimmelfennig for their support and ongoing collaboration. Nuffield College continues to provide the best of all conceivable working environments. The College was also particularly generous in providing grants to attend conferences, workshops, and to do my fieldwork. I am grateful to Jeremy Richardson, Alec Stone Sweet, Adrienne Héritier, Simon Hix, and Gerald Schneider who had to write batteries of support letters to help me secure funding and the smooth progress with my dissertation.

The transition from Ph.D. manuscript to a 'proper' book is a challenge, to say the least. I want to thank my two examiners, Simon Hix and Iain McLean, as well as an anonymous referee for their encouragement and comments to improve the manuscript. I also want to thank Simon for suggesting the title of this book: 'Building Europe's Parliament'. Without Anand Menon's encouragement, I would probably still ponder over whether or not to contact a publisher. At the Press, I wish to thank my editor Dominic Byatt, Claire Croft and my production editor Tanya Dean for their support, as well as for their patience and efficient handling of my queries.

My parents, Irmgard Rittberger-Rückert and Volker Rittberger, and Silke Heinrichs accompanied me in the most difficult and brightest moments of this endeavour. Their dedication and love provided guidance whenever I was close to dropping the pen, and helped me to see the person I am and, more importantly, want to be. It is a custom that the author pay tribute to the loved one who had to suffer most from a partner's long periods of self-inflicted isolation and—for the non-academic—seemingly incomprehensible spleens. I wish I could still write these lines. And whenever I look at this book, I will be reminded of its true price.

Oxford/Tübingen
August 2004   Berthold Rittberger

Contents

List of Figures

List of Tables

List of Abbreviations

CA	Common Assembly (of the European Coal and Steel Community)
CAP	Common Agricultural Policy
CDA	Christen Democratisch Appèl
CDU/CSU	Christlich Demokratische Union/Christlich Soziale Union
CFSP	Common Foreign and Security Policy
CNPF	Conseil National du Patronat Français
COREPER	Comité de représentants permanents des Etats Membres auprès de l'Union Européenne/Committee of permanent representatives of the Member States of the EU
COSAC	Conférence des organes spécialisés dans les affaires communautaires et européennes des parlements de l'Union européenne/Conference of Community and European Affairs Committees of Parliaments of the European Union
CWP	Commission White Paper
EAEC	European Atomic Energy Community (Euratom)
EAGGF	European Agricultural Guidance and Guarantee Fund
EEC	European Economic Community
ECSC	European Coal and Steel Community
ECB	European Central Bank
ECJ	European Court of Justice
ECT	Treaty establishing the European Community (consolidated version)
EIB	European Investment Bank
EMS	European Monetary System
EMU	Economic and Monetary Union
EP	European Parliament
EU	European Union
FDP	Freie Demokratische Partei—Die Liberalen
FT	Financial Times
GCC	German Constitutional Court (Bundesverfassungsgericht)

HA	High Authority (of the European Coal and Steel Community)
IGC	Intergovernmental Conference
IMF	International Monetary Fund
KVP	Katholieke Volkspartij
MEP	Member of the European Parliament
MP	Member of Parliament
MRP	Mouvement Républicain Populaire
N	Nash equilibrium
NAFTA	North Atlantic Free Trade Agreement
NATO	North Atlantic Treaty Organisation
NPs	national parliaments
OECD	Organization for Economic Cooperation and Development
OED	Oxford English Dictionary
OEEC	Organization for European Economic Cooperation
P	Pareto optimal solution
PC	Parti Communiste
PS	Parti Socialiste
PU	Political Union
QMV	qualified majority voting
RKSP	Rooms-Katholieke Staatspartij
RPF	Rassemblement du Peuple Français
RPR	Rassemblement pour la République
SEA	Single European Act
SFIO	Section Française de l'International Ouvrière
SPD	Sozialdemokratische Partei Deutschlands
TCE	Treaty establishing a Constitution for Europe
TEU	Treaty on European Union ('Maastricht Treaty')
UDF	Union pour la démocratie française
UDR	Union des Démocrates pour la République
WEU	Western European Union
WHO	World Health Organization
WTO	World Trade Organization

Introduction: Building Europe's Parliament

In a world in which government authority is derived from representative parliamentary assemblies, Europe cannot be built without such an assembly.

Jean Monnet[1]

Gone are the days when the European Parliament (EP) was still referred to as a talking shop. Article I-20 of the Treaty establishing a Constitution for Europe (TCE), approved by the twenty-five European Union (EU) member states on 18 June 2004, states that the 'European Parliament shall, jointly with the Council, exercise legislative and budgetary functions'; moreover, it shall exercise the function of 'political control' and have the power to 'elect the President of the Commission'. In Article I-46, the Constitution explicitly states that the EU is founded on the principle of representative democracy: 'Citizens are directly represented at the Union level in the European Parliament.' These provisions stand in stark contrast to the relevant articles in the Treaty establishing the European Coal and Steel Community (ECSC) in the early 1950s: the main function to be exercised by the Common Assembly (CA) of the ECSC, the forerunner of the EP, was to control the newly created supranational High Authority (HA) which was later to become the Commission.[2] Akin to international parliamentary assemblies at the time, such as the Consultative Assembly of the Council of Europe, the Assembly of the Western European Union (WEU), or the North Atlantic Treaty Organisation (NATO) Parliamentarians' Conference, the CA of the ECSC was classified as 'talking-shop', 'innocent of legislative power' (Hovey 1966: vii).[3]

Of all international parliamentary assemblies in the post-Second World War era, the CA, however, had a special task to fulfil. It was not—as most international parliamentary assemblies—designed as a consultative body.[4] According to Lindsay (1960: 23), the 'Common Assembly...is neither consultative nor advisory: it aims to supervise and even control an executive.' In the decades to come, this special status of the CA was to be enhanced. While the other international parliamentary assemblies merely retained their consultative status, the 'heir' of the CA, the EP, has developed into an evermore influential parliamentary assembly: in the decades following the creation of the CA, the Community member states bestowed the EP with a kernel of budgetary powers in the Treaty of Luxembourg of 1970, and with the approval of the Single European Act (SEA) in 1986, the EP was given 'real' legislative powers. Since the SEA, the influence of the EP in legislative decision-making in the EU has been extended progressively, prompting commentators to refer to the EP as 'one of the world's more powerful elected chambers' (Hix et al. 2003: 192). In the course of half a century the EP has thus evolved from a 'token talking-shop into a significant player in shaping legislation that applies across a continent' (Corbett et al. 2003: 354).

Equipped with a *trias* of control, budgetary, and legislative powers, it can be hardly controversial to claim that—in terms of its powers and functions—the EP resembles NPs more than its international counterparts. In the light of these developments, comparisons between the EP and NPs assume an evermore prominent place in the literature.[5] Where, then, 'does the contemporary European Parliament stand in comparison to other institutions, others in the genus "legislatures" and "parliaments"?', asks Scully (2000: 229). Comparisons between the EP and NPs commonly take recourse to Mezey's (1979) and Norton's (1998) schemes to classify legislatures. How influential is the EP in comparison to other legislatures? According to Mezey (1979: 25), parliaments are 'salient in the policy-making process to the extent that their presence and prerogatives act as a constraint on the executive'. The power of a parliament to constrain the executive is 'grounded primarily in an ability to exercise a veto over policy proposals, and secondarily in being able to modify them short of veto' (Scully 2000: 236). Norton has advanced a distinction between policy-*making* and policy-*influencing* legislatures to point at the differences displayed by parliaments in their capacity to constrain the executive: policy-making legislatures are able to 'modify or reject government measures' as well as to 'formulate and substitute a policy for that proposed by the government' (Norton cited in Scully 2000: 236), whereas policy-influencing legislatures, while possessing the capacity to reject or amend measures by the government, lack the ability to promote their own agenda vis-à-vis the executive. In terms of its formal powers, since the adoption of the SEA the EP qualifies as a policy-influencing legislature which can amend and, under certain conditions, even reject legislation. Yet, merely looking at the formal powers obscures the fact that the EP, in contrast to most national legislatures, actually uses its formal powers to the fullest possible extent. The separation of the EP from the executive (like in a presidential system) and the absence of a dominant majority or coalition inside the EP enables the EP to exploit its powers much more effectively than national legislatures in other parliamentary systems. Scully (2000: 238–9) thus concludes that 'the policy influence wielded by the EP is surely greater than that of most national chambers in the EU', and that, consequently, the EP 'deserves to be ranked at least towards the upper end of the category of "policy influencer".'

At the turn of the third millennium, it is unlikely to still find scholars who—like Lindsay (1960) and Hovey (1966) in the 1960s—engage in comparisons between the EP and other international parliamentary assemblies. The fact that the EP is now compared to its national counterparts is indicative of the EP's remarkable journey from a talking-shop to a powerhouse. But in spite of this development, half a century after the birth of the ECSC, it remains an unresolved puzzle as to why the idea of parliamentary democracy was raised in the context of the construction of a system of interstate cooperation in the post-Second World War era in Western Europe, finding its expression in the creation of the CA, and why the idea of parliamentary democracy continues to leave its mark on the EU's institutional make-up, mirrored in the progressive increase of the EP's powers, and—as of lately—the growing importance of NPs in EU decision-making.

The aim of this book is thus to explain (a) the creation of the CA and the decision of national governments to bestow it with the power to censure the 'executive' HA, (b) the assignment of budgetary powers in 1970, and (c) of legislative powers as a result of the SEA. Furthermore, the book will also chart the development of the EP's legislative powers from the Maastricht Treaty (Treaty on European Union, TEU) to the TCE.

The 'state of the art' and its shortcomings

After having experienced a brief 'peaking' in the period preceding and following its first direct elections in 1979, literature on the EP has been growing at remarkable pace since the late 1980s, following the European 'relance' in the wake of the SEA (see Hix et al. 2003: 192–3). Besides a set of excellent books by Westlake (1994), Corbett et al. (2000), Costa (2001), Judge and Earnshaw (2003), and Maurer and Wessels (2003), which chiefly focus on descriptions and analyses of the EP's evolution, composition, functions, powers, and internal organization, or interpretations of the literature on the EP, the 1990s have increasingly witnessed theoretically informed original research breaking into the study of the EP: '[R]esearch on the EP has evolved from largely descriptive work on the internal institutions of the parliament (in the 1960s and 1970s), through more detailed work on the EP elections, to highly theoretically and empirically sophisticated research in many areas, including behaviour within the EP, the chamber's internal institutional structure, and the powers of the EP relative to the other EU institutions' (Hix et al. 2003: 193).[6] This literature takes the powers of the EP as exogenous, and hence does not ask why and how the EP acquired these powers in the first place. There is, however, a growing strand in the literature which has vastly improved our understanding of why national governments of EU member states continue to selectively transfer parts of their sovereignty by pooling or delegating powers to 'agents', such as the Commission, the independent European Central Bank (ECB) or other regulatory agencies.[7] However, as I will demonstrate in chapter 1, this literature—which forms part of the new institutionalist turn in political science—has, hitherto, not offered an explanation as to why and under what conditions governments may opt for the creation or empowerment of a supranational parliamentary institution, such as the EP. I will also show that this lacuna can also not be filled by the fast-growing literature on the EU's 'democratic deficit': given that the EP is viewed by many commentators, politicians, and scholars as a crucial element to enhance the EU's democratic credentials, we could actually expect the 'democratic deficit' literature to provide some insights as to why national governments have increased the powers of the EP. Yet, most of this literature does not ask if and how the 'democratic deficit' is perceived by political elites and, consequently, what its behavioural implications are. How, then, can we make sense of the decisions of national governments to create and gradually empower a parliament in a system of interstate cooperation?

The argument: pooling, delegation and the EU's legitimacy deficit

To remedy the shortcomings in the literature, this book will develop a theory of delegation to parliamentary institutions in international polities. The elaboration of this theory will proceed in three interrelated stages. In the first stage, I will specify two conditions under which national governments feel compelled to contemplate the empowerment of parliamentary institutions (at both the supranational level or at the level of the domestic polity) as a necessary corollary of broader international institutional design decisions. As to the first condition, I will argue that the subsequent *pooling*—the adoption of (super)majority voting rules in the Council—and *delegation* of sovereignty to supranational institutions poses challenges to traditional channels of interest representation and accountability at the level of national polities. I will demonstrate that, once pooling and delegation loom, political elites in the member states express concerns about the preservation of domestic democratic procedures which they perceive to be under threat. The concerns voiced by political elites will be the following: once power is delegated, who controls supranational institutions? To whom are they accountable? When sovereignty is pooled by creating (super)majority voting rules in the Council, who can be held to account if 'my' national minister is outvoted by a majority of other national government representatives? What can be done to counter the declining legislative role of national parliaments when evermore legislative decisions are taken at the EU level? While member state governments thus pool and delegate sovereignty primarily to enhance their national polity's problem-solving capacity (see Moravcsik 1998), these transfers of sovereignty produce an asymmetry between *consequentialist* and *procedural* legitimacy: consequentialist legitimacy denotes that compliance with a system of rules is warranted by the efficiency- and welfare-enhancing effects or outputs produced by a polity; procedural legitimacy denotes that compliance with a system of rules is founded on the intrinsic valuation of the rules and procedures whereby actors arrive at decisions. Thus, transfers of sovereignty through pooling and delegation, while improving the problem-solving capacity of a polity (and thereby warranting its consequentialist legitimacy), threaten to undermine its procedural legitimacy by challenging traditional channels of interest representation and accountability, a 'condition' which I will refer to as *legitimacy deficit*. As a result of this perceived legitimacy deficit, I expect that political elites will contemplate institutional solutions as to how the legitimacy deficit can be alleviated. As to the second condition, I contend that during constitutional 'founding moments', when political elites ponder over the creation of a system of 'rules about rules', they display an inclination to voice concerns about matters of procedural legitimacy.[8] In the course of constitution-building processes, political elites not only craft 'lower level' institutions and rules which determine the allocation and distribution of power and resources (decision-making rules, voting weights, and the like) among political actors, but they are also bound to shape 'higher level' institutions which frame political processes, such as the choice of the type of political system to be adopted. Discussions about 'higher level' institutions are hence destined to reflect political elites' views on *procedural* legitimacy: if political elites opt for a democratic constitution, it will be undisputed that the political system cannot do, for instance, without a representative parliamentary institution and separation of powers. Hence, preferences for a particular type of political system ('higher level' institutions) are associated with particular beliefs about the legitimacy of particular *procedures* to 'aggregate preferences' and solve conflicts. These differ, of course, as to whether political elites opt for a system of representative democracy, a monarchy or an autocratic regime.

In the second stage of my theoretical argument, I claim that concerns for procedural legitimacy do not translate automatically into institutional design and reform solutions and are, by no means, uniform across or even within member states. I will, therefore, show that political elites in the member states hold different beliefs about how concerns for procedural legitimacy should be translated into institutional reform solutions. These beliefs are coined *legitimating beliefs* and denote beliefs held by political elites about the appropriateness of mechanisms of interest representation and accountability in a particular situation. I posit that the creation and empowerment of the EP constitutes only one among a variety of potential solutions to tackle the perceived legitimacy deficit: even though political elites share a concern about procedural legitimacy, they may opt either for institutional remedies at the supranational level, for instance by supporting the empowerment of the EP, or they may support remedies which will be implemented at the national level, for instance, by pressing for enhancing the powers of domestic parliaments to influence and scrutinize EU policy-making.

In the third stage, I will illuminate the interaction among national governments at Treaty-amending Intergovernmental Conferences (IGCs). I will ask how the commonly shared perception about the existence of a legitimacy deficit and domestically held legitimating beliefs affect the behaviour of national governments during these negotiations and how they affect institutional reform outcomes. For this purpose, I will present and illustrate the plausibility of a set of competing hypotheses in order to show whether and how the *normative constraints* experienced by political elites—the legitimacy deficit on the one hand and domestically held legitimating beliefs on the other hand—affect the interaction between member state governments. The three competing explanations are based on different modes of action: rhetorical, communicative, and rational. According to the rationalist proposition—which will serve as the 'null hypothesis', political elites will (when 'push comes to shove' at IGCs) not feel bound by the normative constraints defined by the perceived legitimacy deficit and legitimating beliefs. According to the rationalist hypothesis then, decision-making during IGCs is characterized by bargaining about the powers of the EP and the outcome reflects the constellation of preferences and the relative bargaining power of member state governments. Conversely, the communicative action hypothesis predicts that member state governments do not enter the IGC negotiations with fixed, unalterable preferences about how to alleviate the legitimacy deficit. Instead, decision-making is characterized by a truth-seeking discourse on the appropriate role of the EP (and of national parliaments) in the EU polity, as a result of which member state governments reach a reasoned consensus. The third perspective combines a rational logic of action with a normative component: according to rhetorical action hypothesis, based on Schimmelfennig's (2003) ground-breaking work, member state governments act strategically, yet they are constrained since they have to justify their preferences in the light of the normative constraints imposed on them by (a) legitimating beliefs they have subscribed to domestically, and (b) the commonly shared concern about alleviating the legitimacy deficit. Honouring these normative commitments will yield social rewards, while disregarding them will result in social pressure. I will show in Chapters 3–5 that none of these logics of action is dominant in the cases under scrutiny. While communicative action only played a role during the constitutional 'founding moment', the creation of the ECSC (see Chapter 3), rhetorical and rational action capture the interaction among member state governments during IGCs in the two cases concerned with the delegation of budgetary (Chapter 4) and legislative powers (Chapter 5). Figure I.1 represents an overview of the three-staged theoretical argument advanced in this book.

Data, cases, method

The selection of the case studies in this book was guided by the following criteria. First, I have selected cases which mirror the classical policy-influencing powers exercised by legislatures: legislative, budgetary, and executive control/supervisory powers. Consequently, I will explore cases which illuminate why the EP was endowed with this power *trias*. Second, in the light of the existing new institutionalist literature, the cases scrutinized in this book can be viewed as outlier cases, i.e. 'cases poorly

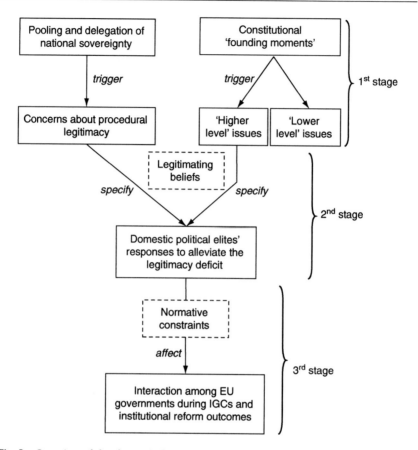

Fig. I.1 Overview of the theoretical argument

explained by existing theories' (Van Evera 1997: 22), a point I have already alluded to earlier and to which I shall return in chapter 1.[9] Since existing theories fare badly in explaining the creation and empowerment of the EP, it has to be assumed that unknown, or poorly specified causes explain the outcome of interest and that, consequently, these causes can be discerned by examining these cases (see Van Evera 1997: 22–3, 86). The theory which I develop to explain instances of the EP's empowerment has to qualify as a *candidate* theory: it was developed in connection with the evaluation and analysis of the cases at hand. Before theories can be *tested* more comprehensively, their plausibility *qua* candidate theories has to be assumed (see Eckstein 1975: 108).[10] Given that there is no prior information on the theory's performance, it seems reasonable to use the cases presented here as 'pilot studies' to see whether these probes confirm the theory's plausibility and hence allow for more extensive data-gathering, theory-refine-ment and, ultimately, theory-testing in future research (see Bennett and George 1997; Odell 2000).

Obviously, the selection of these cases does not represent the universe of cases. To allow for a strong theory-test, two strategies would seem appro-priate: first, we could include all those cases where national governments have pooled or delegated sovereignty and where we would consequently expect a legitimacy deficit to occur, which would then trigger the search for solutions to alleviate the legitimacy deficit. Second, all the cases which resulted in the EP's empowerment could be scrutinized. In all of these instances we would expect to observe that the empowerment of the EP has been accompanied by political elites' perception of a legitimacy deficit.[11] In this book, the following instances of transfers of sovereignty will be analysed in the light of the theory developed in Chapter 2: transfers of sovereignty of the member states, which led (a) to the creation of the CA endowed with control powers vis-à-vis the HA (ECSC Treaty adopted in 1951), (b) the acquisition of budgetary powers (Treaty of Luxembourg of 1970), and (c) legislative powers (SEA signed in 1986). Furthermore, I will look at instances of transfers of sovereignty in the period following the SEA. I will ask whether the continuous pooling of sovereignty has been the prime mover behind member state governments' decisions to empower both the EP as well as NPs in EU decision-making.

A historical work of this kind requires the analysis of a vast array of both primary and secondary sources. Where available, I sought to employ 'hard' primary sources. These carry the advantage of a high degree of reliability.[12] 'Hard' primary sources include, for example, internal government reports, reports of confidential deliberations among important decision-makers, verbatim diary entries and memoirs by crucial participants (see Moravcsik, 1998: 82). In the empirical chapters, I have made extensive use of 'hard' primary sources, collected at the Historical Archives of the European Communities in Florence, in particular with regard to the first two empir-ical chapters, the creation of the CA of the ECSC (Chapter 3) and the assignment of budgetary powers to the EP with the Treaty of Luxembourg in 1970 (Chapter 4). Concerning the more recent instances of the em-powerment of the EP, the SEA and the ensuing Treaty reforms (Chapters 5 and 6), the archives remain inaccessible and, hence, I was confronted with a lack of 'hard' primary source material. Consequently, I relied on 'soft' primary sources (such as public justifications of politicians, e.g. parliamentary debates and publicly accessible official reports, or press reports) and secondary sources offering an analysis of primary sources describing, explaining or interpreting primary sources (e.g., journal articles, academic books, etc.). Yet, secondary sources sometimes also report facts which are based on 'hard' primary sources. Where these 'hard' sources are clearly discernable and not subject to interpretation or evaluation, I also partially relied on this 'methodological compromise', i.e. on the extraction of 'hard' sources from secondary sources (see Moravcsik 1998: 83).

Outline of the book

This book is divided into two major parts. In Part I, the theoretical argument is developed (Chapters 1 and 2). In Part II, I offer three in-depth case studies (Chapters 3–5) to assess the plausibility of the theory developed in Part I. Chapter 6 charts the developments of the more recent instances of the EP's legislative empowerment and the increasing importance of national parliaments in EU decision-making.

Chapter 1 reviews the new institutionalist literature on institution-building and inquires what expectations can be derived from rational choice and sociological institutionalism for explaining the empowerment of the EP. Since concerns about 'democratic legitimacy' are cited frequently in the literature on European integration as ad hoc explanations for the empowerment of the EP, I also turn to the 'democratic deficit' literature and inquire whether this literature offers any cues to improve our understanding of the existence and empowerment of the EP.

In Chapter 2, I develop a three-staged theory to explain the decisions of national governments to create and/or empower a supranational parliamentary institution. In this chapter, I hypothesize that attempts by national governments to pool and delegate sovereignty to manage or solve problems of security or socio-economic interdependence challenge national channels of interest representation and accountability. Consequently, I expect that political elites in the member states will perceive a legitimacy deficit and call for remedies to alleviate it. In the next step, I show that the proposals political elites in different member states advance to alleviate the legitimacy deficit vary within and across member state polities. In a final step, I ask how the concerns about the legitimacy deficit—based on different legitimating beliefs—affect the interaction among member state governments during Treaty-amending IGCs and affect institutional reform outcomes.

Chapter 3 sheds light on the decision of the founding member states of the ECSC to create the CA of the ECSC and to bestow this assembly with the right to censure the supranational High Authority.[13] Chapter 4 looks at the adoption of the Treaty of Luxembourg in 1970 which foresaw the creation of a system of 'own resources' for the Community and, concomitantly, endowed the EP with budgetary powers. The case study presented in Chapter 5 focuses on the third landmark decision in the empowerment of the EP, the delegation of legislative powers as a result of the adoption of the SEA in 1986. In Chapter 6, I shed light on the developments from the SEA leading up to the approval of the TCE. In the concluding chapter, I discuss the broader implications of the findings of this book for the 'state' of parliamentary democracy in the EU and the prospects for parliamentary democracy in international collaborative settings outside the EU. Are concerns for democracy in international polities linked to the degree to which national governments transfer sovereignty to international organizations? Under what conditions can we expect parliamentary institutions to arise and develop outside the EU?

Notes

1. This statement was attributed to Monnet in a meeting between the heads of delegation debating the Schuman Plan (HAEC, AA/PA.SFSP–62, 11 July 1950, author's translation).
2. Article 24 of the ECSC Treaty enables the CA to cast a censure motion asking for the resignation of the HA upon the presentation of its annual report.
3. Lindsay (1960) and Hovey (1966) claim that there were six of them: These are the Consultative Assembly of the Council of Europe, the Assembly of the WEU, the NATO Parliamentarians' Conference, the CA of the ECSC (later the European Parliamentary Assembly of the European Economic Community (EEC), ECSC, and Euratom), the Nordic Council, and the Benelux Inter-Parliamentary Council.
4. See, for example, Rittberger and Zangl (2003: 110) and Marschall (2002: 385–8).
5. See, for example, Scully (2000), Bergman and Raunio (2001), Judge and Earnshaw (2003).
6. Examples for the more recent research on 'behaviour within the EP' and its 'internal institutional structure' include the work on party groups (Hix and Lord 1997; Raunio 1997; Kreppel 2002), the work on Members of the European Parliament (MEP) voting behaviour (Kreppel and Tsebelis 1999; Hix 2001), and on the European Parliament's committee structure (Bowler and Farrell 1995; Whitaker 2001; Mamadouh and Raunio 2003). Examples for the literature on the 'powers of the EP relative to the other EU institutions' include research on the absolute and relative legislative influence of Community institutions, either based on formal models (see Steunenberg 1994; Tsebelis 1994; Garrett 1995; Crombez 1996; Garrett and Tsebelis 1996; Tsebelis and Garrett 2000; Selck and Steunenberg 2004; Selck 2004) or, based on small- or large-empirical

research (Judge et al. 1994; Earnshaw and Judge 1996; Garman and Hilditch 1998; Kreppel 1999; B. Rittberger 2000; Shackleton 2000; Tsebelis et al. 2001).

7. See, *inter alia*, Majone (1996, 2001), Pollack (1997, 1999, 2002, 2003), Moravcsik (1998), Doleys (2000), Stone Sweet (2000, 2002), Thatcher and Stone Sweet (2002).

8. Constitutional founding moments represent a special subset of instances of pooling and delegation.

9. Pollack (2003: chapter 4) labels the EP an 'outlier' since explanations inspired by rational choice institutionalism are unable to account for its empowerment in the legislative and budgetary sphere.

10. See King et al. (1994: 209–12) for a critical appraisal.

11. The latter research strategy has informed a research project supported by a grant from the Thyssen Foundation (2004–6) under the direction of Frank Schimmelfennig and the author.

12. Moravcsik (1998: 81) argues that 'the greater the difficulty of manipulating or concealing evidence of what really occurred at the time, the more reliable (the "harder") the source in retrospect.'

13. I have opted for the ECSC instead of the Treaty of Rome establishing the EEC as the first case in this book because, by the time the Treaty of Rome was negotiated, the institutional blueprint for the new Community was already in place. Although Moravcsik claims that the Treaty of Rome marks the birth of what, today, is the EU, the 'quasi-constitutional institution' (Moravcsik 1998: 2), i.e. the Commission (formerly HA of the ECSC), the Court, the Assembly and the Council, had already been in place as a result of the creation of the ECSC.

PART I

Theory

The Empowerment of the European Parliament: Lessons from the New Institutionalism and Democratic Theory

Since this book is concerned with *explaining* institutional creation and change, a natural starting point for developing an explanation to answer the question of the EP's creation and empowerment is the literature on the 'new institutionalism' (Hall and Taylor 1996).[1] Even though the bulk of this literature focuses on the *effects* of regulative and constitutive institutions on social and political phenomena, different strands of the new institutionalism also offer distinct hypotheses about the creation, design, and change of social and political institutions, treating institutions as *dependent* variables instead of independent or intervening variables. Hence, we would expect some explanatory cues from this literature for answering the question as to why EU member states have delegated and continue to delegate powers to the EP.

In section 1.1, I highlight different strands of the new institutionalist literature and inquire what expectations can be derived for explaining episodes of institutional creation and change. Second, I look at existing institutionalist explanations for the empowerment of the EP, and review and evaluate these explanations in order to identify some of the missing 'building blocks' for a more comprehensive and systematic explanation of its creation and empowerment. An upshot from this literature is that these explanations have to take account of political elites' concerns about the democratic legitimacy of Community governance. Consequently, we would expect that the literature on the EU's 'democratic deficit' can contribute to our understanding of why political elites have delegated and continue to delegate more powers to the EP. This is discussed in the third section.

1.1 Rational choice and sociological institutionalism

Rationalists share the assumption that social actors, their preferences and interests, are the ultimate sources of social action. Social actors are, furthermore, assumed to act instrumentally: rational choice institutionalists assume that social actors only create or change institutions if they help to maximize their (exogenously given) preferences. According to March and Olson (1989, 1998) social action thus follows a *logic of consequentialism*: actors make rational choices among alternative sets of actions by evaluating their likely consequences knowing that all actors do likewise; in interdependent social situations actors behave strategically in order to obtain their most preferred outcome. Accordingly, institutions arise from negotiations among rational actors pursuing personal (or collectively held) preferences in circumstances in which they expect to reap gains from institutionalizing joint action. However, in order to derive concrete expectations as to when and under what conditions actors opt for the creation, maintenance or change of institutions, rationalists make auxiliary assumptions about the goals social actors seek to realize and maximize. In the international relations literature, for instance, Hasenclever and colleagues (1997) distinguish between interest-based and power-based theories to explain international cooperation and hence point at the conditions under which international institutions can be created and maintained. Based on a similar logic, Schimmelfennig (2003) draws a distinction between security-, power-, and welfare-based approaches. From the welfare-based (or interest-based) perspective, states opt for institutionalized cooperation when the economic or efficiency gains expected from cooperation exceed the costs of noncooperation. In contrast, a security-based perspective—such as defensive realism—assumes that states opt for institutionalized cooperation only when they can thus 'balance' effectively against a common external security threat (Waltz 1979).[2] Whereas the different rationalist perspectives differ with respect to the underlying interests states seek to maximize, these accounts share a *functional* logic. Functional explanations 'account for their causes in terms of their effects' (Keohane 1984: 80). Proponents of the functional perspective to institution-building commonly argue that institutions reflect actors' mutually perceived attractiveness of an efficient solution to a given collective action problem.[3] In International Relations theory, functional theory is closely associated with Keohane who has analysed the conditions under which international institutions are created and maintained even after the decline of the power of a hegemon. Explaining the functional logic, Keohane cites the example that businesses' decisions to make investments are made because businesses anticipate their investment to be profitable. In a temporal sense, investment comes before profit, yet in a causal sense, *anticipated* profits (the 'effect') explain the decision to invest (the 'cause'). Based on this logic, Pollack (1997, 2003) has developed a functional theory of institution-building in the EU in which he argues that states opt for creating, maintaining, and reforming European institutions when they face collective action problems that may impede cooperation. His argument is a functional one: collective actors expect joint action or institutionalized cooperation to be mutually beneficial, hence the decision to cooperate, create or maintain institutions. States 'agree to adopt certain institutions primarily to lower the transaction costs of international cooperation, thereby overcoming some basic collective action problems that might otherwise prevent cooperation under anarchy' (Pollack 2003: 21). Institutions are thus 'functional' in helping to reduce transaction costs *ex ante* (e.g. by efficient decision making and provision of information) or *ex post* (e.g. by monitoring compliance and identifying transgressors) which enable states to reap the benefits of joint action. The rationalist perspective would thus expect the creation and empowerment of the EP to follow the logic expressed in the following hypothesis:

Rational choice institutionalist hypothesis
States will create or empower the EP, when the expected mutual efficiency gains which accrue from delegating control, budgetary, and legislative competencies to it exceed the benefits of no or unilateral action.

Whereas rationalists assume an individualist ontology, sociological institutionalists assume a holist and ideational ontology. 'Rather than taking agents as givens or primitives in social explanations, as rationalists tend to do', sociological institutionalists are interested in 'showing the socially constructed nature of agents and subjects' (Fearon and Wendt 2002: 57) by pointing to the *constitutive* role of systemic (inter and transnational) and/or sub-systemic (domestic) norms or ideas. In contrast to rationalists, sociological institutionalists thus 'problematize and endogenize identities, interests—and, ultimately, actors as well' (Schimmelfennig 2003: 69). Furthermore, sociological institutionalists assume that social actors act on the basis of these internalized norms and ideas and thereby emphasize a non-instrumental logic of action, or what March and Olson (1989, 1998) famously dubbed *logic of appropriateness*. According to March and Olson the logic of consequentialism neither considers the role of actors' identities nor the importance of ideas and norms in shaping actor preferences. Subscribing to the logic of appropriateness implies that social action is seen as 'a matching of a situation to the demands of a position' (March and Olson 1989: 23, 1998: 951), both of which are defined by commonly held, internalized ideas and norms. The terminology is thus not one of 'alternatives' and 'choices' but one of 'duties' and 'obligations' which actors feel they have to follow or follow routinely. States do not create or maintain institutions to maximize their exogenously given preferences, rather, institutional creation and change is a response to a perceived lack of resonance between internalized norms and ideas and a social situation which upsets the *match* (or resonance) between 'a situation and the demands of a position.' What is the mechanism which helps us to explain how actors solve this tension originating from a perceived mismatch between internalized norms of appropriateness and the 'demands' of a particular social situation?

One prominent solution to this mismatch problem in the literature is the emphasis on isomorphic processes. Institutions and institutional forms do not necessarily spread because of their 'functional virtues' or because they are an 'efficient' means to solve a certain governance problem, but rather because the broader social environment supports and legitimizes particular institutions and institutional forms (see Finnemore 1996: 329). According to DiMaggio and Powell (1991), isomorphism is a process which forces one unit in a 'population' of institutions to resemble other units that face the same set of environmental conditions. This transfer of institutional forms (isomorphic processes) can be induced through coercion, i.e. formal or informal pressures to conform, such as expectations by 'stakeholders', mimetic adaptation (i.e. by copying institutions which are perceived successful or legitimate) or normative adaptation (i.e. endorsement of institutions and institutional forms) by professionals and networks of experts.[4] From a sociological institutionalist perspective, when would we then expect political actors to push for the creation and empowerment of the EP? For instance, we could expect isomorphic processes to be induced by a mismatch between commonly shared standards of legitimate democratic governance—founded on the principle of representative, parliamentary democracy—and the system of governance of the EU: since member states may perceive of the EU's governance functions as 'state-like', the EU system of governance falls short of conforming to the standard of parliamentary democracy which EU member states subscribe to. Consequently, the mismatch between internalized standards of legitimacy (parliamentary democracy for systems of governance that perform state-like functions) and the actual design of the EU system of governance induce member states to project their internalized standards of legitimacy onto the EU level. Consequently, in the long run, we could expect the EU to resemble a parliamentary democracy.[5]

Sociological institutionalist hypothesis
States will create or empower the EP as a response to a perceived lack of resonance between domestically internalized norms of democratic governance and progressive European integration which generates a mismatch between collectively held norms of democratic governance and governance at the EU level.

In the ensuing two sections, I review existing explanations—based on rationalist and sociological institutionalist assumptions—which address the question of how the existence and ongoing empowerment of the EP can be accounted for.

1.2 Rational choice and sociological institutionalist explanations for the empowerment of the EP

Do rational choice institutionalist explanations help us to grasp national governments' decisions to create and gradually empower the EP? I will now present different accounts which share the underlying assumptions of rational choice institutionalism.

Hix (2002) analyses the switch from the Maastricht Treaty-version of the co-decision procedure ('co-decision I) to the Amsterdam Treaty-version of the co-decision procedure ('co-decision II') which implied an increase in the EP's capacity to influence legislation, making both the EP and the Council 'co-equal' legislators (Tsebelis and Garrett 2000: 15). Hix thus asks why the EP 'won at Amsterdam' and stipulates that an exclusive focus on the Amsterdam Treaty negotiations obscures the fact that the reform of the co-decision procedure was first and foremost the achievement of 'rule interpretation' by MEPs of the Maastricht provisions of the co-decision procedure.[6] At Amsterdam, the member states merely institutionalized formally or *de jure* what was already common practice, i.e. the *de facto* operation of the Maatricht version of co-decision. Simon Hix's argument encompasses three temporally distinct yet, logically interlinked phases:

- First, in the constitutional design-phase, member state governments alter the powers of the EP by changing the Treaty rules. Hix argues,

however, that the 'governments do not expect these new rules to redis-
tribute power to the EP, as the governments expect to retain ultimate
control under the legislative ... procedure' (Hix 2002: 272).

- Second, in the constitutional operation-phase, MEPs seek a favourable
interpretation of the new rules and threaten to jeopardize the legislative
process if the Council is not willing to accept this interpretation. Since
there is at least one member state government which is indifferent
between the *de facto* operation and the *de jure* rules, the intitial status
quo cannot be enforced.
- Third, in the next constitutional reform-phase, the EP proposes to the
member states to formalize the *de facto* operation of the legislative rules.
Hix argues that the 'most integrationist government ... accepts some of
these ideas but recommends some moderate changes, to bring the outcome closer to their own ideal position. This outcome is then preferred
by all the governments to the *de facto* operation, and is hence adopted'
(Hix 2002: 272, emphasis in the original).

It is through this seeming 'automatism' (which Hix calls 'constitutional
agenda-setting through discretion in rule interpretation') that the outcome
of the Amsterdam Treaty negotiations has to be explained. Consequently,
the EP's alleged 'victory' at Amsterdam was actually a formal recognition of
its 'victory' achieved in the post-Maastricht period. Hix qualifies the scope
of the applicability of this 'automatism' by introducing two conditions
which have to be met if the *de facto* operation of constitutional rules is to
be formalized into *de jure* rules: first, there must be no redistribution of
powers between the *de facto* operation of the old and the *de jure* operation of
the proposed new rules; second, there have to be collective efficiency gains
of the new procedure such as greater transparency or greater simplicity in
the actual operation of the procedure (see Hix 2002: 272). If these conditions
are met, even the most recalcitrant government is unlikely to veto a proposal which entails efficiency and transparency gains.

Hix's work constitutes the first systematic attempt to develop a model
which uncovers the conditions under which the EP is able to successfully
challenge the *de jure* Treaty rules. Yet, the two aforementioned conditions
under which the model 'works' are likely to be too restrictive to provide a
fully comprehensive account of the EP's empowerment. The following is
thus only partially a critique of the model *per se*; rather, I intend to point at
the limits of efficiency-based explanations of the empowerment of the EP.

Does Hix convince the reader that member state governments opted for
co-decision-II because they were, at least partially, expecting efficiency

gains? It would surely be desirable to assemble more comprehensive empirical data to test Hix's efficiency hypothesis. In Amsterdam, a considerable number of member state governments were firmly opposed initially to a reform of the co-decision procedure (France, the United Kingdom, Sweden, Denmark, and Spain). Yet, we do not know exactly why these states acquiesced to a reform of co-decision-I: was this due to the expected efficiency-enhancing effects of co-decision reform? Or was it due to other factors? Although Hix's argument about the efficiency-enhancing effects of the 'interpreted' co-decision-I procedure is backed by comprehensive empirical data in other works,[7] there is also evidence that a reform of the co-decision procedure would not have happened in Amsterdam had not three subsequent Council presidencies kept the issue alive: Italy, Ireland, Netherlands were all in favour of the reform proposal.[8] The major critique here is that Hix did not sufficiently address the question why exactly the member states opted for reform. Making a functional argument about the expected efficiency-enhancing effects of co-decision reform is not the same as providing an argument that looks at actors' actual motivations.

Furthermore, in the history of the development of the EP's powers, there is ample evidence—some of which will be presented in the ensuing empirical chapters—that IGCs produced a substantial *redistribution of powers* between the different Community institutions, the beneficiary of which—on a number of occasions—was the EP. In contrast to the expectations derived from the efficiency-based explanation, reforms of legislative decision-making rules do not necessarily result in Pareto-improving bargains. As a result of subsequent Treaty reforms, decision-making efficiency has been substantially hampered by the reform of legislative rules. I will show in chapters 5 and 6 that the introduction of the cooperation procedure and the Maastricht-version of the co-decision procedure cannot be accounted for by an efficiency-based explanation. While Hix has shown that, under certain well-defined conditions, the *de jure* 'empowerment' of the EP has efficiency-enhancing effects (by institutionalizing existing practices and 'completing' incomplete contracts), I claim that there existed a number of occasions where the empowerment of the EP has actually had decision-making efficiency-*reducing* effects and has also led to a redistribution of powers between the Community institutions.[9]

The functional approach to institution-building, however, is not restricted to instances where governments anticipate mutually beneficial efficiency effects of institutional creation or reform. Instead of assuming that actors are motivated by the efficiency-enhancing effects of institutional design choices, Bräuninger and colleagues (2001) pursue a different

route to account for member states' preferences regarding legislative actions of the EP. The argument is still a functional one, that is, causes are
explained in terms of their effects, yet the anticipated effects are not joint
efficiency gains but joint *policy* gains. The authors share the assumption
that actors prefer to create and to sustain those institutions and rules from
which they expect the production of 'policy streams' which help them
maximize their policy preferences under given constraints (such as the
unanimity rules at IGCs). When actors engage in 'constitutional
choices'—choices *on* rules—they will consider the expected utilities from
choosing one set of rules rather than another: policy choice precedes
constitutional choice. Bräuninger and colleagues develop and test hypotheses which reflect this underlying assumption about member states as
'policy-seeking' actors and institutions as instruments for member states
to reap the joint benefits of the 'policy streams' that institutions help to
generate. First, the authors propose that changes in the voting rules in the
Council and EP participation in the legislative process can only come
about when all member states expect to be better off under the proposed
institutional changes; they find that individual member states' net
expected utilities (the gains expected from institutional reform resulting
from the Amsterdam Treaty), even though they vary substantially across
member states, are all greater than zero when compared with the status
quo. Second, the authors propose and find confirmation for the proposition that member states advocate institutional changes along *issue specific
lines* if they expect to be better off as a result (i.e. if they calculate the net
gain from institutional choices in each individual policy area). In their
discussion of the results, Bräuninger and colleagues state that their
models fare well in accounting for the move to a qualified majority or
the retention of unanimity in various policy areas in the Amsterdam
Treaty, yet they are unsatisfactory as far as their power to predict EP
participation in the legislative process is concerned. They argue that
whereas member states 'take into account their individual expected
gains from future policy-making when deciding in the Council's voting
quota for future decision-making', the same does not hold for the EP.
Bräuninger and colleagues (2001: 64) conclude that 'the results on the
EP's participation indicate different reasons for its choice. Commitments
of a certain number of member states do not sufficiently explain the
participation of the EP. We suspect that policy-seeking delegations may
be guided by different "central ideas" when deciding on both voting
rules.' What is meant by 'central ideas'? The notion of the 'democratic
deficit' and associated concerns for democratic legitimacy are employed to

'mop up' unexplained 'variance': '[S]tates may prefer different rules and they may even favour rules for other than policy reasons when relying on consistency with their own idea of (democratic) government, particularly in the case of EP participation' (Bräuninger et al. 2001: 49).[10]

Pollack (1997, 2003) accepts the conclusion that efficiency- and policy-seeking accounts to institution-building do not fare well when we intend to capture the general decision to delegate legislative powers to the EP. Yet, he echoes the results of Bräuninger and colleagues when he argues that the willingness of the member states to support or oppose EP participation in specific policy areas has varied considerably as a result of cross-national variation in substantive policy preferences and the expected consequences of parliamentary involvement in specific policy areas. He stresses that throughout the past Treaty revisions, member states adopted a case-by-case approach to the extension of the respective legislative procedures whereby they took account of the anticipated consequences of EP partici-pation in each individual issue area and the particular 'sensitivities' of each member government.[11] Although we have seen that the existing literature remains sceptical of the capacity of the policy-seeking approach to account for the choice *of* legislative procedures (why the EP was given a role in the legislative game in the first place), there is some evidence that supports the claim that national governments' bargaining over the par-ticipation of the EP in individual policy issues follows the logic of conse-quentialism (Pollack 2003: 257–8). However, we can still conclude this section by arguing that neither the efficiency- nor the policy-seeking approach help us to explain the general decision to improve parliamen-tary participation in the Community's legislative process, let alone the decision to endow the EP with budgetary powers or the rationale behind its creation.[12]

In contrast to rational choice institutionalism, sociological institution-alist approaches about the empowerment of the EP share the assumption that the creation and empowerment of the EP can only be understood by analysing the constitutive effects of domestic norms of democratic gov-ernance on states and their behaviour. Moravcsik and Nicolaïdis (1999), for instance, argue that even though member states may share a concern for assuring the democratic legitimacy of EU governance, their proposals as to how the democratic legitimacy of the EU polity can be assured vary cross-nationally. To explain the reform and extension of the co-decision pro-cedure in Amsterdam, Moravcsik and Nicolaïdis claim that the reform reflects member state governments' concern for the democratic legitimacy of EU decision-making. The authors emphasize 'the long-standing tendency of countries to support or oppose strengthening the EP on the basis of its perceived connection with their own democratic institutions. Before Amsterdam, this typically generated characteristic ideological cleavages pitting the French, British, Danes and Greeks—all opposed to greater parliamentary powers—and others against the Germans, Dutch, Italians and Belgians (Moravcsik and Nicolaïdis 1999: 91). Moravcsik (1998) makes a similar argument, claiming that proposals for reforming structures of democratic governance at the EU-level have their 'sources' in domestic political institutions and traditions.[13] States thus externalize their domestic political practices and norms about democratic governance and advance proposals for institutional reform at the supranational level accordingly. Yet, this 'link' between the domestic and the supranational level, that is, the mechanisms which translate domestic norms in reform proposals and outcomes remains unexplored. In the ensuing paragraphs, I will show that the existing literature—while it is more or less 'silent' on the question of mechanisms—has provided detailed analyses of the content of domestic norms that provide political actors with prescriptive guidance for the *democratic* construction of the Community polity. This literature thus goes a step further than what has been said hitherto, offering more refined accounts of the preferences about the powers of the EP.

In an attempt to specify underlying member states' preferences for the EP's powers, Wagner (1999, 2001, 2002) dismisses some of the rationalist strands in international relations which posit, as argued in the preceding section, that institution-building accounts have to be compatible with underlying security motives which induce states to seek to maximize autonomy or influence. While Wagner dismisses the autonomy-motive out of hand and for obvious reasons, the influence-oriented argument fares equally poorly since any empowerment of the EP equals a loss of state influence over legislative outcomes (Wagner 1999: 426).[14] Wagner thus turns to sociological institutionalism to derive possible explanations about the strengthening of the EP's legislative powers. Wagner argues that political elites in the member states employ notions of 'appropriate parliamentary legitimation' (Wagner 1999: 427) which states derive from domestic political culture. The 'political culture' of a state is operationalized by identifying 'those worldviews and principled beliefs—values and norms—that are stable over long periods of time and are taken for granted by the vast majority of the population' (Risse-Kappen quoted in Wagner 1999: 427). Thus, states' domestic political institutions serve as a proxy for its political culture. Member states will 'respond to the question of supranational democracy in the same way they have addressed the question of *sub-national* democracy' (Wagner 2002: 29, emphasis in the original). More concretely, Wagner argues that we should expect 'support for direct parliamentary legitimation by those countries whose policy at the regional level has been legitimized by directly elected regional parliaments, i.e. by federal states. ... [C]ountries whose regional-level policy has been legitimized indirectly by the national parliaments, i.e. unitary states..., are expected to prefer indirect parliamentary legitimation for the EU' (Wagner 2002: 29). Hence, federally-organized member states such as Germany and Belgium in which regional policy is directly legitimized through the involvement of regional parliaments are expected to be in favour of a strengthening of the EP's powers while unitary states, such as France, are less inclined to support its empowerment. Although Wagner's theoretically derived expectations are largely corroborated in his work, his approach is, nevertheless, causally incomplete. The causal mechanisms linking political culture and the preferences held by political actors remain obfuscated: how does political culture 'get' to decision-makers and their preferences? Furthermore, Wagner's definition of political culture misses some major variation in domestic support or opposition for the strengthening of the powers of the EP. Jachtenfuchs's work, which I introduce in the ensuing paragraphs, has demonstrated convincingly that support and/or opposition to empowering the EP varies not only across but also *within* national polities.

In several works, Jachtenfuchs (1999, 2002) and colleagues (1998) have specified the content of shared beliefs about a 'legitimate political order' (*polity ideas*) which play an important role in the constitutional development of polities (see Jachtenfuchs et al. 1998: 410). They show that variation in polity ideas helps to explain why not only different EU member states, but also different political parties *within* a member state polity hold different preferences for the 'appropriate' scope of policy integration, form and powers of EU institutions. Jachtenfuchs and colleagues argue that polity ideas have to be sufficiently detailed and relevant to influence actors' preferences: they have to prescribe concrete modes of action[15] and they also have to be articulated by the relevant actors in a polity. According to Jachtenfuchs and colleagues (1998), national political parties are the major 'carriers' of polity ideas: they are articulated in national party manifestoes and records of parliamentary debates during which governments have to justify their foreign policy behaviour before their domestic audience. Four analytically distinct polity ideas are identified: (a) *intergovernmental cooperation* ('Staatenbund'), (b) *federal state* ('Bundesstaat'), (c) *economic community* ('Wirtschaftsgemeinschaft'), and (d) *network*

('Netzwerk'), which offer alternative prescriptions for action. Depending on which polity idea an actor adheres to, the answers he or she will give to questions such as the sources of legitimate governance, the desirability and possibility of democracy at the supranational level, supranational citizenship, etc. will vary substantially. This argument also applies to the question about the empowerment of the EP: whether or not political elites within and across EU member states support or oppose EP empowerment depends on the polity idea that respective political elites hold. Contrary to Wagner, Jachtenfuchs and colleagues thus offer a more nuanced analysis of those normative beliefs or polity ideas which define what actors consider 'appropriate' governance structures, pointing at the observation that political culture is not interpreted uniformly within each member state.

Even though Jachtenfuchs's account is more precise in specifying the content of alternative polity ideas and their behavioural prescriptions, his own and the explanations discussed hitherto, do not offer a full explanation for the creation and empowerment of the EP. First, none of the works discussed explains the *timing* of constitutional reform decisions in general and those reforms affecting the powers of the EP in particular. Second, while Jachtenfuchs is focusing on the formation and content of actors' preferences, nothing is said about the way constellations of preferences translate into outcomes, that is, concrete institutional or policy choices. Third, analyses of co-variance tell us little about the causal mechanisms linking polity ideas, actor behaviour, and institutional outcomes. I will address these problems in Chapter 2.

Does rational choice institutionalism or sociological institutionalism fare better in capturing the member states' decisions to create and empower the EP? The literature discussed in this chapter allows us to be highly sceptical about the explanatory power of the rationalist hypothesis which posits that member states will only support EP empowerment if the benefits of empowerment (measured by the expected gains of increasing decision-making efficiency and the realization of preferred 'policy streams') outweigh the costs of delegating sovereignty (giving up control of certain national policy-making prerogatives). There is neither evidence that supports the proposition that parliamentary empowerment reduces the transaction costs of decision-making (efficiency-seeking argument); nor can the argument be sustained that national governments have continuously empowered the EP because of anticipated joint policy gains. Approaches informed by sociological institutionalism ascribing an important role to polity ideas in shaping actors' preferences and guiding action, have improved our understanding about the source of political

Table 1.1 Rational choice institutionalism, sociological institutionalism, and the EP

	Factors driving institutional choice decisions	Empowerment of the European Parliament
Rational choice institutionalism	⬩ Anticipated efficiency-enhancing effects ⟶	⬩ EP participation tends to reduce decision-making efficiency
	⬩ Anticipated effects of locking in mutually beneficial 'policy streams' ⟶	⬩ Politicized nature and periodically changing composition of the EP after elections makes it difficult for governments to predict a stable policy preference over a long period
Sociological institutionalism	⬩ States externalize domestic norms of governance to propose solutions to the legitimacy deficit of systems of supranational governance ⟶	⬩ Federally-organized states support EP empowerment, because of their experience with vertically diffused power (regional assemblies); political parties adhering to the *Federal State* polity idea support a strong EP

elites' preferences about what are the 'appropriate' powers and the 'appropriate role' for the EP. However, as I have mentioned, sociological institutionalist approaches fall short of offering a causally complete explanation of the creation and empowerment of the EP. Table 1.1 provides an overview of the literature discussed in this chapter.

Before I offer an explanation for the creation and empowerment of the EP which overcomes the shortcomings of existing accounts, the ensuing section will point to one large body of literature which could potentially provide additional cues to explain EP empowerment—the literature on the EU's 'democratic deficit'. Since both rational choice institutionalists and sociological institutionalists agree that any account of the EP's empowerment has to address political elites' concerns about the EU's democratic credentials, there are thus good reasons to expect that the vast body of the 'democratic deficit' literature addresses this issue.

1.3 Democratic theory and the empowerment of the European Parliament

Since the early nineties, in the wake of the Treaty-amending bargains struck at Maastricht, Amsterdam, and Nice, the number of newspaper and academic articles addressing the question of the Community's democratic credentials has increased remarkably. Figure 1.1 lists the total number of newspaper articles published in the Financial Times (FT) of the United Kingdom (UK), containing the terms 'democratic deficit' together with 'European Union' or 'European Community'.[16] The data show that, prior to 1990, there was virtually no discussion in the media about the Community's democratic credentials. Yet, with the IGC leading towards Political Union (PU) and Economic and Monetary Union (EMU), the democratic deficit has established itself firmly on the public and media agenda. Figure 1.2 lists the number of articles published in academic journals per year containing the terms 'democratic legitimacy' or

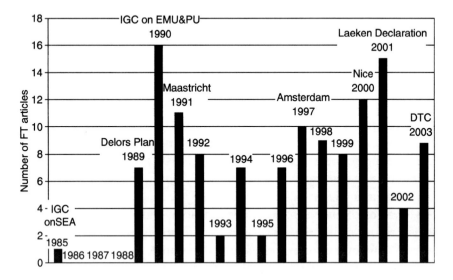

Fig. 1.1 FT newspaper articles on EU/EC's 'democratic deficit'
Source: Lexis Nexis, Executive News Service

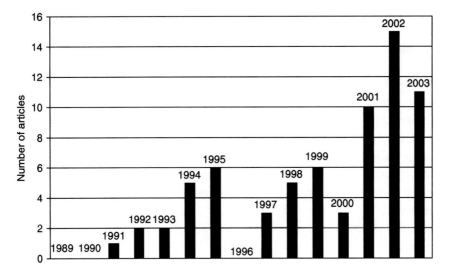

Fig. 1.2 Academic journal articles on 'democratic legitimacy' and the 'democratic deficit' in the EC/EU

Source: BIDS-IBSS database

'democratic deficit' (related to the EU polity and EU politics) until 2003.[17] The data show that prior to 1990, the question of the quality of democratic governance in the EU had not (yet) entered the academic debate.

According to Majone, the literature on the democratic credentials of the EU can be best characterized by its individual and collective efforts in 'standard setting'. Majone (1998: 6) claims that 'we are still groping for normative criteria appropriate to the *sui generis* character of the European Community... Since the legitimacy debate is still in the standard-setting state, current evaluations start from different normative premises to reach different, even contradictory, conclusions.' Majone's point can be easily illustrated by looking at a selection of the literature on the EU's democratic credentials. Much of this scholarship derives standards for demo-cratic legitimate governance in the EU from the three core principles that Abraham Lincoln has espoused in his Gettysburg address as core tenets for legitimizing governance: according to Lincoln, legitimacy de-rives from 'government *of* the people, *by* the people, *for* the people.'[18] While the first principle (government *of* the people) presupposes that there exists a definition as to who 'the people' are, thereby engendering questions of exclusion/inclusion (the boundaries of the polity) and its social identity, the principle of government *by* the people rests on the intrinsic importance attributed to procedural mechanisms for participation, interest representation, and accountability. The third principle (government *for* the people) proclaims that political choices—in order to command legitimacy—need to effectively solve the problems the citizens of a polity collectively care about.[19] In the ensuing paragraphs, I will illustrate Majone's point about the consequences of exercises in 'standard-setting': the adoption of alternative democratic theories provides a variety of possible standards or benchmarks against which the democratic legitimacy of the EU can be assessed. It comes as no surprise that not only the assessments as to whether or not the EU 'suffers' from a democratic deficit vary considerably across and even within the different dimensions of government *by*, *for*, and *of* the people, but that equally the prospects for alleviating the democratic deficit display substantial variation.

On the government-*by*-the-people dimension, Hix (1998), for instance, has offered a set of benchmarks for democratically legitimate governance in the EU which relate to the 'inputs' of the political process, the electoral process, and party competition. He argues that the main sources of the EU's democratic deficit lie in the nature of elections to the EP and the lack of party competition at the European level. At present, elections to the EP are national contests fought by domestic political parties on national manifestoes, not European ones. EP elections are thus 'second order' elections: they serve as 'beauty contests' for national parties, with domestic parties in government usually experiencing electoral punishment and domestic parties in opposition and smaller parties experiencing a boost (mid-term election phenomenon). Consequently, the present system of EU governance discourages the formation of rival policy agendas by European political parties since political parties in the EP are not seen to be competing for executive political office and candidate selection is still in the hands of domestic party executives. Hix now asks what institutional procedural reforms can be brought about to render EP elections 'first order' and to ensure party competition with rival European agendas. What is of importance for my argument is not the actual institutional solution which Hix advances to render EU governance more democratically legitimate. What is important is to elucidate the assumption upon which his argument is based: the democratic deficit can be alleviated by 'manipulating' institutions that affect the inputs into the political process. For Hix, institutions are procedural rules serving as incentive structures which—if reformed—directly affect actors' 'payoffs' for choosing a particular course of action. Hence, institutional reforms affect actor behaviour in the short-term since actors seek to modify their behaviour in the light of the new payoff structure.

On the government-*for*-the-people dimension, Majone's own work offers an instructive example of 'standard-setting'. His work mainly focuses on the conditions under which regulatory credibility can be achieved in the EU polity, and argues that transfers of sovereignty through delegation are conducive to improve the common welfare of EU citizens by strengthening and expanding the EU's regulatory capacity. Compared with the degree to which the EU exercises redistributive and stabilization functions, the regulatory function is unrivalled.[20] Regulatory credibility, however, is conditional upon certain institutional design conditions being met. For example, the 'time inconsistency' problem may render the delegation of regulatory functions to *non-majoritarian* institutions, such as independent regulatory agencies or an independent central bank, necessary to enhance policy coherence and credibility.[21] Majone (2000) has argued that the EU's regulatory system is increasingly coming under threat. The increasing politicization and parliamentarization of the Commission progressively threatens the successful fulfilment of the Community's regulatory function by gradually undermining its character as a non-majoritarian institution. Not only does the exposure to national political pressures threaten the coherence and credibility of Community policies, the enhanced powers of the EP in the investiture of the Commission and an increasing tendency to call for a 'parliamentary' Commission—whose policy programme should be supported by parliamentary majority—'threaten' to bring 'politics' (majoritarian decision-making and the pressure of party politics) into a sphere, where non-majoritarian solutions deliver more credible and sound policies. Whereas—as some may argue—adopting the model of parliamentary democracy for reform efforts may enhance the legitimacy of the EU polity from the perspective of government *by* the people, this 'solution' runs counter to regulatory efficiency or government *of* the people.[22] In sum, Majone sees the EU's institutional setting to produce efficient policies whose continuous production is, however, potentially undermined by making calls for institutional reforms to make the EU procedurally more 'democratic' (adopting the template of parliamentary democracy).

Finally, on the government-*of*-the-people dimension, Cederman (2001) has offered an insightful discussion of different perspectives about the possibility of the construction of a European *demos*. He distinguishes between a constructivist and essentialist logic of identity formation.

Whereas, according to the former, different ethnic cores produce distinct political identities, the constructivist logic proclaims the existence of an 'active process of identity formation entailing manipulation of cultural symbols' whereby political activists play an important role in selecting 'the ethnic cleavages to be mobilized or suppressed' (Cederman 2001: 142). It is thus not difficult to conceive that from the essentialist and constructivist perspectives, different conclusions can be drawn about the potential of creating an EU demos. The dominant strand of essentialist thinking assumes the existence of a national identity as the point of departure. For such 'ethno-nationalists', national identities are fixed and are there to remain. In its famous decision on the constitutionality of the Maastricht Treaty (BVerfGE 89, 155), the German Constitutional Court (GCC) proclaimed that democracy is unthinkable without a demos ('Staatsvolk'). Consequently, democracy, or as Weiler and colleagues (1995: 3) put it, 'parliament without a demos is conceptually impossible, practically despotic.' Weiler (1995) outlines the ethno-nationalist overtones of the GCC's 'Maastricht decision' in the following way: 'How sad...to observe the Bundesverfassungsgericht...looking backwards, like Lot's Wife, to a polity based on the tired old ideas of an ethno-culturally homogeneous Volk and the unholy Trinity of Volk-Staat-Staatsangehöriger as the exclusive basis for democratic authority and legitimate rule-making.' In contrast to this 'thick' identity-conception shared by ethno-nationalism, 'post-nationalism' assumes a 'thin' political identity 'detached from the nation while at the same time redefining the notion of democracy itself' (Cederman 2001: 155). This perspective is informed by a constructivist logic of identity formation: it departs from the assumption that nationalism is essentially a modern invention (Hobsbawm 1990) and proclaims that political identities are not necessarily national identities. Post-nationalism, which is closely associated with Habermas's work, attempts to circumvent the EU's 'no demos' problem by 'promoting a "thin" political identity detached from the nation' (Cederman 2001: 155) so that even culturally heterogenous polities have a potential for 'community-building' (Zürn 1998). Detaching democracy from the nation state, post-nationalists thus place their aspiration on the democratic process and put particular emphasis on 'deliberative democracy'. Proponents of deliberative democracy argue that democratic legitimacy is spurred by processes of deliberation and not by 'fixed conceptions of the common good...[or] from the aggregation of preferences of all' (Eriksen and Neyer 2003: 8).[23] Democracy is thus conceived of in a more abstract fashion, not as a principle that prescribes a particular organizational form (a representative democracy for instance) but as a legitimation principle which lays out the conditions necessary for finding out what constitutes the 'common interest' and, more generally, a community or common identity.

Even half a decade after Majone's bemoaning of the state of the 'democratic deficit' literature, the key challenge perceived by most scholars remains that of finding adequate standards. Eriksen and Neyer (2003: 6) voice Majone's concern: 'Where can a normative standard be derived from if neither nation state democracy theory nor the minimal normative standards in IR theory are directly applicable?' What conclusions can we draw from the discussion of these exemplary treatises of democratic governance in the EU and the democratic deficit? It is evident that the benchmarks against which democracy at the EU-level are measured, and, consequently, the means through which the democratic deficit should be remedied depend on the researchers' assumptions of what constitutes democratically legitimate governance. Yet, whatever these assumptions and benchmarks, the literature on the EU's democratic credentials has hitherto suffered from one serious shortcoming: by conceptualizing the democratic deficit as a value of the *dependent variable*, the literature has masked an important question. The observation that the democratic deficit occupies the minds not only of ever more scholars, but also of the public and political elites, makes us ask why there is so little systematic research on the potential *behavioural implications* of the democratic deficit on political elites who may perceive the democratic deficit as problematic? Hence, by conceptualizing the democratic deficit as part of the *explanans*, it should be possible to 'test' some of the implicit claims made by the myriad of pieces written on the democratic deficit. If the democratic deficit *matters* to political elites, we should be able to observe that it affects the design and reforms EU institutions. In order to subject this claim to empirical scrutiny, we need a systematic treatment of the democratic deficit as *explanans* or *independent variable*: when and under what conditions do actors perceive a democratic deficit? What do they intend to do about it? When political elites are conscious of the democratic deficit, what are the possible institutional design implications?

The data in Figures 1.1 and 1.2 on the public and academic 'awareness' of the EU's democratic deficit suggests that the democratic deficit is of rather recent origin. According to the data, prior to 1990, the democratic deficit was a non-issue in scholarship and media commentary. This, however, does *not* necessarily imply that questions of democratically legitimate governance in the EU were non-issues in the period before Maastricht. To conclude that concerns for democratic legitimacy are a product of the early nineties is problematic on both empirical as well as on theoretical grounds, as I will demonstrate in the ensuing chapters. The literature has persistently overlooked the fact that the foundations of the EP's powers have been laid long before the single market programme was launched and long before the Maastricht Treaty was negotiated and entered into force. Before the adoption of the Maastricht Treaty, the EP was already in full enjoyment of its famous power *trias*: legislative powers, budgetary powers, and 'executive' control or supervisory powers (vis-à-vis the Commission). Whatever the origins of the recent rise of scholarly interest in EU democracy and the democratic deficit, the creation and successive empowerment of the EP suggests that political elites' concerns about democratically legitimate governance structures played an important role in constructing the EU polity long before the public, media, and social scientists became interested in the issue.

Notes

1. See Aspinwall and Schneider (2000), Schneider and Aspinwall (2001) for a discussion of applications of the 'new instituionalisms' to the study of the EU.
2. See Schimmelfennig (2003: 28–30) for an overview.
3. See, for instance, Keohane (1984) and Knight (1992, 1995).
4. Some recent contributions which identify isomorphic processes or 'transfer of institutions' within an 'organizational field' include Mark Thatcher's account of the creation of independent regulators in telecommunications where several European countries followed the British example (Thatcher 2002) or the proliferation of competition authorities whose spread was exemplified as an 'orgy of borrowing' (Wilks and Bartle 2002). Whereas isomorphic processes mirror homogenizing pressures within certain 'organizational fields' or policy areas, these pressures are often mediated by institutional legacies at the national level (Thatcher and Stone Sweet 2002). These legacies range from alternative formal requirements for constitutional change or the number of 'veto players' (e.g. Tsebelis 1995, 2002), different regulatory models in a given policy area (Héritier et al. 1996), to actors' cognitive or normative constraints (e.g. Katzenstein 1993).
5. Heinrich Schneider (2002) speaks of the possibility of a 'staatsrechtlicher Reflex' which could be interpreted as a form of isomorphism with member states projecting domestic political institutions onto the EU level.
6. See Rasmussen (2000) and Farrell and Héritier (2003) for a similar argument.
7. See, for example, Maurer (1999, 2002), Maurer and Wessels (2003).
8. Interview with Michael Shackleton, European Parliament Secretariat, 13 March 2000.
9. The effects of parliamentary participation on decision-making efficiency have been addressed in a paper by Schulz and König (2000). They ask whether legislative reform in the EU actually enhances decision-making efficiency. If this was the case, does this

support the functional, efficiency-based hypothesis that member state governments engaged in legislative reform in anticipation of efficiency-enhancing effects? The conclusion drawn by Schulz and König is unambiguous. They argue that 'the reason for providing the EP with the power to influence legislative outcomes was to reduce the EU's much lamented "democratic deficit". Our results specify the costs of increasing the democratic accountability of EU institutions in terms of decision-making efficiency: giving the Parliament a formal role in the legislative process significantly increases the duration of the decision-making process' (Schulz and König 2000: 664).

10. Starting from a similar set of assumptions, Steunenberg and Dimitrova (1999) develop a rational actor model of 'constitutional choice' with which they aim to explain the extension of the co-decision procedure at Amsterdam to new policy areas. As in the case of Bräuninger and colleagues (2001), their core assumption is that states will opt for a legislative procedure which maximizes the individual and joint preferences in a given policy area. Based on the calculation of a strategic power-index (measuring an actor's power to affect outcomes in a particular procedure) and an inertia-index (measuring the likelihood of a procedure ending in gridlock thereby obstructing any policy change), they come to the conclusion that co-decision fares best given, that in the case of 'inertia', 'a qualified majority in the Council and approval of Parliament is sufficient for the passing of a proposal' (Steunenberg and Dimitrova 1999: 17). While the model helps explain why member states (should) prefer one legislative procedure over another, it does not improve our understanding—as the authors readily concede—on the issues central to this book: why did the legislative procedures evolve the way they did, and, more specifically, why did the member states decide to endow the EP with a prominent legislative role (Steunenberg and Dimitrova 1999: 22)?

11. Pollack (2003: Chapter 4) refers to Jupille's work to back up his arguments (see Jupille 2004). See also Steunenberg and Dimitrova (1999: 21). They quote Moravcsik's (1993, 1998) argument that 'when the consequences of institutional decisions are politically risky, calculable and concrete, national positions will be "instrumental" reflecting the expected influence of institutional reforms on the realization of substantive interests.'

12. In the literature, we can evidence further attempts to explain the extensions of the EP's powers grounded in a policy-seeking approach. Moravcsik and Nicolaïdis's (1999) take on the question of why the EP 'won at Amsterdam' is as follows: Social democratic parties and governments in the Council supported an increase in the EP's legislative powers given that at the time of the Treaty negotiations there existed a left-wing majority of MEPs in the EP. This seemingly 'in-built' left-wing majority rendered the decision to increase the legislative powers of the EP 'easy' for the mainly social democratic chiefs of government during the Amsterdam negotiations. This argument, however, is not supported by data. More fundamentally, however, if the decision of the predominantly left-wing chiefs of government was based on the instrumental calculation that a left-wing majority in the EP would (help) produce legislation closer to the respective governments' ideal points than a right-wing dominated EP, Moravcsik and Nicolaïdis assume that governments are all but far-sighted and have little understanding of the logic of European parliamentary

elections as 'second order national contests' which tend to benefit those parties domestically in the opposition. Hix (2002: 269) thus argues that 'by strengthening the EP's power, the centre-left governments increased the likelihood of centre-right policies at the European level. Hence, Moravcsik and Nicolaïdis's explanation only holds if it includes the assumption that the governments negotiating the Treaty of Amsterdam made a major miscalculation about the future political make-up of the EP.'

13. Moravcsik (1998: 70) argues that '[s]ome national public, elites, and parties are more federalist; others are more nationalist. National positions concerning institutional form reflect these beliefs rather than the substantive consequences of transferring sovereignty.... Such ideas and ideologies may reflect distinctive historical memories of World War II, partisan positions, preferred styles of domestic governance, or broad geopolitical calculations.'

14. V. Rittberger (2001), Baumann and colleagues (1999, 2001) develop a set of predictions congruent with recent developments in rationalist 'neorealist' International Relations theory. They abandon Waltzian 'system level' predictions for state interests derived from the anarchical structure of the international system, and turn to 'unit level' predictions.

15. 'Polity ideas' resemble closest to what Goldstein and Keohane have defined as *principled beliefs*. Principled beliefs are commitments to certain shared values and 'translate fundamental doctrines into guidance for contemporary human action' (Goldstein and Keohane, 1993: 9), for example, by prescribing how an appropriate political order is supposed to look like.

16. This data was retrieved from the Lexis Nexis database (Executive News Service).

17. This data was retrieved from the Bath Information and Data Services—International Bibliography of the Social Sciences (BIDS-IBSS) database.

18. See <http://www.loc.gov/exhibits/gadd/4403.html>, accessed on 05/02/2004, emphasis added.

19. The literature on the EU's democratic credentials is too vast to be adequately summarized here. For some more recent exemplary treaties of the 'government *of* the people' dimension refer to Cederman (2001) and Kielmansegg (2003); for the 'government *by* the people' dimension, see Hix (1998) and Decker (2002); for the 'government *for* the people' dimension, see Majone (2000) and Crombez (2003). For a combination of the different dimensions, see Zürn (1996), Scharpf (1997, 1999, 2001), Höreth (1999), and Moravcsik (2002).

20. Following Majone, the redistribution function 'includes all transfers of resources from one social group to another, as well as the provision of merit goods'; the stabilization function 'is concerned with the preservation of satisfactory levels of economic growth, employment and price stability' through fiscal and monetary policy, labour market policy, and industrial policy. And last, the regulatory function 'attempts to increase the allocative efficiency of the market by correcting various types of market failure: monopoly power, negative externalities, failures of information or an insufficient public good provision' (Majone 1996: 55).

21. See the overviews by Blinder (1987) and Mankiw (1990) for reasons why elected politicians may wish to remove certain decisions from *majoritarian* decision-making mechanisms by creating and delegating powers to *non-majoritarian* institutions.

22. Majone (2000: 289) argues that '[a] less technocratic, more political Commission may enjoy greater democratic legitimacy, but eventually it will have to face the same commitment problem of all democratic governments.'

23. See also Eriksen and Fossum (2000). On deliberative democracy more generally, see Elster (1998), Dryzek (2000), Fishkin and Laslett (2003).

2

Parliamentary Institutions in International Polities: What are the Conditions?

In this chapter I ask whether the democratic deficit, as perceived by political elites, carries behavioural implications and, consequently, affects the way member state governments go about designing and reforming the institutions of the EU polity. To answer this question, we have to know under what conditions political elites are likely to *perceive* that there is a democratic deficit and what they intend to do about reducing or alleviating it. This research strategy does not add another 'standard-setting' perspective to the democratic deficit debate. Rather, by conceptualizing the democratic deficit—as perceived by political elites—as *explanans*, this chapter develops a set of hypotheses which address the behavioural implications of the democratic deficit for instances of institutional design and reform. Furthermore, once it has been established whether or not political elites perceive a democratic deficit and intend to do something about it, we have to know what they will propose for remedying the democratic deficit and how the decision-making process and outcomes of institutional reform endeavours can be accounted for.

This chapter is organized as follows: in Section 2.1, I argue that the democratic deficit, as it is perceived by political elites, can be understood as an asymmetric combination of procedural and consequentialist legitimacy. Throughout the history of political order, legitimacy has been a multi-dimensional concept, composed of different combinations of beliefs in tradition, value-rationality or means-ends calculations. I argue that the notion of *democratic* legitimacy—founded on a combination of procedural and consequentialist legitimacy—is of rather recent origin. In order to understand why not only domestic political systems but equally systems of international institutionalized cooperation may suffer, in the

eyes of political elites, from an asymmetry between procedural and consequentialist legitimacy (the legitimacy deficit), I offer two possible pathways to illuminate the question of *why* and *when* political elites will be
concerned about the legitimacy deficit. According to the first pathway,
transfers of sovereignty from the domestic to the European level, through
acts of pooling and delegation, produce an asymmetry between consequentialist legitimacy and procedural legitimacy: transfers of sovereignty,
while they are considered to enhance the problem-solving capacity of a
polity, nevertheless help undermine democratic mechanisms of interest
representation and accountability at the level of the domestic polity in the
individual member states. I argue that political elites will be aware
that, while enhanced problem-solving capacity increases its consequentialist legitimacy, it does so at the expense of procedural legitimacy. The
resulting asymmetry between procedural and consequentialist legitimacy
thus produces a legitimacy deficit. The second pathway emphasizes the
uncertainty about the possible payoffs of establishing specific institutional
rules on the one hand, and the *type* of institutional issue at stake on the
other. Following Jillson and Eubanks (1984), I distinguish two types of
institutional issues: 'lower level' issues relate to the distribution of power
resources whereas 'higher level' issues relate to the fundamental norms
that provide guidance for the creation of the general institutional structure of a polity. It will be argued that when 'higher level' issues are at
stake—first and foremost during constitutional 'founding moments'—
considerations that reflect the exigencies of procedural legitimacy are
likely to loom large and influence the way political elites think about
and act upon institutional issues. Conversely, when 'lower level' issues
are negotiated (such as decision-making procedures, weighting of votes
etc.) the potential distributive implications of adopting alternative institutional rules are much more easily discernable than in the case of 'higher
level' issues. Consequently, questions about procedural legitimacy are less
pertinent.

In Section 2.2, I push the argument a step further by exploring
political elites' responses to the perceived legitimacy deficit. What will
national governments and political parties propose for its remedy? It will
be shown that political elites hold different views not only on the proposed remedies but also on the perceived intensity or severity of the
legitimacy deficit. This variation is founded on different, analytically
and empirically distinct, legitimating beliefs which allow us to compare
and predict patterns of political elites' responses to alleviate the legitimacy
deficit.

Section 2.3 addresses the question how the perceived legitimacy deficit and the proposed remedies affect the decision-making process and the outcomes of institutional reform instances. What drives governmental decision-makers during IGCs to push for or oppose institutional solutions to the legitimacy deficit? I offer a set of competing explanations based on different modes of action: rational, communicative, and rhetorical.

2.1 Legitimacy and the construction of political order

The maintenance of a system of rule—'the probability that a command with a specific content will be obeyed by a given group of persons' (Weber 1968: 212)—is fatefully dependent on the wilful compliance of the ruled with those exercising domination (see Weber 1992: 7–8). According to Weber (1968: 212), system of rule ('Herrschaft') 'may be based on the most diverse motives of compliance: all the way from simple habituation to the most purely rational calculation of advantage'. Following Weber, democratic theorists have argued for long that compliance with and obedience to systems of rule does not automatically ensue from the '[p]urely material interests and calculations of advantages' (Weber 1968: 213, emphasis in original) stemming from specific policies or political decisions. According to Weber, 'the legitimacy of an order can be guaranteed in two principal ways': the first follows a 'purely subjective' route based on tradition, affection, religion or value-rationality, and the other way is denoted by 'the expectations of specific external effects, that is, by interest situations' (Weber 1968: 33). As in any type of common-purpose organization, the stability and survival of a political system cannot be achieved by negative and positive sanctions, but equally depends on the degree to which its citizens feel bound to obey to authority.[1] For Weber, tradition, custom, affectual ties, material interests, as well as value-rational ('wertrationale') motives play an important role to produce system compliance. Whereas these different motivations for compliance apply to any kind social system, Weber (1968: 213) introduces the concept of *legitimacy* to address the question of compliance in a system of political rule:

[C]ustom, personal advantage, purely affectual or ideational motives of solidarity, do not form a sufficiently reliable basis for a given domination. In addition there is normally a further element, the belief in legitimacy.

Experience shows that in no instance does domination voluntarily limit itself to the appeal to material or affectual or ideal motives as a basis for its continuance. In addition every such system attempts to establish and to cultivate the belief in its legitimacy.

How, then, can political domination be legitimized? Weber advances his famous *trias* of motivations that lead social actors to belief in the legitimacy of systems of rule: rationally grounded, traditionally grounded, and charismatically grounded legitimacy.[2] Each 'pure type...of legitimate domination' (Weber 1968: 215), however, is rarely sufficient to produce legitimacy in and of itself. Weber himself admits 'that "ruling organizations" which belong only to one or another of these pure types are very exceptional' (Weber 1968: 262). Hence, "ruling organizations" (systems of rule) command legitimacy from different sources, albeit to different degrees and combinations:

[I]t should be kept clearly in mind that the basis of every authority, and correspondingly of every kind of willingness to obey, is a *belief*, a belief by virtue of which persons exercising authority are lent prestige. The composition of this belief is seldom altogether simple. In the case of 'legal authority', it is never purely legal. The belief in legality comes to be established and habitual, and this means it is partly traditional. Violation of the tradition may be fatal to it. Furthermore, it has a charismatic element...For republics...striking victories may be dangerous in that they put the victorious general in a favorable position making charismatic claims (Weber 1968: 263).[3]

Democratic theorists[4] underwrite the argument that the legitimacy of political order and, hence, compliance with a given system of rule—domestic and international—is founded on alternative motives which have already been defined in the Introduction: procedural and consequentialist legitimacy. Johnston (1999) and Hurd (1999) argue that if political actors in international politics were only interested in maintaining international political orders as long as they produce certain material benefits or reduce the costs of sustaining cooperation (for instance by lowering transaction costs), we should observe much less compliance with these international political orders. In a study addressing the determinants of domestic elite support for the EU polity, Jachtenfuchs and colleagues (1998) underline the relevance of these two dimensions of democratic legitimacy by referring to Easton's distinction between *diffuse* and *specific* support. Political systems need not only specific support 'caused by interests in relation to a particular policy... [P]olitical systems [also] needed "diffuse support" which may, among other things, originate in the belief of the members of a political system that the latter is legitimate' (Jachtenfuchs et al. 1998: 412). With the terminology introduced here, it can be argued that procedural legitimacy (i.e. the maintenance of political order for reasons that have to do with placing intrinsic value on upholding and promoting democratic procedures) is the difference between compliance based on material incentives (or: consequentialist legitimacy) and the overall degree of compliance with a system of political rule. Compliance C is hence a function F of both procedural legitimacy PL and consequentialist legitimacy CL.

$$F(C) = PL + CL$$

Figure 2.1 presents this argument graphically, adding time as dimension. When the consequentialist legitimacy of a polity decreases over time (e.g. when decisions to transfer sovereignty generate increasing opposition by actors who feel disadvantaged by these decisions) by factor x, the overall amount of compliance decreases only by factor x−y where y is the amount of procedural legitimacy.

In Johnston's own words, procedural '[l]egitimacy is the stickiness that keeps members of an in-group complying with the rules of the power hierarchy even as the material benefits supplied by the power status quo drop off' (Johnston 1999: 6). From this perspective legitimacy requires that potential losers 'accept either that their losses are not so important . . . or that they think there are existing channels and methods for recouping their losses' (Johnston 1999: 6), whereby the relevance of the *procedural* dimension of legitimacy is emphasized.

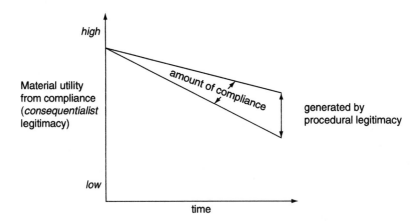

Fig. 2.1 Sources of legitimacy and system compliance
Source: adapted from Johnston (1999)

2.1.1 The legitimacy of political order: past and present

Whereas in present-day democracies the belief in consequentialist and procedural legitimacy generates system compliance, throughout the history of mankind beliefs in the legitimacy of systems of rule have been highly variable. Changes in the content of these beliefs have led to the most profound of transformations in the organization and legitimacy of systems of rule. Hennis (1976) has argued that the legitimacy crises of the sixteenth and seventeenth centuries which have occurred in the context of the English and French religious civil wars have resulted in a struggle to replace the *Divine Rights Theory*[5]—the justificatory basis of absolutist monarchical rule—with the *Consent Theory*, which—for the first time in Stuart England—saw the justification of political rule in the rule of law guaranteed by acts of the English Parliament (e.g. Kluxen 1983 and Ferejohn 1993). The replacement of the Divine Rights Theory with Consent Theory fundamentally altered the foundations of the justification of authority, rendering legitimacy to the argument that the monarch could actually 'do wrong'. Throughout Western Europe, the relevance of the Divine Rights Theory as justificatory basis of political rule gradually eroded and was replaced by the doctrines of the rule of law, popular sovereignty, and nationalism, in different combinations and with varying emphases (e.g. von Beyme 1999: 15–21). Alluding to nationalism and the rivalling legitimating beliefs of popular sovereignty and the monarchic principle, Kielmansegg contends that '[t]he conviction in the legitimacy of a given political order has, practically always, different roots.' (Kielmansegg 1997: 390, author's translation) Returning to Weber's *trias*, Kielmansegg also argues that—in order to understand the persistence of specific legitimating beliefs—the Weberian notion of traditionally-grounded legitimacy is of particular relevance. For example, popular sovereignty, a legitimating belief which is inherent in the notion of the 'democratic constitutional state' ('demokratischer Verfassungsstaat') can today be considered the unrivalled legitimating belief for systems of rule (Hennis 1976: 20); it has achieved a status of taken-for-grantedness:

Decisions taken and regarded legitimate in the past are espoused by way of tradition, in the course of which the original motivation to adopt a certain legitimating belief can vanish from the active consciousness of the populace, and it is tradition which congeals these initial motivations. All social orders lean towards this state; every legitimating belief which persists for a considerable period of time will reach this state so that traditionally-grounded legitimacy reflects the 'stability phase' of a legitimate political order (Kielmansegg 1997: 378, author's translation).

It was in revolutionary America that the double legitimacy requirement combining the notion of popular sovereignty—'government *by* the people' as an expression of procedural legitimacy—and the state's effective promotion of the welfare of its citizens—'government *for* the people'[6] as an expression of consequentialist legitimacy—found its expression in the newly established constitutions of the former colonies declaring their independence from the British Crown. For most Americans, the Revolution meant the abolition of despotic, tyrannical government embodied by colonial rule and its replacement with republican government founded on the rule of the people. These ideas found their most famous expression in a resolution published by Continental Congress on 15 May 1776 and, more famously, in the Declaration of Independence of 4 July 1776.[7] Republicanism in eighteenth-century America equated popular government with the pursuance of the public good and common welfare. As Woods (1998: 56) puts it, '[s]ince in a free government the public good was identical with the people's welfare . . . and founded on the "Common Consent" of the people, the best way of realizing it . . . was to allow the people a maximum voice in the government.' Republican thought in the revolutionary period hence assumed a mutuality of interests between the population and their representatives: 'government *by* the people' thus guaranteed 'government *for* the people'. The Philadelphia Convention of 1787–8 and the adoption of the Constitution for a *United* States of America upheld these two components of legitimacy, while seeking to improve on the deficiencies of the state constitutions, for instance, by instituting a clear separation of powers that would enable an 'energetic' yet not despotic executive (see, for example, Rakove 1997) which Madison espoused elegantly in the Federalist No. 47 (Rakove 2003).

In the aftermath of the Second World War, the state as an agent of wealth redistribution and as public goods provider marks the latest stage in the development of the modern state, covering the way from the state as guarantor of the 'rule of law' to the democratic state with (full) popular participation and representation ('demokratischer Rechtsstaat') and, finally, the modern welfare state ('sozialer Wohlfahrtsstaat').[8] Scharpf employs the terms of *input* and *output* legitimacy to refer to the composite condition for the compliance and maintenance of political order (Scharpf 1970). Input-oriented—or procedural—legitimacy denotes that '[p]olitical choices are legitimate if and because they reflect the "will of the people"— that is, if they can be derived from the authentic preferences of the members of a community' (Scharpf 1999: 6). On the other hand, output-oriented—or consequentialist legitimacy—denotes that 'political choices are legitimate if and because they effectively promote the common welfare of the constituency in question' (Scharpf 1999: 6).

Why is the distinction between procedural and consequentialist legitimacy important for the discussion about the creation and empowerment of the EP? The answer is relatively straightforward: with the gradual growth of the policy-making powers concentrated at the supranational level, the EU has come to exercise functions that, traditionally, belonged to the domain of nation states. Against this background, Robert Dahl has observed that the process of European integration presents the European public and its political leaders with a 'fundamental democratic dilemma' (Dahl 1994: 23) which can be summarized as follows. Wherever and whenever democratic polities are subjected to significant external socio-economic or security challenges which they cannot meet unilaterally, they face a trade-off between, on the one hand, enhancing the capacity of their polity to deal with these challenges effectively by increasing the size of their political unit (through inter-/supranational cooperation) and, on the other hand, the ability to influence the government through direct or indirect participation (which decreases with unit size):

That larger political systems often possess relatively greater capacity to accomplish tasks beyond the capacity of smaller systems leads sometimes to a paradox. In very small political systems a citizen may be able to participate extensively in decisions that do not matter much but cannot participate much in decisions that really matter a great deal; whereas very large systems may be able to cope with problems that matter more to a citizen, the opportunities for the citizen to participate in and greatly influence decisions are vastly reduced (Dahl 1994: 28).[9]

Zürn has aptly described this trade-off as *denationalization* of national polities in a world of complex interdependence (Zürn 1998, 2000). Denationalization defines a state in which spaces constituted by dense transactions transcend national borders and results in a 'weakening link between territorial states and their corresponding national societies' (Zürn 2000: 187). We have seen that Scharpf described the same process in the EU by emphasizing that, with the creation of the internal market and the concomitant dismantling of barriers to the free flow of goods, services and capital, national polities have given up 'boundary control' in order to enhance the output capacity of the larger unit—the EU (see Scharpf 1997, 1999, 2001). What Dahl, Scharpf, Zürn, and other scholars suggest is that in the outgoing twentieth century, democratic self-determination at the national level has, to a large degree, lost its effectiveness. However, to 're-claim' policy-making effectiveness on the European level, for instance, by harmonizing certain social, welfare or taxation policies, the EU still lacks legitimacy given the absence of a collective identity which would make majority rule in the policy areas mentioned appear less threatening. Yet, whatever the actual prospects for this form of transnational legitimacy are, I show in Section 2.2 that political elites are well aware of the asymmetry between consequentialist and procedural legitimacy at the supranational level and have developed alternative conceptions to address this problem.

2.1.2 Pooling, delegation and the legitimacy deficit

Increased transfers of sovereignty have left national democratic processes not unchallenged. The centralization of policy-making at the Community level has increased remarkably since the early days of European integration.[10] Whereas in 1957 only seven out of a possible twenty-eight policy areas had been subject to some policy decision-making on the European level (almost exclusively issues falling into the economic issue arena), fifty years later, Donahue and Pollack (2001: 107), applying the same framework, find that in *none* of the twenty-eight arenas do member states enjoy exclusive national competences. They also show that, in eleven out of the twenty-eight areas, policy decisions are now either taken 'mostly' or 'exclusively' on the Community level whether economic, socio-cultural, politico-constitutional issue or issues relating to the EU's international and external relations. This development has taken place against a background of increasingly potent and powerful supranational institutions, such as the Commission and the European Court of Justice, which are 'marked by an astonishing autonomy... from direct democratic control' (Wessels 1999: 2). This point is underlined by Wessels who argues that the Community's supranational institutions 'are *de jure* and to a large degree *de facto* independent of national governments... [T]his implies that "sovereign" states have to deal with political actors which are outside their immediate control' (Wessels 1996: 21). This state of affairs 'naturally raises the democratic question of how the system of institutions exercising this power is to be controlled and held accountable' (Wessels 1999: 2). The far-reaching competencies of Community institutions, therefore, should pose a formidable concern to national policy-makers with regard to the democratic legitimacy of the evolving European polity. Asked about their satisfaction with the working of democracy in the EU, 50 per cent of the respondents among members of *national* parliaments asked in 1996 (from eleven EU countries) were 'not very satisfied' (40%) or 'not satisfied at all'

(10%). In contrast, when asked about the working of democracy in their own countries, only 20% of the respondents among these national MPs were not satisfied (Wessels 1999: Table 1). The European Commission (1998) has published the results of a survey conducted in 1996 among 'top decision makers'[11] which mirror the perceived (albeit cross-nationally variable) need to reform the Community institutions and make them more democratic (European Commission 1998: 14–15, 31–6 and A.14–A.21). Hence, what is of concern here is not the theoretical or actual possibility of a European transnational democracy, but rather the *belief* or *perception* of political elites that *something has to be done about the perceived 'legitimacy deficit'*. What this 'something' means, however, is the subject of sturdy contestation since different actors perceive the problem of democratic legitimacy through different lenses, a point which will be explored in Section 2.2.

Thus far, it has been argued that legitimacy is a two-dimensional concept: for a polity to command the compliance of its subjects, it has to be considered legitimate from both a procedural and consequentialist point of view. Recurring voluntary decisions by EU member states to transfer sovereignty to a new level of governance have put the existing equilibrium between procedural and consequentialist legitimacy into jeopardy, both at the national level as well as on the level of inter-/supranational governance: while the states fuelled consequentialist legitimacy by pooling and delegating policy competencies thereby endowing supranational institutions with unprecedented decision-making powers, citizen participation and popular self-determination came increasingly under stress in the member states. I have presented some descriptive data which indicates that political elites are aware of the challenges of increased socio-economic cooperation with regard to procedural legitimacy. Consequently, we will expect the pooling or delegation of policy-making competences to be accompanied by proposals of political elites to institute mechanisms to mitigate the perceived loss of democratic self-determination (procedural legitimacy). For example, as a result of the replacement of the unanimity principle (the conventional decision rule in international or intergovernmental bodies) by qualified majority rule, governments of member states can be outvoted; although decisions based on majority rule may improve the decision-making efficiency and policy-making effectiveness, they are likely to trigger a myriad of responses and critical questions about their procedural legitimacy: is the principle of popular sovereignty and democratic self-determination violated when national representatives (legitimized through popular elections) cannot be held accountable (by their electorates) for decisions taken by a 'hostile' majority? Who controls supranational actors to whom decision-making powers have been delegated? The following hypothesis expresses the expected link between transfers of sovereignty through pooling and delegation, the increase in the looming gap between consequentialist and procedural legitimacy.

Hypothesis 1a: legitimacy deficit
Delegation and pooling of national sovereignty will produce an asymmetry between consequentialist and procedural legitimacy (legitimacy deficit).

What are the observable implications of this hypothesis? We have to ask whether transfers of sovereignty through pooling and delegation actually occurred: have the member states transferred decision-making competencies from the realm of their domestic polity to supranational institutions (delegation)? Or have member states committed themselves to sharing of decision-making competencies by adopting mechanisms of majority rule (pooling)? If the answer to either of these questions is positive we would expect political elites in the member states to express concerns about a looming asymmetry between consequentialist and procedural legitimacy. Hence, if the legitimacy deficit hypothesis holds, we would expect member states' political elites to make references to the some of the following questions in periods when decisions to transfer sovereignty loom large:

- *Delegation of sovereignty*: who are supranational institutions accountable to? Who will control them? Can delegation be justified solely by referring to the material gains from cooperation (economic, security, etc.)?
- *Pooling of sovereignty*: how does pooling affect the channels of democratic participation and national parliamentary prerogatives? To whom are national governments accountable when portions of their decision-making powers are pooled?

2.1.3 'Higher' and 'lower level' issues and institution-building

Constitutional design is concerned not only with the question of how institutions can be created to enhance certain individual or collective policy-preferences or the problem-solving capacity of a polity. Constitutional 'founding moments'—the formation of novel systems of 'rules about rules'—are also particularly likely to prominently reflect concerns about matters of procedural legitimacy. Studying the negotiations leading to the adoption of the US Constitution, Jillson and Eubanks argue that the choice of so-called 'higher level' institutions—choices that involve, for instance, the type of political system which is adopted—have little in common with 'lower level' institutional questions which induce actors to compute the distributive implications of alternative institutional choices, such as decision rules, voting rules and rules for representation:

At the "higher" level, the constitution-maker wrestles with general questions concerning the scope, scale, and form appropriate to government. "Will the government have a legislative or an executive focus? Will its legislature be bicameral or unicameral?" As the general institutional design and the relationships that will pertain among its component parts become clear, the constitution-maker moves closer to the realm of practical politics. The questions that dominate this "lower" level of constitutional design concern the regulation of political behavior through rules governing such specific matters as suffrage and voting, eligibility to office and representation.... [Q]uestions at this level are much more likely to be decided with direct reference to the political, economic and social characteristics of the chooser than with reference to philosophical principles' (Jillson and Eubanks 1984: 438).

Studying the motivations of the individual states at the Philadelphia Convention in 1787, Jillson (1988) demonstrates that, in designing the Constitution's fundamental institutions ('higher level' institutions), the participating delegates advanced competing philosophical ideas. A new form of republicanism inspired by the Scottish enlightenment and espoused by the likes of James Madison, Alexander Hamilton, James Wilson, and Governor Morris who advocated a strong central government (*nationalists*) clashed with more traditional versions of republicanism which bred a 'small republic vision' (*localists*). The pursuit of *distributive* goals was an equally important concern for these constitution-makers, especially when they voted on issues affecting the distribution of power and influence within the new government institutions. When, for example, delegates debated the representation of the individual states in the legislature, the smaller states preferred equal representation whereas the larger ones opted for proportional representation in the legislature. The discussion of different types of issues therefore produced different coalitions of states which formed either around an ideological cleavage (e.g. pitting *nationalists* against *localists*) or a material/distributional cleavage (e.g. pitting *large* against *small* states).

Such divisions are familiar in constitution-making episodes in the EU. For example, the re-weighting of votes in the Council, the number of Commissioners per member state, or the number of seats in the EP allocated to each member state cause governments to divide along a distributional cleavage pitting large against small member states. Yet, as will be demonstrated in the ensuing chapters, the question about creating and enhancing the powers of the EP in the supervisory, legislative, and the budgetary realms caused and continues to cause member states to divide along an ideological cleavage pitting proponents of different 'legitimating belief' against each other (see Section 2.2).

Jillson's attempt to demonstrate empirically that political actors do not only calculate the expected distributional consequences of alternative institutions and rules ('lower level' institutional choices), but are also guided by the prescriptive properties of shared beliefs about 'appropriate' and legitimate institutions ('higher level' institutional choices), is theoretically backed-up by Vanberg and Buchanan. While most of the theoretical institutional choice literature sustains the divide between idea-based and material interest-based explanations, they argue that '[h]ow a person chooses among potential alternatives is not only a matter of "what he wants" but also of "what he believes", and for some kinds of choices, an actor's beliefs or theories may play a most crucial role. We suggest that the second element is particularly important for constitutional choices, that is, choices among rules' (Vanberg and Buchanan 1989: 51). Vanberg and Buchanan hence distinguish between an interest-component and a belief- or theory-component 'in almost any choice' and argue that—compared to most ordinary market choices—the belief-component plays a particularly important role in constitutional choices because people's beliefs or theories 'about the working properties of alternative rules or rule-systems, and not just their interests in expected outcomes, are of crucial relevance to their choice behaviour' (Vanberg and Buchanan 1989: 51). Returning to the example from the Philadelphia Convention, the 'extended republic men' (*nationalists*) and 'small republic men' (*localists*) held different beliefs or theories about the optimal scope of government. Conflicts of interests, such as the conflict between small and large states over representation in the legislature, are thus more likely to reflect a rational mode of action which is characterized by distributive bargaining among actors. In contrast, conflicts between alternative shared beliefs or theories about the form of government are more likely to be characterized by actors engaging in a 'discourse about legitimate political ends and means' (Schimmelfennig 2003: 158) in which they bow to the force of the better argument (see Risse 2000).[12] During the construction and reform of constitutional orders, political actors constantly shift between these two levels of debate and conflict. The existing literature about 'constituent assemblies', such as the Philadelphia Convention in 1787 (see Jillson and Eubanks 1984; Jillson 1988; Elster 1994, 2000), the Assemblée Constituante in Paris from 1789–91 (see Elster 1994, 2000) and, equally, the deliberations resulting in the creation and reform of 'Europe's constitutional system' (see Chapters 3–6), underwrites this claim. Hence, where 'constitution-makers' face decisions to delegate or pool sovereignty they will feel compelled to reflect about the *procedural* legitimacy of their institutional choices and, in doing so, they will be guided by 'legitimating beliefs', 'polity ideas' (Jachtenfuchs et al. 1998; Jachtenfuchs 1999) or 'democratic values' (Katz 2001) which provide 'road maps' or 'signposts' for action by guiding political elites' preferences for alternative 'higher' level institutional solutions (see Goldstein and Keohane 1993; B. Rittberger 2001). The following hypothesis summarizes the main claims made in this section:

> *Hypothesis 1b: 'higher level' and 'lower level' institutions*
> When political elites face novel situations—during episodes of constitutional formation—in which constitutional principles ('higher level' issues) have to be established, concerns about procedural legitimacy are likely to feature prominently in political elites' institutional design choices. As a corollary, where institutional choices which have obvious distributive implications are the subject of debate and reform ('lower level' issues), concerns for procedural legitimacy are not likely to be prevalent.

Even if it is possible to conjecture from empirical evidence that political elites perceive the existence of a legitimacy deficit as problematic, or when concerns for procedural legitimacy loom large during constitutional founding moments, this says nothing about how these shared concerns translate into concrete institutional (reform) goals and behaviour. Section 2.2 demonstrates that member state governments and political parties perceive the asymmetry between consequentialist and procedural legitimacy quite differently and consequently advance different proposals as to how the problem should be tackled.

2.2 Legitimating beliefs as prescriptions to alleviate the legitimacy deficit

The main argument of this section runs as follows: when transfers of sovereignty loom, member states provide different interpretations regarding the severity of the legitimacy deficit and also advance different proposals as to how the legitimacy deficit should be alleviated. In this argument, beliefs about legitimate and appropriate forms of supranational governance (legitimating beliefs) are endowed with a crucial role in explaining the formation of actors' goals. Legitimating beliefs are likely candidates to guide actors' institutional choices as they 'express a world view that influences behavior not only directly, by setting standards of appropriateness for behavior, but also indirectly through selective prefabricated links between values that individuals or collectivities habitually rely upon to address specific problems' (Katzenstein 1993: 267).[13] I have argued in the preceding section that—once we view the construction and reform of political orders not *solely* as an exercise which produces benefits which are judged by their instrumental value, but also by its intrinsic value, as an endeavour to produce procedural legitimacy—we have to be receptive to those arguments which policy-makers advance to justify political order: legitimating beliefs. As emphasized above, throughout history legitimating beliefs have varied enormously temporally and across polities.[14] Yet, whereas the notion of liberal democracy, today, is the predominant legitimating belief in the 'developed' world, this by no means implies that the interpretation of this principle for the construction and reform of political orders is necessarily uniform: Peter Katzenstein has argued that '[n]orms work their effects through historically created institutions and experiences' (Katzenstein 1993: 268), and it is obvious that these institutions and experiences differ across countries and even across different groups within societies.

How, then, do legitimating beliefs affect actors' responses to the perceived legitimacy deficit? Recent scholarship has provided students of European integration with extensive material regarding the classification of different legitimating beliefs and their prescriptive value for behaviour ('if actor *A* holds 'legitimating belief' *X*, he is likely to propose *Z*'). Jachtenfuchs and colleagues have developed a taxonomy of legitimating beliefs based on qualitative content analysis of party manifestoes (see Jachtenfuchs et al. 1998; Jachtenfuchs 1999, 2002; Diez 1999). They present four analytically distinct legitimating beliefs labelled: (a) *federal state*, (b) *intergovernmental cooperation*, (c) *economic community* and (d) *network governance*. These four legitimating beliefs are considered ideal types and allow us to derive propositions about the responses political elites are likely to make when they confront situations of pooling and delegation and the concomitant legitimacy deficit.[15] For those adhering to a *federal state* legitimating belief, legitimacy is the expression of popular sovereignty which can be shared across different levels of governance (the state and federal/union level). The *federal state* legitimating belief thus prescribes the establishment of a popularly elected assembly (representing the *people*) alongside mechanisms to represent the composite states at the federal/union level.

In contrast, the *intergovernmental cooperation* legitimating belief is founded on the conception of 'social' legitimacy which vests legitimate rule in the nation. Interstate cooperation and integration is desirable as long as it is protective of a nation's autonomy and does not undermine national democratic process and institutions. The procedural legitimacy of international polities is guaranteed by the representation of member state governments in the European Council and Council of Ministers— other institutional venues and mechanisms to promote procedural legitimacy such as an international or supranational parliamentary body—are not considered desirable.

According to the *economic community* legitimating belief, the legitimacy of a supranational polity is founded upon effective and efficient solutions to allocative problems that can best be solved either via the market mechanism or through delegation to *non-majoritarian* institutions such as independent regulatory agencies.

Turning from content analysis of party manifestoes to survey data of national Members of Parliaments (MPs) on the conceptions of EU democracy, Katz (2001) distinguishes between two ideal types, a 'populist' version of democracy (based on the notion of popular sovereignty and the maximization of the 'public interest' through representative institutions) and a 'liberal' version of democracy (based on the 'Madisonian' idea of limiting power against abuse).[16] For example, support of the populist notion of democracy is indicated by MPs backing of the proposal that the Commission should be chosen by the EP rather than by the national governments. Katz observes that MPs who hold these two different conceptions of democracy come to completely different assessments of the EU's democratic deficit:

> With many political issues, there is agreement regarding the nature of the problem to be solved, even though there may be disagreement concerning the appropriate means or the priority the problem should be accorded. . . . In the case of EU democracy . . . there appears to be disagreement over the proper meaning of democracy, and therefore not simply over what reforms would most improve democracy but indeed over whether particular reforms would make the Union more or less appropriately democratic (Katz 2001: 74).[17]

It follows that supporters of a populist version of democracy or the *federal state* legitimating belief tend to see the empowerment of the EP as a solution to alleviate the legitimacy deficit in order to compensate for the weakening of NPs' control and policy-making functions as response to increased transfers of sovereignty. From this perspective, political elites put a strong emphasis on questions of procedural legitimacy. In contrast, supporters of the *economic community* legitimating belief tend not to perceive the relationship between consequentialist and procedural legitimacy particularly asymmetric as long as pooling and delegation promote the abolition of barriers to trade and enhance economic and decision-making efficiency. Here, political elites put stronger emphasis on consequentialist legitimacy. For adherents of the *intergovernmental cooperation* legitimating belief, issues of procedural legitimacy loom large—as they do for proponents of the *federal state* legitimating belief—yet, the institutional design implications are strikingly different. Among those subscribing to the *intergovernmental cooperation* legitimating belief, proposals for reducing the legitimacy deficit will not be directed at establishing democracy at the supranational level, but rather tend to emphasize that any form of government derives its legitimacy from the domain of national politics, directly through the national parliamentary channel and indirectly through national governments. Table 2.1 contrasts the different legitimating beliefs across different dimensions.

The juxtaposition of different legitimating beliefs shows that it is unlikely that the legitimacy deficit will be uniformly interpreted among political elites and that consequently, the proposals for its reduction are likely to differ substantially. *Hypothesis 2* summarizes the main tenets of this section.

Hypothesis 2: legitimating beliefs
Alternative proposals to create and reform institutions with a view to reducing the asymmetry between procedural and consequentialist legitimacy (the legitimacy deficit) are likely to reflect differences in legitimating beliefs held by different political elites.

In order to empirically scrutinize this hypothesis, we have to find an answer to the question as to *where to look for legitimating beliefs*. In their research, Jachtenfuchs and colleagues have argued that political parties are the primary carriers of legitimating beliefs: not only do political parties themselves constitute markers for alternative legitimating beliefs, political parties also make legitimating beliefs behaviourally relevant since they provide prescriptions for action and political parties have the capacity to pursue them (Jachtenfuchs et al. 1998: 115). The data to assess the legitimating beliefs of parties in government will be mainly based on parliamentary debates on foreign and European policy for the following reasons: first, in contrast to party or election manifestoes which usually provide a

Table 2.1 Legitimating beliefs, democracy, legitimate governance, and the nature of the 'democratic deficit'

Legitimating belief	Federal state	Intergovernmental cooperation	Economic community
Source of legitimacy	Popular sovereignty at state and union/federal level of governance	National sovereignty (sovereignty indivisible)	Economic effectiveness and efficiency
Conception of democracy at the inter-/supranational level	Parliamentary assemblies on state and union/federal level; intergovernmental institution to represent states	Intergovernmental institutions representing member state governments	No particular democratic structures required on supranational level
Nature of the legitimacy deficit	Delegation/pooling produce accountability gap and weaken NPs	Delegation/pooling produce accountability gap and weaken NPs	Economic effectiveness and efficiency guarantee legitimacy
Remedies for the legitimacy deficit	Representative element at EU level considered too weak: EP should be empowered	Legitimacy deficit to be solved domestically (e.g. increasing scrutiny power of NPs)	Indifferent to EP empowerment as long as effectiveness-and efficiency-goals are not hampered

political party's broad outlook on their preferred EU level policies and institutional reform choices, the question of whether or not to support a strengthening of the EP is usually too specific to be covered in these documents. And even if this were the case, party or election manifestoes rarely provide *reasons* for why the EP should or should not be empowered. Politicians are more likely to provide norm-based arguments for or against the empowerment of the EP during parliamentary debates, thereby providing a reliable indicator for both the content of individual legitimating beliefs and the presence of the link between prospective pooling and delegation and the deployment of legitimating beliefs to infuse the discussion about the perceived legitimacy deficit with content.

Second, during parliamentary debates, members of government may feel compelled to declare their goals for prospective European negotiations and consequently pre-commit to a certain course of action. Domestic parliamentary debates thus also reflect exchanges of arguments and attempts by domestic political parties to commit their governments to a particular course of action.

Thus far, I have argued that the creation and empowerment of the EP can be understood by pursuing the avenues as laid out in the earlier sections. Where sovereignty is transferred through pooling and delegation, political elites will be aware of the challenges pooling and delegation pose to domestic channels of interest representation and accountability, producing what political elites come to perceive as the legitimacy deficit. Yet, actors' interpretation of the legitimacy deficit is likely to differ depending on which legitimating belief guides behavioural responses. Alternatively, in times of constitutional 'founding moments' or comprehensive constitutional reformulation or change, where actors will not only be concerned with institutional adjustments on a 'lower level' but face institutional questions of more abstract constitutional nature ('higher level' issues), legitimating beliefs provide *road maps* or *signposts* for actors' institutional preferences.

In this and Section 2.1, I have been chiefly concerned with how political elites come to define their goals in situations where major portions of sovereignty are pooled and delegated either during IGCs or, more 'dramatically', during constitutional founding moments. The argument, thus far, assumes that when political elites encounter such situations they act in accordance with the logic of normative action. Normative action implies that the goals actors choose to pursue are 'the result of [their] normative reasoning and thus a matter of reflective and purpose choice' (Schimmelfennig 2003: 158). Political elites thus reflect on the situation and make a conscious choice about what their preferences are and what type of behaviour is associated with it: 'In making these assessments and choices, the actors do no start from their individual needs and interests and do not calculate how to advance them but reason normatively about what to want and what to do...' (Schimmelfennig 2003: 162). In doing so, actors remain 'within the parameters established by the dominant institutional values' (Peters 1999: 29). I have argued in the preceding sections that these 'parameters' are defined by two components: first, since all member states are liberal democracies, their political elites share the view that the decision-making process at the new level of governance must conform to standards of democratic governance that respect procedures for interest representation and accountability. The translation of these standards of democratic governance into proposals for institutional reform is, however, not uniform: political elites are thus, second, constrained by domestically propagated legitimating beliefs which help them to specify their goals and guide their behaviour geared towards institutional reform.

2.3 Institutional reform outcomes and social action

In this section I will elucidate the interaction among national governments who come together during IGCs to negotiate institutional reforms affecting the EP's control, budgetary, and legislative powers. More specifically, I ask how the commonly shared perception among political elites' about the existence of a 'legitimacy deficit' and domestically held legitimating beliefs impact on the behaviour of national governments during these negotiations and how they affect reform outcomes.

I have argued that normative action best captures political elites' responses to the legitimacy deficit: they reflect on the consequences of transfers of sovereignty for traditional channels of interest representation and accountability by 'borrowing' from both Community-wide and domestically held beliefs about legitimate and appropriate mechanisms of supranational governance. In the remainder of this chapter, I present a set of hypotheses which illuminate the impact of these normative constraints (the legitimacy deficit and domestic legitimating beliefs) on the interaction between member state governments.

2.3.1 The rationalist 'null hypothesis'

The rationalist 'null hypothesis' posits that once national governments enter the negotiations at IGCs, their capacity to act will not be affected by normative constraints such as prevailing community or domestic standards of legitimacy, that is the prevailing concerns about the legitimacy deficit and domestically held legitimating beliefs. Hence, even though representatives of individual member state governments may have felt compelled to express their commitment to a particular standard of legitimacy prior to or during an IGC, absent material threats to push them into compliance, they are likely to pursue their own egoistic or altruistic, ideational or material preferences. The 'null hypothesis' is based on the assumption that interaction among national governments will reflect bargaining and the exchange of threats and promises and that the outcome will mirror the constellation of the preferences of member state governments and their relative power (Schimmelfennig 2003: 158). The relative power of actors rests on resources which can be 'extra-politics', that is, they exist independently of the political system (see Elster 2000: 392) and can be attributed to the characteristics of a particular actor or situation—such as the degree of impatience and salience or the availability of outside options—or they arise out of the negotiating context at hand, such as opportunities for issue-linkages and logrolling.

Hypothesis 3: The 'null hypothesis'
Decision-making is characterized by bargaining about the powers of the EP and the outcome reflects the constellation of preferences and relative bargaining power of member state governments.

2.3.2 The communicative action hypothesis

While the 'null hypothesis' discards the role and effectiveness of norm-based arguments in convincing other actors about one's preferred courses of action, the communicative action hypothesis posits just that: actors argue 'to convince each other to change their causal or principled beliefs in order to reach a reasoned consensus... Successful arguing means that the "better argument" carries the day, while one's (material) bargaining power becomes less relevant' (Risse 2000: 9). In the communicative mode of action actors' interests and identities are no longer fixed, 'but subject to interrogation and challenges and, thus, to change.... Since the validity claims of identities and interests are at stake in theoretical and practical discourses, an argumentative consensus has constitutive effects on actors' (Risse 2000: 10). The difference to the rational mode of action is evident: while in the communicative mode actors are prepared to change their preferences, interests, and identities given the power of better argument, in the rational mode actors' identities and preferences remain fixed.

Hypothesis 4: Communicative action
Decision-making is characterized by a truth-seeking discourse on the appropriate role of the EP in the Community polity as a result of which member state governments reach a reasoned consensus.

2.3.3 The rhetorical action hypothesis

The rhetorical mode of action combines elements of the rational and communicative action hypotheses. Since I have placed such strong emphasis on norms or 'standards of legitimacy', typified by the claim that political elites share the perception of a legitimacy deficit, once transfers of sovereignty loom and advance domestically held legitimating beliefs to propose remedies to this deficit, we should expect that these 'standards' affect the interaction among member state governments at IGCs. The logic of rhetorical action, according to Schimmelfennig (2003: 193), 'draws on a strategic conception of rules that combines a social, ideational ontology with the assumption of rational action; it postulates that social actors use and exchange arguments based on identities, values, and norms institutionalized in their environment to defend their political claims and to persuade their audience and their opponents to accept these claims and to act accordingly.'

'Why is rhetorical action relevant in politics?' asks Schimmelfennig (2003: 206) and argues that rhetorical action—the strategic use of norm-based arguments—gains relevance for three reasons:

- First, political actors live and act in a 'community environment' (Schimmelfennig 2003: 206) which is defined by the values and norms shared by the members of the community. These norms and values determine, in turn, the prevailing standard of legitimacy which determines the type of political purposes, programmes, and actions considered desirable and acceptable within the community. Consequently, political actors are seen to pursue legitimate goals to the degree that their political behaviour and goals conform to the standard.
- Second, in a community environment, actors need legitimacy to act successfully. The logic of rhetorical action does not require political actors to have internalized a particular standard of legitimacy. Whatever goals political actors pursue and whether they are motivated egoistically or altruistically, in a community environment, they must pay tribute to the prevailing standard(s) of legitimacy in order to effectively pursue their goals. Hence, 'the more legitimate the actors and their goals are (or

appear) in the light of the community standard, the better they are able to realize their political objectives. Conversely, actors regarded as illegitimate and pursuing illegitimate goals . . . will face severe difficulties in inducing other actors to support them and cooperate with them' (Schimmelfennig 2003: 207)

- Third, when actors pursue particular actions or goals, they strive to make their actions or goals appear legitimate by using arguments in a strategic fashion and thereby aim at persuading the audience of the legitimacy to support their actions and goals. Thus, '[b]y skilfully manipulating the community's standard of legitimacy through rhetoric, political actors are able to gain and advantage over their competitors . . . On the other hand, political actors come under pressure if their competitors are able to demonstrate, and to persuade the public, that they violate the community's standard of legitimacy' (Schimmelfennig 2003: 208). Rhetorical action thus 'changes the structure of bargaining power in favour of those actors that possess and pursue preferences in line with . . . the standard of legitimacy' (Schimmelfennig 2003: 208).

How does rhetorical action work? In the absence of formal sanctions or material threats, why do states comply with the arguments advanced by their opponents instead of disregarding them? Johnston observes that conformity to norms may come 'from a recognition that there are social rewards or punishment that come with either accepting or ignoring these norms. That is, there are cognitive and social "goods" that actors would like to maximize (self-esteem or status, for example) and that can only be maximized if they engage in behavior that is observed and rewarded by those who have internalized in-group norms and values' (Johnston 1999: 8–9). Schimmelfennig advances a similar argument to illuminate the question why standards of legitimacy exercise a powerful effect on state behaviour even though they may hold interests that deviate from these standards. He thus also argues that the compliance problem cannot merely be reduced to the presence of material threats or sanctions:

[I]t is often assumed that actors comply with the rules in order to avoid coercive sanctions imposing potentially infinite costs on them. In the public choice perspective, political actors operate under the constraint that voters may not reelect them if they deviate from the standard of legitimacy. Both perspectives, however, do not capture the core of the compliance problem in international relations. . . . [M]ost international political issues are exempt from the reelection constraint either because voters are not sufficiently informed about or interested in these issues or because they escape effective control by national constituencies and legislatures. (Schimmelfennig 2001a: 64)

The decision of member states to support or oppose the creation and empowerment of the EP constitutes only one of many sets of decisions that are likely to be taken during an IGC. Consequently, it is reasonable to assume that, for example, NPs shun away from threatening non-ratification over a single issue among a larger package even if government representatives refrained from behaving in line with the behaviour prescribed by the domestically prevalent legitimating belief on the EP question. Hence, when material threats (like the non-ratification threat) do not explain why governments comply with a legitimating belief, *soft* mechanisms of social influence may help us account for pro-norm behaviour *in the absence of sanctions and material threats.* According to Johnston (2001: 499), '[s]ocial influence refers to a class of microprocesses that elicit pro-norm behavior through the distribution of social rewards and punishments.' On the reward side, psychological well-being, status, a sense of belonging, a sense of well-being derived from conformity with role expectations belong to this class of microprocesses; some of the microprocesses on the punishment side include shaming, shunning, exclusion, humiliation, and dissonance derived from actions inconsistent with role and identity. Thus, social influence "works"—it produces social pressure—because members of a community are 'concerned with their image and reputation in the community and do not want to be regarded as...illegitimate' (Schimmelfennig 2003: 218).[18] Among the microprocesses inducing compliance with a standard of legitimacy, *shaming* features among the most prominent. Shaming refers to the 'public exposure of illegitimate goals and behaviors' (Schimmelfennig 2003: 219). For shaming to be effective, actors must have committed to a particular standard of legitimacy, yet, it is irrelevant whether this commitment is motivated by instrumental reasons or a belief in the rightfulness of the standard of legitimacy. When actors find themselves in a decision-making situation in which their self-interest conflicts with the prevailing standard of legitimacy other members of the community will shame them into complying with the prevailing standard of legitimacy. They do so by 'exposing the discrepancy between their declared commitment and their current preferences and behaviour' (Schimmelfennig 2003: 219). The actors shaming recalcitrant members of the community into compliance do not necessarily have to be, in the case at hand, other member state governments, but can be domestic actors—such as parliamentary party groups—who wish to see *their* government comply with the domestically prevailing standard of legitimacy. Hence, it is not only likely that governments feel compelled to justify their actions before various audiences but also that these audiences may strive to shame governments who do not support *their* standard of legitimacy into compliance.

How can an actor who was shamed into compliance be identified? Schimmelfennig (2003: 220) argues that shamed rhetorical actors try to evade disapproval by other community members and seek to refrain from conforming to 'legitimate' behaviour, that is, behaviour prescribed by the prevailing standard of legitimacy: 'They may, for instance, downplay the community values and norms or reinterpret them to their advantage, question their relevance in the given context, or bring up competing community values and norms that back their own preferences.'

The effectiveness of social influence is affected by a number of conditions:

- First, states are sensitive to the social rewards and punishments of a group to which they belong or aspire to belong, that is social influence is 'only effective *inside the actor's in-group or community* (Schimmelfennig 2003: 218, emphasis in original).
- Second, social influence is effective the more legitimate the members of a community perceive a particular standard of legitimacy to be. The degree of legitimacy is affected by the prior commitment of actors to this standard, the specificity of the standard (does the standard offer clear behavioural prescriptions?),[19] and the authoritativeness of its source.
- Third, resonance affects the effectiveness of social influence and consequently enforces the compliance-pull of a particular standard of legitimacy: according to Schimmelfennig (2003: 218–19), 'social influence is most effective if actors truly believe in, or are seriously committed to the community values and norms... [S]ocial influence to promote international rules will be easier also if a state's domestic values and norms match or harmonize with these rules.'

In the case at hand, *two communities* can be identified which constrain the range of possible actions and outcomes. Within the two communities different standards of legitimacy operate which can be either complementary or conflicting. On the one hand, the member states form a *community of states* which is 'founded on the principles of liberty, democracy, respect for human rights and fundamental freedoms, and the rule of law' (Article 6 of the Treaty on European Union, TEU) and thereby they can be considered to share a set of fundamental values and norms (see Schimmelfennig, 2001b: 7). The observation that all member states of the EU are liberal democracies suggests that one standard of legitimacy shared by all member states posits that state-like polities should be democratically organized: they should conform to standards of democratic governance that respect procedures for interest representation and accountability.[20] On the other hand, each member state is also part of a *domestic community* which defines its own standard of legitimacy. As demonstrated in Section 2.2, domestic political parties hold different legitimating beliefs against which government action is assessed and evaluated, and in the light of which each government has to justify its action. It is conceivable that governments may be caught between conflicting legitimating beliefs on the level of the community of states and the domestic community. As a result, governments may find themselves in a situation where they have to justify their behaviour before different audiences—one interstate, one domestic—and potentially employ different arguments in order to appear compliant with the standards of legitimacy operating on different levels.

With a view to the *interstate level*, it can be expected, for instance, that states which committed themselves to the empowerment of the EP employ the argument that—as a result of transferring sovereignty to the supranational level—the supranational polity has to conform to standards of democratic governance (a standard of legitimacy shared across members of the interstate community) and that the EP needs to be strengthened as a result. In turn, this argument is likely to put social pressure on recalcitrant member states—the proponents of the *intergovernmental cooperation* and *economic community* legitimating belief. However, they can be expected to counter claims that strengthening the EP is the only solution to pay tribute to standards of democratic governance.

On the *domestic level*, national governments face a domestic parliamentary audience which evaluates their actions against the benchmark of domestically prevailing legitimating beliefs. For instance, we can expect that where government and domestic audience are proponents of the *federal state* legitimating belief, the domestic audience is likely to be most pleased with the outcome of an empowered EP. Where institutional reform outcomes are at odds with the legitimating beliefs held by a government and its domestic audience, the government does not only have to suffer from the unpleasant experience of having been shamed into compliance by other states, it also has to explain the reform outcome to a critical domestic audience. This is most likely to be the case for governments and audiences holding an *intergovernmental cooperation* or *economic community* legitimating beliefs. Consequently, it can be expected that where national governments have domestically committed to the *intergovernmental cooperation* legitimating belief, they are likely to downplay transfers of sovereignty, stress the material benefits of cooperation, emphasize that domestic channels of democratic representation and accountability have not been negatively affected by integration, and argue that whatever powers the EP has acquired, they can be considered negligible. Where governments have committed to the *economic community* legitimating belief, transfers of sovereignty will be justified by the expected economically desirable results and by their efficiency-enhancing effects. Any attempt to 'democratize' Community institutions will be downplayed and presented as negligible as far as it affects the effectiveness of policies and/or efficient decision-making.

> *Hypothesis 5: Rhetorical action*
> Decision-making is characterized by the strategic use of arguments through which member state governments seek to justify and realize their own preferences regarding the powers of the EP. Proponents of the *federal state* 'legitimating belief'—appealing to community values—exercise social pressure on recalcitrant states with the aim to shame them into acquiescing to the EP's empowerment. Recalcitrant member states will downplay the outcomes, question their relevance or reinterpret them to their advantage in the light of domestic opposition.

2.4 Summary

In this chapter, we have travelled a considerable distance: in Section 2.1, the question has been addressed when and under what conditions we can expect political elites and national governments to perceive a legitimacy deficit which triggers the search for behavioural responses. In Section 2.2, I have argued that the behavioural responses by national governments are likely to reflect or be rooted in domestically held legitimating beliefs. In Section 2.3, it has been argued that when member states governments 'talk the talk' which is expected of them by their domestic audience (such as political parties in government), they may also be forced to 'walk the walk' as a response to social influence (rhetorical action hypothesis). However, the possibility cannot be discarded that national governments reach a reasoned consensus on the question of the empowerment of the EP mirrored in a convergence of initially diverging preferences derived from alternative legitimating beliefs (communicative action hypothesis). It is also conceivable, however, that the negotiations among member state governments is characterized by bargaining, the outcomes reflecting the constellation of preferences and relative bargaining power of member state governments (rational action hypothesis).

The arguments presented in this chapter are summarized in Table 2.2. The theory developed in this chapter will be subjected to empirical

Table 2.2 Summary of the main arguments

1st theory building-block Why and when do political elites perceive a legitimacy deficit?	*Hypothesis 1a: Legitimacy deficit* Delegation and pooling of national will produce an asymmetry between consequentialist and procedural legitimacy (legitimacy deficit). *Hypothesis 1b: 'Higher level' and 'lower level' institutions* When political elites face novel situations – during episodes of constitutional formation – in which constitutional principles ('higher level' issues) have to be established concerns about procedural legitimacy are likely to feature prominently in political elites' institutional design choices. As a corollary, where institutional choices which have obvious distributive implications are the subject of debate and reform ('lower level' issues), concerns for procedural legitimacy are not likely to be prevalent.
2nd theory building-block How do political elites evaluate the legitimacy deficit and what remedies do they propose?	*Hypothesis 2: Legitimating beliefs* Alternative proposals to create and reform institutions with a view to reducing the asymmetry between procedural and consequentialist legitimacy (the legitimacy deficit) are likely to reflect differences in legitimating beliefs held by different political elites.
3rd theory building-block What mode of action drives decision-making between member state governments at IGCs? How do modes of action affect institutional reform outcomes?	*Hypothesis 3: 'Null hypothesis'* Decision-making is characterised by bargaining about the powers of the European Parliament and the outcome reflects the constellation of preferences and relative bargaining power of member state governments.

(Continues)

Table 2.2 (*Continued*)

Hypothesis 4: Communicative action Decision-making is characterised by a truth-seeking discourse on the appropriate role of the European Parliament in the Community polity as a result of which member state governments reach a reasoned consensus.
Hypothesis 5: Rhetorical action Decision-making is characterised by the strategic use of arguments through which member state governments seek to justify and realise their own preferences regarding the powers of the European Parliament. Proponents of the *Federal State* legitimating belief – appealing to community values – exercise social pressure on recalcitrant states with the aim to shame them into acquiescing to the Parliament's empowerment. Recalcitrant member states will downplay the outcomes, question their relevance or reinterpret them to their advantage in the light of domestic opposition

scrutiny in the subsequent chapters by employing three case studies, each covering a landmark in the development of the EP's powers. Chapter 3 will look at the initial creation of the EP's 'forerunner', the CA of the ECSC and the delegation of control powers vis-à-vis the HA (predecessor of the Commission). One additional comment concerning Chapter 3 is neces- sary: the notion of a constitutional 'founding moment' (an instance dur- ing which debates about 'higher' level institutions feature prominently) undoubtedly applies to the creation of the ECSC; not only was a new institutional setting with 'quasi-constitutional institutions' (Moravcsik 1998: 2) introduced (a parliamentary institution, a court of law, an 'execu- tive' authority), the ECSC also established a systems of 'rules about rules', by which is meant a set of rules was laid down which governed the making of 'secondary' rules such as regulations which were binding on the mem- ber states. *Hypothesis 1b* has been introduced to demonstrate the applic- ability of theories of constitutional choice from the domain of domestic politics to the sphere of international politics. Hence, the ECSC case will show that the literature on constitutional choice developed in the context of the founding of the French and US constitutions helps us to explain the type (and sequence) of institutional choices made in establishing the ECSC.

Notes

1. In *Political Man* (1960), S. M. Lipset has brought this line of thought back in the political science literature.
2. These three pure types of legitimate rule are considered sufficiently familiar; thus they will not be explored here in detail. The *locus classicus* is Weber (1968: Chapter III).
3. Schmitter (2001: 1) has defined legitimacy as 'a shared expectation among actors in an arrangement of asymmetric power, such that the actions of those who rule are accepted voluntarily by those who are ruled because the latter are convinced that the actions of the former conform to pre-established norms.' According to Schmitter, legitimacy thus converts power into authority—*Macht* into *Herrschaft*—and thus establishes an obligation to obey and a right to rule.
4. Many democratic theorists argue that the maintenance of and compliance with systems of governance is ensured by balancing the *procedural* and *consequentialist* legitimacy of political order (Weber 1968; Scharpf 1970, 1999; Schmidt 2000). *Procedural* (or input-oriented) legitimacy emphasizes the condition of 'government by the people' which stipulates that '[p]olitical choices are legitimate if and because they reflect the "will of the people"—that is, if they can be derived from the authentic preferences of the members of a community' (Scharpf 1999: 6), while *consequentialist* (or output-oriented) legitimacy emphasizes the condition of 'government for the people' which defines that 'political choices are legitimate if and because they effectively promote the common welfare of the constituency in question.' (Scharpf 1999: 6). With a view to assess the democratic credentials of the EU, Carter and Scott (1998) and Hix (1998), for example, emphasize the *procedural* dimension of the democratic deficit (or 'non'-deficit) whereas Majone (1996, 2000) advances a *consequentialist* interpretation of the Community's democratic credentials, and Scharpf (1997, 1999, 2001) opts for an 'integrated' approach which combines both *procedural* (input) and *consequentialist* (output) elements.
5. The so-called *ius divinum* stipulates that the monarch's authority is derived directly from God.
6. To use Abraham Lincoln's famous 'trilogy' in his Gettysburg address of 19 November 1863, during the American Civil War: 'It is rather for us to be here dedicated to the great task remaining before us—that from these honored dead we take increased devotion to that cause for which they here gave the last full measure of devotion—that we here highly resolve that these dead shall not have died in vain; that this nation shall have a new birth of freedom; and that this government *of* the people, *by*

the people, *for* the people, shall not perish from the earth' (see <http://www.loc.gov/exhibits/gadd/4403.html>, accessed 6 September 2002, emphasis added).

7. In the resolution of 15 May 1776, the Continental Congress resolved that 'the Exercise of every kind of Authority under the . . . Crown should be totally suppressed, and all the Powers of Government exerted under the Authority of the People of the Colonies' (Adams Electronic Archive, Autobiography of John Adams, <http://www.masshist.org/digitaladams/aea/cfm/doc.cfm?id=A1_35>, accessed 4 July 2004). Asked whether the resolution is 'a Machine for the fabrication of Independence', John Adams writes: 'I said, smiling, I thought it was independence itself. . . . '

8. See Guggenberger (1995).

9. Dahl and Tufte (1973) and Dahl (1989, 1999) have made similar points in earlier works. Dahl (1989: 319) argues that a 'country's economic life, physical environment, national security, and survival are highly, and probably increasingly, dependent on actors and actions that are outside the country's boundaries and not directly subject to its government. Thus the members of the demos cannot employ their national government . . . to exercise direct control over external actors whose decisions bear critically on their lives.'

10. See Schmitter (1996), Fligstein and McNichol (1998), and Donahue and Pollack (2001).

11. In the Commission survey, the group of 'top decision makers' comprises elected politicians, such as members of NPs and the EP, senior national civil servants in all member states, leaders of business and labour associations, individuals playing a leading role in the academic, cultural or religious life of their respective countries.

12. See, for example, Elster (1994, 2000) for a discussion and application of 'bargaining' and 'arguing' modes in constituent assemblies.

13. See also DiMaggio and Powell (1991). Abromeit (1995, 2000), Jachtenfuchs et al. (1998), and Jachtenfuchs (1999, 2002) emphasize that variation in justifications of legitimate political order stems from alternative 'doctrines of sovereignty' (Abromeit) or 'polity ideas' (Jachtenfuchs and collaborators) which vary across or even within nation states as a result of different political cultures.

14. See, for example, Hennis (1976), Kielmansegg (1997) and Ferejohn (1993).

15. See Jachtenfuchs (1999: 129–37). The discussion will be limited to the first three 'legitimating beliefs' (excluding the *network* legitimating belief) because, thus far, they have provided the most prominent *signposts* for political actors' preferences towards institutional design and reform (see Jachtenfuchs et al. 1998; Jachtenfuchs 1999).

16. See Riker (1982) for an analogy of these two versions of democracy.

17. A survey commanded by the European Commission among European 'Top Decision Makers' in which questions were asked with regard to the balance of power between the EU institutions corroborates these findings (European Commission 1998). For example, when top decision makers were asked about whether the EU should have a government responsible to the EP, there is a stark split not only on an aggregate level but also within individual member states. Whereas the founding member states appear to be more 'populist' by having a majority of its top decision makers supporting this idea, the Nordic countries, Ireland, and the UK show opposition to this idea (European Commission 1998: A.18).

18. 'I believe the answer is X, but everybody else said Y, and I don't want to rock the boat, so I'll say Y'. Or to paraphrase Schimmelfennig (2003: 218): 'If community member P is able to demonstrate that member O violates the community standard of legitimacy to which he subscribed, O will be induced to conform with the standard.'

19. The more specific a particular standard of legitimacy, the better actors understand the concomitant behavioural prescriptions and prohibitions (see Legro 1997: 34).

20. This argument is also in line with the first hypothesis presented in Section 3.1.

PART II

The European Parliament's Power Trias

3

The Origins of the Common Assembly of the European Coal and Steel Community

Initially dismissed as a democratic window-dresser and talking shop which possessed only few 'negative' powers, such as the right to censure the High Authority of the ECSC (HA), and no 'positive' powers, such as to actively influence the policy-making process, over time the EP developed into an institution possessing far-reaching powers in the budgetary and legislative sphere. Despite its seemingly inconsequential 'infancy' years, the EP would not possess the powers presently at its disposal if the founding 'Six'[1] had not considered the inclusion of a parliamentary body in the first place. In stark contrast to other international parliamentary assemblies, the CA must appear as an 'oddity': its main function was that of scrutinizing, controlling and, if deemed necessary, censuring a supranational institution, the HA, forerunner of the Commission. Which other parliamentary institution in the universe of institutionalized international cooperation exercised tasks of similar kinds? In this chapter, I explain why, from the start of the European integration 'enterprise', the founding states contemplated the creation of the CA, and why this body was endowed with supervisory powers rather than budgetary and legislative powers at the outset. In Section 3.1 of this chapter, I demonstrate that the prospect of delegation of national sovereignty to a supranational institution, the HA of the ECSC, triggered concerns among government representatives negotiating the treaty about the procedural legitimacy of the new supranational polity and it will be conjectured from the empirical evidence that political elites perceived a legitimacy deficit that they wished to alleviate. In Section 3.2, it will be shown that—among the 'Six'—concerns about the legitimacy deficit were all but uniform. I thus investigate the different solutions that were brought forward to alleviate the legitimacy deficit. In Section 3.3, I ask how the behaviour and inter-action among the different delegations can be best accounted for during the negotiations leading to the adoption of the Treaty of Paris on 18 April 1951.

3.1 The Schuman Plan and the legitimacy deficit

In the ensuing paragraphs, I assess the value of the independent variable in *hypothesis 1a*: did the 'Six' transfer sovereignty to the supranational level? If the answer to this question is positive, we expect this to trigger political elites to express concerns about the procedural legitimacy of domestic and Community level governance.

> Hypothesis 1a: legitimacy deficit
> Delegation and pooling of national sovereignty will produce an asym-metry between consequentialist and procedural legitimacy (legitimacy deficit).

3.1.1 A way out of the intergovernmental trap: 'A Bold, Constructive Act'

The Oxford English Dictionary (OED) defines the term *supranational* as 'having power, authority, or influence that overrides or transcends national boundaries, governments, or institutions.'[2] According to Thie-meyer, the ECSC was the first supranational organization in the history of international cooperation where national governments decided to delegate 'previously national competencies in the coal and steel sectors [to the new organization]' (Thiemeyer 1998: 6).[3] Much has been written on Monnet's *Schuman Plan*, its 'intellectual predecessors' and the motives that drove the key actors towards proposing and accepting it.[4] I will offer only a cursory overview of some of the personal and contextual forces that had an effect on the content and timing of the Schuman Plan.

In his *Memoirs*, Monnet, the mastermind behind the Schuman Plan, has made ample references to the deadlock experienced as a result of post-war efforts to establish a lasting and effective system of international cooper-ation. The various security and economic challenges Western Europe faced at the time were not met with adequate international 'organizational' responses. One of the major 'culprits' identified by Monnet which obstructed progress in this respect was the intergovernmental nature of existing organizations:

It was while I was in Washington on that occasion that the Convention establishing the OEEC [Organization for European Economic Cooperation] was drafted and signed in Paris. When I studied it, I could not help seeing the intrinsic weakness of a system that went no further than mere co-operation between governments. One single line in Article 14...prevented any kind of joint action: 'Unless the Organization otherwise agrees for special cases, decisions shall be taken by mutual agreements of all the members'. (Monnet 1978: 271–2).

Not only the OEEC, also the Council of Europe proved to be a 'lame duck' despite the fact that it attracted all the 'mighty' powers of the European concert of states. When the preparations were being made for a great congress at The Hague in May 1948 under the chairmanship of Winston Churchill, Monnet—in hindsight—confessed that he paid 'little attention to the Hague Congress' and claimed that 'its enthusiastic resolutions; which a year later led to the founding of the Council of Europe, confirmed my belief that this approach would lead nowhere' (Monnet 1978: 273). However, the Council of Europe evoked hopes. As Monnet's long-term assistant and biographer Duchêne (1994: 187, emphasis in the original) noted:

A romantic even as pragmatic as Spaak believed for a short while, when the Council of Europe's Consultative Assembly was set up in 1949, that it was a *"constituante"*, meaning...an echo of the Third Estate, which in 1789 seized power from the limp hand of Louis XVI. In fact, the British insistence on the national veto in the Council of Ministers left the limp hand to the Consultative Assembly, not the governments. Though the assembly attracted glittering names, it soon became a byword as talking-shop.

On paper, the Council of Europe consisted of a Consultative Assembly and a Committee of Ministers and thus 'appeared to be an embryonic federal government', while 'in reality it was a discussion group of national leaders' (Scalingi 1980: 14).[5] Scaligni has argued that from the moment of its inception 'the Assembly had no authority to convert proposals into laws, no constituency to whom it could appeal for support, and no executive to implement decisions.... [T]he Consultative Assembly lacked any constitutional basis for expanding its powers or for substituting elected delegates for appointed ones' (Scalingi 1980: 14–15). Real decision-making power was vested in the intergovernmental Committee of Ministers where decisions were taken by unanimity. As far as the unanimity decision rule was concerned, Monnet did not hide his scepticism. 'At the Council of Europe', he argued, 'spectacular resolutions had been passed amid great acclaim. "The aim and goal of the Council of Europe", said one of them, "is the creation of a political authority with limited functions but real powers." This text was proposed by a British Labour Party delegate, R.W.G. Mackay. It was sent to the Committee of Ministers, and there disappeared without trace' (Monnet 1978: 281–2). A proposal to establish a Public Authority for European Steel by Paul Reynaud[6] submitted to the Council of Europe's Consultative Assembly suffered a similar fate.[7]

Monnet's verdict on the decision-making capacity of the above-mentioned organizations in general, and the 'intergovernmental method' in particular was damaging: for Monnet (1978: 281), 'inter-governmental systems, already weakened by the compromises built into them, were quickly paralysed by the rule that all decisions must be unanimous.' What could be done to overcome the paralysis of unanimity? Monnet states his solution clearly and unmistakably: *'National sovereignty would have to be tackled more boldly and on a narrower front'* (1978: 274, emphasis added). The 'Monnet Method', which essentially implied a sector-by-sector, gradual delegation of national sovereignty, was born. For Monnet, the attributes 'sectoral' and 'gradual' were the key to make cooperation and delegation manageable.[8] In a conversation with German Chancellor Konrad Adenauer, shortly after the French Minister for Foreign Affairs Robert Schuman announced the plan on 9 May 1950, Monnet defended his sectoral approach, claiming that '[o]ne of the problems of the past undertakings was the attempt to construct a federation of national sovereignties. Instead one should create a supranational authority...The nation states would not accept to transfer a part of their sovereignty unless for a common good, for a clearly defined task.[9] But, which sectors to opt for? Where would national governments be most willing to give up a portion of their national sovereignty? For Monnet, the choice of coal and steel was driven by a combination of economic and security motives (Lynch 1988). In his memoirs, Monnet expressed these concerns lucidly, referring to the international political situation and the yet uncertain role Germany was going to play in the midst of the looming block-confrontation between East and West.

I can read in [my notes] the anxiety that weighed on Europe five years after the war: the fear that if we did nothing we should soon face war again. Germany would not be its instigator this time, but its prize. So Germany must cease to be a potential prize, and instead become a link... What could be done to link France and Germany, and implant a common interest between them, before it was too late? (Monnet 1978: 289).

The plan elaborated by Monnet was also in pursuit of economic objectives which were, however, closely linked to concerns about 'relative gains' and, thus, matters of security: if the German economy recovered and modernized faster than the French, this would not only be an economic but also a potential security threat to France. A key objective for the French was to 'decartelize' the production of coal and steel in Germany, 'not so much to encourage competition, which could only strengthen the German economy over the long run, but to break up a potential concentration of monopoly' (Gillingham 2003: 25).[10] Lynch (1988: 119–20) writes that the greatest concern for the French government was that it saw itself powerless 'to increase coal production in the Ruhr. The controls which had existed since the war... could only fix the quantity of coal and coke available for export. They took no account of what coal Germany might import... Monnet's fear was that Germany would have every incentive to limit its own coal production and be in a stronger position than France to import coal from the United States.' How could France square its economic-and security-induced concerns of a rising German economic power in an unsettled international economic and security environment? Lynch (1988: 120) writes that '[i]f the French government was powerless to influence what happened in the Ruhr, the French steel industry was in an even weaker position. Some control had to be found which was above governments and was stronger and more permanent than cartels. It was Paul Reuter who provided the legal answer in the form of a supranational High Authority whose decisions would be binding on governments.'[11]

Given these economic-and security-induced pressures for closer cooperation among the Western European nations in general, and France and Germany more specifically, numerous proposals to establish closer cooperation between France and Germany—including proposals for cooperation in the coal and steel sectors—had been launched on both sides of the Rhine since the late 1940s,[12] yet none of these gained the necessary momentum. With time pressing for a French foreign policy initiative towards Germany in the light of British and US proposals to ease restrictions on German steel quotas (which appeared particularly threatening to French security and its economy), Monnet launched his initiative just before the allied foreign ministers met in London on 10 May 1950 (Küsters 1988: 74). Schuman, who was burdened to present his allied counterparts with a proposal regarding the 'German problem', was delighted to have the Schuman Plan, drafted by Monnet, ready at hand for presentation. According to Duchêne, the Schuman Plan came 'as a shock' although it seemed to have been launched 'on a thousand lips' (Duchêne 1994: 203). The plan, officially announced by Schuman on 9 May 1950 in the Quai d'Orsay, combined economic and security-driven motives to establish a new form of supranational, sector-driven interstate cooperation combining different elements that had been floating around for some time, but which hitherto had never been put together in the 'right' way and presented at the 'right' time. Schuman and Monnet referred to the plan as a 'bold, constructive act'[13] and Duchêne labelled it a 'break with the past' in the light of its supranational quality (Duchêne 1994: 205). The *conditio sina qua non* of the plan was that the prospective member states of the ECSC accept the *delegation* of sovereignty (in the respective policy sectors) to a supranational HA which was to have the power to issue decisions which were binding for the member states. The relevant passage of the Schuman Plan declaration of 9 May 1950 reads as follows:

Par la mise en commun de productions de base et l'institution d'une Haute Autorité nouvelle, dont les décisions lieront la France, l'Allemagne et les pays qui y adhéreront, cette proposition réalisera les premières assises concrètes d'une Fédération européenne indispensable à la préservation de la paix.[14]

3.1.2 The nature of the perceived legitimacy deficit: To whom is the High Authority accountable?

If *hypothesis 1a* holds, we would expect that the traditional notion of accountability of national governments in international political cooperation would be subject to challenge and redefinition. Accountability of national governments in decision-systems based on unanimity is considered relatively unproblematic since national governments can ultimately exercise their unconditional right to veto decisions whenever they see their 'national interest' threatened. One of the central aims of the Schuman Plan was to overcome the paralysis of unanimity by establishing a supranational body whose decisions would be *binding* for the partaking states. Yet, given the lack of any prior experience, there was no 'blueprint' as to who this new supranational institution should be accountable to. The accountability question was first advanced by the Belgian and Dutch governments. Following a conversation with Monnet on 24 May 1950, roughly one month before the Schuman Plan negotiations were to kick-off, the designated leader of the Dutch delegation, Spierenburg, expressed great concern about the HA by asserting that it could potentially resemble a congregation of experts who were going to exercise some form of dictatorship over the coal and steel industries (Spierenburg and Poidevin 1994: 16). While received enthusiastically in Germany, the institutional clauses of the Schuman Plan met with great reservations in the Benelux countries. During several meetings with representatives from the Benelux governments, a key point of contention was the degree to which the HA should be allowed to act autonomously and without interference from national governments. Within the Dutch government, the scepticism was so pronounced that the government's official answer to the French 'invitation' to the Schuman Plan negotiations made its participation conditional on an 'acceptable' solution to the accountability question (Griffiths 1990: 265–6). The Dutch government hence suggested that a ministerial council should be instituted to which the HA should be ultimately responsible (Griffiths 1990: 266). Reactions of a similar kind echoed from Brussels: the HA had to be held at bay and could not go uncontrolled. Three weeks before the Schuman Plan conference was to start, the Benelux countries demanded to circumscribe the supranational character of the HA and, in turn, increase the influence of national governments (Küsters 1988: 78–9). The vigorous expression of these concerns prior to the beginning of the Schuman Plan conference led Monnet to reflect more intensely on accountability and control mechanisms that could be instituted vis-à-vis the HA (see Lappenküper 1994: 418). He began to see clearly that the transfer of sovereignty to the HA would not be considered acceptable without instituting adequate control and accountability mechanisms (see Küsters 1988: 79). Arguments employed to counter the assertion of the HA becoming a potential technocratic 'dictatorship' and reflections on possible accountability mechanisms were also voiced by Schuman in a declaration to the Anglo–American press in early June 1950:

It can be anticipated that certain decisions taken by the High Authority could be regarded as dangerous. An international recourse mechanism is hence considered. But before which body? It is too soon to tell. The Council of Europe? Not in its present form. An elected European Parliament? Not necessarily. It is possible to envisage an organism created by the governments, under the condition that—once created—it is free from the interference of national governments, like it is the case for the International Court of Justice.[15]

An internal document to coordinate the French negotiating position drafted for a meeting on 12 June 1950 bears proof that two new ideas to tackle the accountability problem were taken on board: the first stipulated that the HA should be held to account by a parliamentary assembly of elected members of NPs, while the second envisaged that this parliamentary assembly should be able to censure the HA (Küsters 1988: 79–80). During a meeting with the German delegation, Monnet explained his ideas about the role and competencies of a parliamentary assembly: it should be given the right to debate an annual report submitted by the HA, and it should be allowed to pose questions to the HA on matters arising in the report, and, if deemed necessary, have the power to censure the HA by a majority of two-thirds.[16] The following day, Monnet admitted that, initially, he had not considered a parliamentary body as part of the institutional set-up of the ECSC; however, he was now convinced that it was necessary to include one.[17]

During a debate in the French National Assembly, Schuman emphasized time and again that the delegation of sovereignty to a new supranational HA required flanking mechanisms against potential abuse while, at the same time, these mechanisms should not undermine the supranational body's independence. Alluding to the creation of a parliamentary assembly, Schuman drew a clear connection between the delegation of sovereignty from the domestic to a new, supranational level of governance and the perceived necessity to endow a supranational parliamentary body with the power to control the HA.[18] At the end of the first week of the negotiations, Monnet presented a working document (*Document de Travail*) as the basis of subsequent rounds of discussion. The idea of the parliamentary control body found its way into the French document and its inclusion was celebrated as a step without precedent: 'For the first time, an international assembly will become more than a purely consultative body; the [national] parliaments which will give up a fraction of their sovereignty will...exercise this sovereignty jointly.'[19] These statements provide evidence for the existence of a perceived link between the delegation of sovereignty and the creation of flanking mechanisms to ensure the procedural legitimacy of the new polity, embodied by a parliamentary assembly. The statements also point at the novelty of this institutional arrangement and institutional design consequences: given the lack of *supra*national institutions, the question about including a body to ensure democratic control and accountability had not arisen hitherto. Yet, the new logic of supranational interstate cooperation required the inclusion of new institutional features (such as a parliamentary institution to hold the 'executive' HA accountable).

How much influence was the HA supposed to exercise over the coal and steel sectors? Who would it be accountable to and who would control it? How much sovereignty would national governments have to relinquish? While questions of this type were nagging for all partaking governments, the fact that they were asked and vigorously discussed demonstrates that all negotiators shared the accountability concern. The prospective member states of the ECSC shared the belief that the supranational HA had to be answerable to 'someone', a parliament, a ministerial council, etc. The evidence presented hitherto thus supports *hypothesis 1a*. Yet, despite the common perception that there existed a 'problem', the national delega-

tions were yet far from reaching an agreement over the appropriate mechanisms of control and accountability vis-à-vis the HA: After a week-long
recess, following the first round of negotiations in late June, the different
delegations came back to Paris and utterly disagreed over the question as to
how control over the HA should be exercised and to *who* exactly it should be
accountable. The leader of the Belgian delegation, Max Suétens, claimed
that his government would not accept a parliamentary control organ constituted by members of NPs, arguing that 'national parliaments are the
ultimate locus of responsibility and not some randomly selected groups
of parliamentarians. To the contrary, the ministers . . . constitute the con-
trol-organ for the HA.'[20] Similarly, the head of the Dutch delegation, Spierenburg, stated that he would like to see the HA answerable to a Council of
Ministers emphasising that 'the governments are responsible for the general economic policy . . . [I]t is thus dangerous to transfer excessive powers
to a council of technicians [the HA].'[21] Monnet, who found support from
the heads of the German and Italian delegations (Walter Hallstein and
Paolo Emilio Taviani respectively), underlined the importance of a supranational body capable of taking decisions without interference from other
Community institutions. He recalled that the creation of the ECSC would
go beyond cooperation in two economic sectors as it was the groundwork
of a European *federation* comprising *inter alia* a parliament and a body
representing the interests of the constituent states.[22] How can we then
explain the variation in the preferences expressed by the different national
delegations as to *how* the HA should be controlled and held accountable?

3.2 How to ensure accountability?[23]

First of all, I argue that political elites' motivations for cooperation,
whether status- or security-related, or driven by economic motives, cru-
cially affected the degree to which the partaking governments perceived
procedural legitimacy to be a problematic issue that had to be dealt with
during the Schuman Plan negotiations. It has already been mentioned
that the ECSC was the first *supra*national system of interstate cooperation
and, as such, there existed no predecessors which could assist as 'blue-
prints' for this novel organizational form. Given the creation of this new
institutional arrangement, the Schuman Plan negotiations can be considered a constitutional 'founding moment', which led to the creation of an
entirely novel systems of 'rules about rules' and a set of 'higher level'
institutions which framed political processes. *Hypothesis 1b* reflects this
link between alternative motives for cooperation and concerns for pro-

cedural legitimacy which are likely to be reflected in the construction of 'higher level' institutions:

> *Hypothesis 1b: 'higher level' and 'lower level' institutions*
> When political elites face novel situations—during episodes of constitutional formation—in which constitutional principles ('higher level' issues) have to be established, concerns about procedural legitimacy are likely to feature prominently in political elites' institutional design choices. As a corollary, where institutional choices which have obvious distributive implications are the subject of debate and reform ('lower level' issues), concerns for procedural legitimacy are not likely to be prevalent.

I also, in a second step, answer the question of why concerns about procedural legitimacy did not result in a uniform response to the perceived legitimacy deficit.

> *Hypothesis 2: legitimating beliefs*
> Alternative proposals to create and reform institutions with a view to reducing the asymmetry between procedural and consequentialist legitimacy (the legitimacy deficit) are likely to reflect differences in legitimating beliefs held by different political elites.

3.2.1 *Preferences for cooperation and institutional design implications: some theoretical remarks*

According to Andrew Moravcsik, most of the literature on European integration ascribes the underlying preferences in favour of, or against international cooperation to security- or status-related as well as economic motivations. Whereas the former category reflects perceived threats (military or ideological) to a country's security and status, the latter reflects the imperatives induced by economic interdependence and opportunities for cross-border economic transactions (Moravcsik 1998: 26, 1993). It will be demonstrated in this section that an answer to the question of how national governments sought to solve the procedural legitimacy problem was conditional on whether or not their underlying motivation for cooperation was induced by security or status concerns on the one hand, or by economic motives on the other hand. Hence, variation in preferences for cooperation correlates with different emphases on the problem of procedural legitimacy. The key to grasping this correlation lies in the type of the cooperation problem and how it is perceived by different actors. For actors who are predominantly concerned with overcoming a *security* dilemma through cooperation by creating co-binding 'commitment' institutions (Ikenberry 1998, 2001),[24] the key concern lies in securing the mutual gains from cooperation by overcoming the notorious 'defection problem'. The actual distribution of the gains from mutual cooperation through 'commitment' institutions may be less important either because of the *symmetrical* nature of their distribution or because the exact payoffs themselves may be *uncertain*. This is illustrated by the game form portrayed in Figure 3.1. In the situation depicted here, different actors share a mutual interest in cooperation, but given the lack of enforcement institutions, of mutual trust, or of a reputation of honouring agreements, defection will be the actors' dominant strategy. However, if actors can agree on enacting institutions that enforce agreements by sanctioning non-compliance, the 'defection problem' can be overcome. For example, states can do so by delegating powers to supranational institutions which are given the power to monitor and sanction transgressors.

When, however, an actor's motivation to cooperate is induced by the prospect of reaping the expected economic benefits from joint action, such as from free trade or regulatory harmonization in specific sectors of the economy, governments will be less willing to subscribe to an international constitutional settlement that fails to specify *ex ante* the sectors which will be subject to cooperative efforts as well as the distribution of gains from joint action. Where economic interests are at stake, pooling and delegation will be *selective*. States will only agree to transfer sovereignty in those issue areas where the expected gains from cooperation are highest and are most certain to materialize. Therefore, states will be expected to advocate an exact and specific elaboration of the provisions of a prospective agreement before general consent to the agreement is given. Such a rationale for cooperation correlates strongly with institutional preferences that focus on 'lower level' issues, that is, on the question of how competences have to be allocated among international institutions so that actors can reap the benefits of cooperation. Figure 3.2 illustrates a coordination game with

Actor A/ Actor B	Cooperation	Defection
Cooperation	3 / 3 (P)	1 / 4 (no agreement)
Defection	4 / 1 (no agreement)	2 / 2 (N) (no agreement)

(P) Pareto optimal outcome   A - column actor
(N) Nash equilibrium   B - row actor

Fig. 3.1 The 'defection problem'.

ActorB/ Actor A	Solution I	Solution II
Solution I	<3 / 3 (P,N)	No agreement
Solution II	No agreement	3 / <3 (P,N)

(P) Pareto optimal solution   A - column actor
(N) Nash equilibrium   B - row actor

Fig. 3.2 The 'coordination problem'

distributional conflict. Actor A and B prefer the two cooperative soluton (Solution I – Solution I; Solution II – Solution II) over the two non cooperative solution (Solution I – Solution II; Solution II – Solution I). Among the two cooperative solutions, however, Actor A prefers Solution I – Solution I over Solution II – Solution II since the first situation will leave Actor A with a payoff of '3' while the latter situation will leave her with a payoff of '<3'. Conversely, Actor B will prefer Solution II – Solution II over Solution I – Solution I since former will endow her with a payoff of '3' and the latter arrangement with a payoff of only '<3'. Both cooperative solutions represent the respective ends of a 'contract curve' connecting Actor A's and Actor B's most preferred outcomes. Which of the two cooperative solutions will be chosen? It is conceivable that, for instances, the distribution of bargaining power among the two actors will determine the division of the spoils of cooperation, for example, how competences are distributed between different political institutions, how seats are allocated in the lefislature, how voting rights are distributed, etc.

How do economically and status/security-induced preferences for co-operation translate into preferences for institutional solutions to alleviate the legitimacy deficit problem? Depending on whether economically or status/security-induced preferences inform the behaviour of national governments, 'lower level' choices in the former and 'higher level' choices in the latter case will dominate the respective governments' agendas in a constitutional bargain. When governments are primarily driven or constrained by economic concerns, economic cooperation will be pursued in sectors where the gains of cooperation are highest, most certain, and most concentrated. Consequently, governments are most likely to support pooling (through the adoption of qualified majority voting in specific sectoral policies) and delegation (by providing supranational institutions with agenda-setting or adjudicating powers) within an international institutional structure to 'lock-in' these prospective gains from cooperation. With reference to institutional questions, governments will be most strongly concerned with problems such as which policy areas should be included into a cooperative arrangement, or how competences should be distributed between different decision-making institutions ('lower level' concerns). 'Lower level' institutions thus are the *means* or devices through which governments promote their ends. As a corollary, we would expect 'higher level' concerns about procedural legitimacy to feature little in the discussions about 'lower level' institutions. Yet, whenever 'higher level' issues or concerns about procedural legitimacy are subject to debate, they will be scrutinized as to their implications for 'lower level' concerns. For example, the general constitutional principle of supranationality introduced in the ECSC was—from the perspective of those governments with economically-driven preferences for cooperation—acceptable only in so far as it exclusively applied to those issue areas in which the gains from delegating and pooling were most visible and in which they were in line with *a priori* specified policy goals. Wherever the application of the supranational principle threatened to interfere with cherished domestic policy objectives, competences of the Community organs had to be curtailed and closely circumscribed.

When status-related or security-induced preferences for cooperation motivate governments' actions, mutual institutions through which economic goals can be realized are merely one possible solution to lock-in mutual commitments. The question as to which institutions should be created in order to lock-in cooperative arrangements is more likely to be open to debate: actors driven by status-related or security-induced concerns will face a higher degree of *uncertainty* with regard to the expected distribution of gains from the cooperative arrangement; consequently, 'higher level' issues and concerns about *procedural* legitimacy of the constitutional order are likely to feature more prominently. Overall, different motivations for cooperation are likely to correlate with different logics of institution-building ('higher' versus 'lower level' institutions) and furthermore allow different emphases on questions of procedural legitimacy. Still, we do not know which constitutional principles actors are likely to advance when contemplating their responses as to how the perceived legitimacy deficit can be alleviated. I have argued in Chapter 2 that in order to fill this 'void' political actors are most likely to be guided by legitimating beliefs.

3.2.2 *Assessing preferences for cooperation: the creation of the ECSC*

In a first step, the preferences of the governments participating in the ECSC negotiations are assessed, before the implications for questions of constitutional design and, more specifically, solutions for the perceived legitimacy deficit are illuminated.[25]

3.2.2.1 France: anticipated decline of security and economic power

In the French case, the decision to opt for institutionalized cooperation in the early 1950s was induced by both security/status and economic considerations which proved to be mutually reinforcing. The anticipation of a decline of military and economic power in the medium to long term (asymmetric economic interdependence and increasing security threats), a lack of outside options to assure French economic and security goals in the medium to long run, as well as insulation of the negotiators during the Schuman Plan negotiations from domestic organized interests (of the coal and steel industries) exerted a strong influence on France's preferences for cooperation.

As the basis for a cooperative agreement, coal and steel were considered policy areas which would be most conducive to integrative efforts, not only because of their symbolic value—coal and steel were considered the base-material of the 'war industry'—but first and foremost, because Monnet expected that Franco–German integration in this sector would produce positive security and economic externalities which would also serve prolong to the efforts for economic modernization spelled out in the Monnet Plan (Lynch 1988: 124–6). France had a number of interconnected reasons to 'lock-in' cooperation with Germany: The prospect of industrial recovery of (West) Germany and disagreement among the allies—especially between the United States and France—on whether or not to allow a speeding up of Germany's industrial recovery was connected with the fear that Germany, once freed from allied control, would pose a threat to French security given its economic superiority. Furthermore, rising tensions with the Soviet Union in the context of the Cold War induced the French government to support efforts which would bind Germany to the 'West' (Lappenküper 1994: 406).[26] The conclusions that French diplomats drew from the assessment of this multifaceted situation was the following: Germany had to be institutionally bound to a system of cooperation in Western Europe. A Quai d'Orsay document from 18 April 1950 reads as follows:

We pronounce that the re-enforcement of the links between Germany and occidental Europe is inseparable from reinforcing cooperation on a European scale. With this in mind, we declare our will to endeavour to create a political organization of supranational character.[27]

Monnet's assessment of France's state of the economy and security broadly coincided with that of the Quai d'Orsay. Fears of a revitalized, economically powerful Germany which would be in the midst of a potential confrontation of the two 'blocks' were also vivid. Monnet recognized the threat of German industrial domination vis-à-vis France, lamenting that '[i]f only the French could lose their fear of German industrial domination, then the greatest obstacle to a united Europe would be removed' (Monnet 1978: 292). In the literature, Monnet's proposed coal and steel pool is seen as a means to protect French security and promote economic reconstruction through the international control of Germany's heartland of heavy industry, the Ruhr (Gillingham 1991: 229).[28] With France being— at the time—the world's largest importer of coal and coke (Lynch 1988: 119), a common market for coal and steel promised to ensure sufficient and cheap supply of German combustible material for French industry and for the realization of the French economic plan for modernization (Lynch 1988: 125). With the creation of the ECSC, issues such as the control over the Ruhr (and also the Saar) would cease to be a concern because '[w]ar between France and Germany would be ruled out since neither could fight without an independent coal and steel industry. Thus the ECSC would constrain Germany and enhance French security' (Milner 1997: 183).

Was France able to rely on outside 'help' to assure that her economic and security problems would be solved in the framework of a multilateral organization? To meet the fear of an economically evermore powerful Germany, and given the prospect of an end to the allied occupation of Germany, Monnet and Schuman held the view that a solution had to be found sooner rather than later. This was evermore pressing for two reasons. First, existing cooperative efforts did not prove promising, as mirrored by the disappointing performances of the OEEC and the Council of Europe whose ambitions were paralysed by the burden of unanimity. Yet, the question remains why Monnet and Schuman opted for May 1950 to present their plan about supranational cooperation between France and Germany? Bernard Clappier, Schuman's *chef de cabinet*, told Monnet that the foreign minister was looking for a concept which he could present to the conference of allied foreign ministers in London on 10 May 1950, and Monnet presented his plan to Schuman on 28 April in a memorandum to which Schuman was reported to have said: 'I have read the plan, I will join in.'[29] Second, time was 'against' France. According to Milward (1984: 378), '[i]t was better for France to negotiate now while the West German state was in tutelage, before the extent of the Ruhr Authority's powers were fully discovered, and before the Federal German Republic was admitted more fully into the system of military alliances.' Consequently, France saw its 'outside options' rapidly disappear.[30]

To what degree did domestic industry influence the drafting of the Schuman Plan? The role of the French coal and steel industry can be described as very circumscribed. It was only *after* the announcement of the plan that the steel industry launched fierce campaigns against the way the negotiations were conducted, yet they were mostly excluded from the talks, mainly as a result of the industry's lack of a concerted stance.[31] Diebold claims that there was no initial 'push' on behalf of industry to integrate these sectors of the economy (Diebold 1959: 16–17). The pressure to cooperate or 'integrate' did thus not originate from the economic arena. Although French producers (represented by the *Chambre Syndicale de la Sidérurgie Française*) looked favourably upon a Franco–German rapprochement and particularly supported all measures facilitating the flow of cheap German combustibles to France, they also feared that the proposal would force them to compete with Germany on unfavourable terms (Gillingham 1991: 236). Even though the producers demanded to be involved in the Schuman Plan negotiations, this never happened in practice.[32] The hostility of French steel industry was also fuelled by the 'French plan's own investigations [which] invariably depicted the industry as better able to compete than it was prepared to admit' (Gillingham 1991: 237). Shortly after the announcement of the Schuman Plan, 'the steel syndicate whipped up opposition to the Schuman Plan within industry, launching a campaign through the Conseil National du Patronat Français (CNPF)...By the end of the year, protests of Monnet's conduct of the negotiations were registered by nearly every chamber of commerce in France' (Gillingham 1991: 237). However, the French coal and steel industry was strongly divided in its approach towards the Plan (Mioche 1988). The French delegation, supported by a *troisième force* majority[33] in the National Assembly hence had considerable leeway in proposing an institutional structure that was destined to solve the pressing economic and security concerns.[34]

The motivation of the French governing elite to tie Germany's coal and steel industry to a supranational coal and steel pool was thus clearly not driven by the primacy of sector or issue-specific demands articulated by affected organized interests, but rather from domestic economic policy objectives which were spelled out in the Monnet Plan. However, these economic concerns existed alongside geopolitical and security concerns

(Abelshauser 1994: 7). The pursuit of both socio-economic and security objectives in reaching economic and security-related goals was mutually reinforcing rather than mutually exclusive. The prime means to realize these status- and security-related goals was to bind Germany to a supra-national organization in which cooperative agreements were facilitated and rendered enforceable, unlike previous unanimity-based institutional arrangements such as the OEEC or the Council of Europe. To achieve this goal, France and Germany had to commit themselves institutionally and thereby reduce incentives for defection inherent in international cooperation lacking adequate enforcement institutions. Furthermore, with regard to the economic goals of cooperation, a supranational HA with the authority to issue binding decisions would have the potential to help France create a 'level playing field' in the production of steel, especially with regard to price adaptation (Lynch 1988: 125).

3.2.2.2 Germany: primacy of 'politics' over 'economics'

The initial response by the German government to the Schuman Plan strongly mirrors the primacy of security- and status-related preferences for cooperation and relegated the economic considerations to second rank. Given its position in the international community after the Second World War Germany possessed only limited external and internal sovereignty (the majority of political decisions had to be approved by the allied High Commission). Therefore, the prospect of international cooperation signalled an opportunity to regain domestic and foreign policy-making capacity. In the eyes of the German government, the Schuman Plan offered an immediate opportunity to become an 'equal' member in the European concert of states. However, Germany could also expect its status as occupied power to ease in the medium to long run. Consequently, enthusiasm to unconditionally abide by the French proposal without specifying the actual terms of the cooperative agreement was considered increasingly unpopular by a significant part of the German political and economic elite as soon as alternative avenues for cooperation opened up. Opposition to the plan was mainly on economic grounds, yet Germany's governing political elite was initially relatively autonomous from domestic economic pressures in forging ahead with Schuman's proposal (though the major opposition force in the Bundestag, the Social Democrats, actually opposed the Schuman Plan).

The Schuman Plan was received enthusiastically by the German Chancellor, Adenauer.[35] When Adenauer was informed about the plan he replied to Schuman on 8 May 1950, the day before the plan's official announcement, by stating 'I can already assure you of Germany's willingness to participate in the preparation of all necessary organisational steps.'[36] In his *Erinnerungen* (memoirs), Adenauer recalls that 'Schuman's Plan corresponded entirely with my feelings about linking the European key industries. I told Schuman immediately that I offered my unfaltering support to his proposal' (Adenauer 1965: 332, author's translation). The supranational principle enshrined in the institution of the HA was readily accepted as were economic concessions in order to regain sovereignty through participation in the ECSC project. On the side of Adenauer and his aides, it was not a very difficult decision to renounce those aspects of national sovereignty that fell into the HA's jurisdiction: the prospective coal and steel pool opened a path to more international influence and the regaining of national policy-making prerogatives in other fields through the weakening of the occupation status (Küsters 1988: 78; Lappenküper 1994: 411–13). The early reactions to the Schuman Plan mirror the German government's unfaltering commitment to the plan, by accepting the setting up of a general institutional structure before any 'lower level' concerns would be tackled. However, it was precisely the 'technical' issues which proved to be highly 'political'. In the course of the negotiations, the German delegation did not shy away from pressing for concessions and clarifications, especially with regard to the prospective competencies of the HA. Hence, the dominance of security- and status-related concerns in informing the German government's stance towards cooperation and the initial acceptance of the principle of supranationality (with relatively little by way of specification of how supranationality would impact upon 'lower level' issues) was weakened during the course of the negotiations: economic considerations found their way into the German negotiating position as a result of a change in external circumstances. The Korean War, which was accompanied by discussions about the potential remilitarization of Germany,[37] and mounting political opposition, especially from the 'free-marketeers' in the ministry of economics, left their mark on the government's calculation of its strategy.[38] This prospect rendered the Schuman Plan in its initial form (with little in terms of the details on issue-specific cooperation) much less beneficial in the government's view, especially since the regaining of sovereignty could be attained at lower costs (through US-supported remilitarisation of Germany). This was immediately reflected in a hardening of Germany's bargaining position and a closer focus on 'lower level' issues. Consequently, the willingness to make economic concessions in order to attain status-related goals (foremost that of sovereignty) declined. As Gillingham (1991: 233) stated:

The chancellor was hardly a starry-eyed idealist. A shrewd calculation underlay his apparent acquiescence to the French. Adenauer questioned neither the vigour of his producers nor their ability to stand up for their interests and was certain that time was on his side.

Gillingham's position, however, is not unanimously supported in the literature. Adenauer's approach was still stressing the primacy of 'politics' over 'economics'. Under mounting domestic opposition, Adenauer was still able to assure that the proposed ECSC did not get its final blow over rows on issues of industry deconcentration. Milward has argued that 'Adenauer insisted throughout on the prime political priority for the Federal Republic on the removal of the Ruhr Authority and the weakening of the Occupation Statute' (Milward 1984: 413) to bolster German sovereignty. Furthermore, with a view to potential opposition from the industry itself, the German Iron and Steel Manufacturers' Association was informed by the government that 'the political aim was in the foreground, and economic aims were more or less subordinate to it' (Milward 1984: 413). The question of the dissolution of the German steel cartels is instructive in order to assess whether—even under intense pressure from industry—Adenauer would be able to commit to the issue of deconcentration. Duchêne (1994: 218) asked the crucial question: 'Adenauer's goodwill was not in doubt, but who held the power?' Despite massive opposition from industrialists and labour unions who alluded to the spectre of unemployment, Adenauer succeeded in imposing the crucial elements of the Schuman Plan. Milward (1984: 390) concludes that 'without Adenauer's autocratic imposition of his own foreign policy on the Federal government [the French] proposals would surely not have been made.'

The primacy of status-related interests for cooperation suggests that the German government united with France in its attempt to establish an institutional structure and general agreement for cooperation before 'lower level' choices over how decision-making powers between the different institutions were to be tackled. The government's commitment to cooperation and its willingness to make economic concessions thus stemmed predominantly from the expected benefits of the gradual elimination of the occupation status and the prospective regaining of sovereignty as well as from Adenauer's ability to impose his preferences on domestic opposition. The key to 'lock-in' cooperation was seen in the acceptance of the HA (considered by the French as the *conditio sine qua non* for cooperation). Consequently, the focus on 'higher level' choices permitted negotiators to reflect, in a relatively unconstrained fashion, the shape of an appropriate institutional structure, the heart of which was to become the HA. Innovative proposals as for how an 'appropriate' solution to the 'separation of powers' problem was to be achieved featured strongly among the German and French delegations.

3.2.2.3 The Benelux countries: Primacy of 'economics'

The Benelux countries based their agreement to join the coal and steel pool on a calculation of the expected economic benefits from such an enterprise. Although early objections were made to the envisioned powers of the HA, there was no general disagreement whether or not to surrender a certain 'portion' of national sovereignty. The primacy of economic interests is mainly reflected in the *selective* approach towards cooperation taken by the Benelux countries. Rather than accepting an *a priori* commitment to a supranational community, the respective governments sought cooperation in policy areas in which the expected joint-gains would be highest and existing domestic social and economic policies would not be negatively affected. The willingness of the Benelux governments to commit themselves institutionally 'in the dark' was thus much less pronounced than in the case of France and Germany. Hence, agreement as to whether the supranationality principle was acceptable was conditional on a satisfactory solution to 'lower level' issues. This stemmed from the perceived need to protect those areas where unilateral (domestic) socio-economic policies required safeguards. In turn, cooperation was sought in those areas were joint-gains of cooperation would be most beneficial without damaging domestic policy objectives. Consequently, the severe scepticism on behalf of the Benelux delegations with regard to the Schuman Plan was easy to envisage: a poorly specified treaty endowing the HA with far reaching powers and insufficient control mechanisms to check its power was simply unacceptable unless the details as to how the powers were to be distributed among the institutions and as to which issue areas would be covered were spelled out precisely.

Although the Benelux countries welcomed the Schuman Plan as a 'breakthrough in French policies towards Germany' (Kersten 1988: 287) and saw in it an opportunity to profit from Germany's economic strength without being threatened by it, there was a considerable degree of scepticism as to the powers envisaged for the HA. Subscribing to a coal and steel pool under the terms set by France was not considered an overly attractive option. The Dutch government, in particular, had a very strong interest in the abolition of quantitative restrictions on trade and hence tabled the 'Stikker Plan' in June 1950 which intended to appeal not just to a core Europe but to all OEEC members with a view to creating a common market, making trade liberalization binding and easing the removal of quantitative restrictions to trade. Yet, given that the prospect for even a very modest degree of economic integration within the framework of the OEEC was gradually disappearing, the Schuman Plan was all there was left on the table. Its political importance could not be denied, and rather than being left out, the Benelux countries decided to join the negotiations. However, they strongly signalled that they were not willing to provide *a priori* commitment towards cooperation before the terms of the prospective agreement had been elaborated in detail. In the following paragraphs, I will demonstrate that security-and status-related concerns featured much less in informing the Benelux governments' preferences for cooperation than this was the case for France and Germany. For the Benelux governments, economic policy constraints mattered much more strongly.

How can the primacy of economic over status-and security-related preferences for cooperation be accounted for? One crucial argument refers to the position of the respective industries in the domestic economies and the impact of the envisaged policies 'imposed' by the HA on other key sectors in the Benelux economies. For example, Dutch import dependence on the one hand, Belgium's and Luxembourg's export dependence with regard to coal and steel on the other hand, led the respective governments to press for low common tariffs. The Benelux delegations thus advocated that the HA should *not* be given the opportunity to set a tariff level which, so the Benelux countries feared, would probably be higher than the one that the three countries had negotiated among themselves. Especially Belgium and Luxembourg were more dependent on the steel market for their exports than the other negotiating partners because steel amounted to one-fifth of their total exports: 'For them the issues, economically, were more crucial than for France or Germany' (Milward 1984: 415–16).

Another issue area that caused much disagreement and thus manifested that the Dutch were more inclined to 'sort out the details' before they were willing to provide general agreement to cooperation was the area of wage policy. In this policy area, pronounced differences in the productivity and wage costs among the different countries existed. The possibility envisaged in the French *Document de Travail* that the HA should be empowered to equalize living conditions and prevent countries that wished to catch up economically from pursuing a low-wage strategy, was rejected by the Dutch government whose low-wage policy was a cornerstone to its post-war recovery policy (see Griffiths 1990: 271: Gillingham 1991: 244). Griffiths argues that any powers delegated to the HA to influence wage levels 'were inimical to the Dutch, who interpreted them as a fundamental threat to their newly enforced system of national wage bargaining' (Griffiths 1988: 40). Similar examples could be provided for the highly contested questions about investment control, price levels, cartels/restrictive practices, and transitional agreements.

I have already mentioned that Monnet had envisaged a rapid negotiation process by limiting the agenda to discussing the general institutional settlement which was to 'assemble' around the supranational HA—'the technical details would either be worked out in a separate convention after the Treaty's ratification or left entirely to the [High Authority].'[39] With respect to the socio-economic implications of the Schuman Plan on prices, production quotas, investments, and salaries, the Benelux delegations demanded that the powers of the HA had to be specified and controlled 'because of the effects of its decisions in these areas upon national and social policies' (Kersten 1988: 289). Only in those areas where the Benelux governments expected economic gains from cooperation did they push for delegation. The negotiators of the Benelux countries made it clear that no 'blank cheque' would be signed for the HA. Table 3.1 provides a summary of the arguments advanced in this section by drawing attention to the link which is established between preferences for cooperation and their institutional design implications. Having assessed the different governments' preferences for cooperation, we are now in a position to derive expectations with regard to the institutional design implications and concerns about procedural legitimacy.

3.2.3 Institutional design implications: which constitutional structure for the ECSC?

In the ensuing paragraphs, evidence is presented to subject the expectations advanced earlier to empirical scrutiny. Did different motives for cooperation connect with different concerns about how the institutional structure of the ECSC should be designed? Did France and Germany attach more weight to the problem of procedural legitimacy (and hence 'higher level' institutional choices) than their Benelux counterparts?

Table 3.1 Preferences for cooperation and the construction of the ECSC

	Status- and security-related preferences for cooperation	Economically-induced preferences for cooperation
Motives for cooperation	Realization of security externalities from cooperation; securing or improving one's position of influence in international relations through co-binding 'commitment institutions'	Realization of economic benefits and domestic policy goals through economic integration in sectors where the joint gains from cooperation are high
Expectations about constitutional design	Focus will be on 'higher level' institutions—questions of procedural legitimacy are likely to loom large; debates on 'lower level' institutions are of minor relevance where the likely distributional effects are considered negligible or uncertain	Focus will be on 'lower level' institutions (how will the 'spoils' of cooperation be divided?); questions of procedural legitimacy will be secondary ; conflicts about 'higher level' institutions are only likely to occur when they potentially affect the division of gains from cooperation
Country-specific expectations	France and Germany	Benelux countries

3.2.3.1 'A leap in the dark'

'But what form should be given to a decision-making authority common to Germany and France? History offered no precedent' (Monnet 1978: 294). Given the relative autonomy of the French negotiators, there was considerable space to 'innovate' institutionally and propose an institutional structure that would crack the impasse induced by unanimous decision-making which Monnet despised so heavily (Monnet 1978: 281–2; Duchêne 1994: 205; Parsons 2003: 59). Given Monnet's strong belief in the unsuitability of unanimous decision-making bodies which could impede France's strive for economic recovery and security, the idea of a supranational institution to issue binding decisions for all participating states seemed highly attractive. The idea of a supranational HA has to be seen in the light of Monnet's and Schuman's motivation to *bind* Germany institutionally and to ensure that Germany would not have a competitive advantage by charging prices for coal which would force the French government to heavily subsidize the consumption price for coal (Lynch 1988: 125). Although the intentions of Monnet and the French negotiators were mainly 'political', they bore a strong economic element that, nevertheless, produced positive security externalities.[40] The French approach to create a supranational HA came to be dubbed metaphorically as 'a leap in the dark':

Few people realized how true the metaphor was. They [the British] tended to think that the technical aspects of the plan had been meticulously prepared [...]. That seemed sheer common sense, but it led to many misunderstandings—beginning in London, where on their arrival Schuman and Clappier [Schuman's chief of staff] were bombarded with questions about the power of the High Authority, the fate of a particular coalfield, or how prices were to be fixed (Monnet 1978: 305).[41]

And quite so, they were unable to provide an answer. It was Monnet's pronounced goal to set up a treaty and the HA as quickly as possible in order to effectively bind Germany, and only then should 'the technicians...go to work' to fill in the details (Monnet 1978: 310). Adenauer recalls that he and Monnet agreed that, for the Schuman Plan conference, technical experts should be excluded from the different delegations to avoid the danger of the plan being 'talked to death' ('*zerredet*') before it even saw the light of day (Adenauer 1965: 340). However, this proved to be wishful thinking. In the early phases of the negotiations, the Benelux countries made it very clear that they would not consent to any treaty unless it spelled out precisely the scope of competences attributed to the supranational HA (Kersten 1988: 295). This concern led directly to the question of how much decision-making competency the HA should possess, in which issue areas, and how it could be assured that it would be held at bay ('lower level' institutional questions).

Consequently, the expected economic implications of decisions made by the HA and their effects on areas sensitive to national socio-economic policies led the Benelux countries to call for an approach to institution building that differed from the one adopted by France and Germany. The dominance of economically-induced preferences and the way in which they informed preferences for institutions can be best grasped by the reaction of Belgium's chief negotiator Max Suétens and the Belgian Minister of Foreign Affairs, Paul van Zeeland. In addressing Monnet, the former claimed that 'you see the solutions to our problems in the High Authority. We see the High Authority in the light of the problems and their solution.'[42] Similarly, van Zeeland stated that the 'political' aspect should follow 'economic' considerations and not vice versa.[43] The Benelux delegations all agreed that the potential 'lower level' implications of an *a priori* agreement to accept a powerful HA without specifying the limits of its power and the scope of its influence had to be studied with scepticism (Spierenburg and Poidevin 1994: 15).

Three weeks before the actual negotiations began (20 June 1950), the Dutch delegation, supported by the delegates from Belgium and Luxembourg, addressed the problem of the HA's accountability. As indicated previously, Spierenburg put the issue bluntly: Does the HA embody a dictatorship of experts? Given the Benelux preoccupation with domestic socio-economic policy-making objectives, the powers of the HA, in their view, had to be closely circumscribed so as not to interfere with the cherished national policy objectives (Küsters 1988: 79). The US Ambassador to Belgium, Robert Murphy, summarized the Belgian (and equally the Dutch) position by referring to their two key demands: first, a more flexible and limited jurisdiction for the HA—on an issue-by-issue basis— should be put in place. Second, the HA should share its decision-making powers with an intergovernmental organ.[44] Spierenburg added to this view that the intergovernmental body, a committee of ministers, should be able to block decision made by the HA.[45]

With the demand for a tight circumscription of the HA's competencies, the Benelux countries had in mind an effective *ex ante* control mechanism. Furthermore, *ex post* control of the HA was supposed to be exercised partly by the member states (in the proposed interministerial council) and partly by a court. The inclusion of the member states—as stated earlier—was considered vital because the decisions made by the HA could affect domestic economic policy decisions and potentially annexed policy objectives.[46] Furthermore, a court as appellate body seemed the obvious solution to ensure *ex post* control. The inclusion of a court was strongly supported by the Benelux countries. As far as the Court's control competencies were concerned, the Benelux countries argued that they should be limited to those of an international court (such as the International Court of Justice in The Hague) before which *only member states* should be allowed to bring charges, thereby limiting its role to ensure that the HA would not abuse its powers vis-à-vis member states. The German delegation's demand that private litigants should be allowed to bring charges before the court was rejected by the Benelux delegations. They expressed the fear that this would limit the competencies of national courts and undermine national sovereignty even further (Küsters 1988: 94). Despite initial French and (to a lesser extent) German disapproval of the Benelux proposal of an interministerial council, both delegations eventually responded positively to this institutional innovation to the Schuman Plan early in the negotiations. Especially the German delegation welcomed this intergovernmental element as a building block of a federal constitution which ought to comprise both representation at the state level (the member states in the Council) and the union level (embodied by a supranational parliament representing the member states' peoples). According to Kirsten Gerçek (1998), it came as no surprise that it was the German delegation which 'reinvented' a role for the Council within the Community by resorting to the conception of a supranational federal state ('Bundesstaat'). However, the German delegation was also eager to point out that a prospective Council of Ministers—if it was to resonate with the *federal state* conception—could not be given the same rank as the HA because this would jeopardize the Schuman Plan's underlying conception of a HA above the member states, capable of issuing binding decisions ('Überordnungslösung'). The Council-idea, however, was warmly welcomed: it would be a body representing the national governments ('Staatenhaus') as one chamber of a bicameral parliamentary institution (Mosler 1966: 373).

3.2.3.2 Democratic accountability: Why and by whom?

Mosler, member of the German delegation to the legal affairs committee of the Schuman Plan negotiations, recalls that 'during the course of the first days of the conference of delegates it became apparent that . . . the grand issues of constitutional politics must not be neglected: the distribution of functions between governing organs . . . The necessity to control the High Authority was immediately obvious. All partaking governments were parliamentary democracies' (Mosler 1966: 369, author's translation). In a similar vein, Monnet argued that '[i]n a world where government authority is derived from representative parliamentary assemblies, Europe cannot be built without such an assembly.'[47] Documentary evidence shows that in late May and early June 1950 intensive discussions among the French negotiators took place touching upon the questions of democratic control and accountability of the HA which found its way into the *Document de Travail*.[48] Pierre Uri's draft of 7 June 1950 mentions that the HA should be responsible to an *Assemblée de l'Union Européenne*. It was foreseen that the main function of this assembly was to debate the HA's annual report.

Furthermore, the Assembly was supposed to possess the right to censure the HA (by a two-thirds majority). The name of the parliamentary assembly of the ECSC, *Assemblée Commune*, was used for the first time in a French working document of 21 June 1950 (Gerçek 1998: 105, fn. 22). During the very first days of the Schuman Plan negotiations the idea of a CA was already a subject of discussion among the 'Six'. Talks between Monnet and members of the German delegation on 22 June 1950 indicated that Monnet had become very receptive to idea of including a parliamentary body in the organizational set-up:

Initially we [the French delegation] have not considered such an organ. However, the High Authority is a body that partially fuses states' sovereignty and, from a democratic point of view, its existence therefore cannot be envisaged without the inclusion of a control body. It is for this reason that the French initiators of the plan have thought of a parliamentary control organ comprised of the members of the different national legislatures . . . This rudimentary assembly is not supposed to have decision-making and executive functions. The High Authority has to be accountable to the assembly. If the assembly is not satisfied with the way the High Authority fulfils its duties, it shall censure the High Authority.[49]

It was plain from the start of the negotiations that the concern about 'executive control' was unanimously shared among all participating delegations. Yet, it was also obvious, that the delegations' views differed as to *how* executive control mechanisms should be designed and *to whom* the HA should be accountable to. It has been hypothesized that when 'higher level' concerns are dominant, the solution to the problem of (executive) accountability is likely to be contemplated in the light of 'appropriate' democratic institutional solutions which are present in national political systems, and that concerns about procedural legitimacy are likely to dominate those of efficiency and effectiveness. In contrast, when 'lower level' concerns are paramount, control mechanisms have to be effective, i.e. their 'appropriateness' is measured against the background of the achievement or protection of policy goals. This is exactly what could be observed in the discussions surrounding the role of the CA. Whereas the Benelux countries only accepted those 'higher level' institutional solutions that did not negatively affect their dominant 'lower level' concerns, the German and French delegations were less constrained by 'lower level' concerns in proposing a design of the structure of the new constitutional order. The German delegation's proposals in this respect were inspired by the *federal state* analogy. Time and again, Walter Hallstein, Carl-Friedrich Ophüls, and other members of the German delegation justified their institutional proposals by taking recourse to the *federal state* legitimating belief. Although the French delegation led by Monnet and the German delegation attached similar importance to 'higher level' institutions and were aware of a legitimacy deficit if the HA was not subjected to some form of parliamentary control, their arguments to support or oppose certain control mechanisms differed. The head of the German delegation to the Schuman Plan negotiations, Walter Hallstein, was reported to have expressed these differences with remarkable boldness:

The Common Assembly cannot be viewed as an organ representing the interests of different individual states, but is—by its very nature—a unitary organ, because control over a unitary organ [the High Authority] can only be ensured by a unitary organ, otherwise one denies the supranational nature of the High Authority. On the other hand, the ministerial committee represents the interests of states... The European Union, whatever it is to look like in the future, will have a federal state-like character, in which the representation of individual states' interests is, after all, legitimate. Despite making references to the example of the United States of America, it was difficult to make some of the French Gentlemen understand the concept of a federal state, given that they— understandably—start from the tradition of the French unitary state.... [T]here was agreement that the Common Assembly had to be strengthened... beyond what the French working document envisaged. To justify this necessity, Hallstein drew attention to the logic of a federal constitution, in which the state-element had to be balanced by a federal-element unless one wanted to end up with the status of a confederation.[50]

While the French and German delegations thus agreed on basic constitutional principles (parliamentary accountability of the HA), their views clashed over the exact institutional design implications: The German delegation firmly adhered to a *federal state* legitimating belief, while the French delegation did not view the institutional set-up through an equally well-defined *Leitbild*, although—on a number of occasions—Monnet underlined that the ultimate goal was to create a *federal* institutional set-up.[51] As the documentary evidence amply demonstrates, the German delegation intended to move towards a *federal state*-like institutional set-up which was, however, only partly taken up by Monnet and his collaborators as a result of their (alleged) 'unfamiliarity' with a federal system (Küsters 1988: 84–5). In an internal memorandum of the German delegation on the state of the institutional debate, it reads:

Germany supports the idea of a strong *federal* level ['starke Bundesgewalt'] by employing the federal idea from German constitutional practice. It strongly encourages the creation of a directly elected Common Assembly... France equally supports a strong *central* level ['starke Zentralgewalt'], yet it has little appreciation for the German federal state-conception ['bundesstaatliches Denken'] and considers organs such as the Council of Ministers and... the Common Assembly as "incomplete" European [organs].[52]

The centrality of the *federal state* legitimating belief in informing the German delegations' proposals for 'higher level' institutions was furthermore reflected and exemplified in the German delegation's proposal for a unicameral or, alternatively, bicameral *Montan-Kongress*.[53] It was envisaged that the Montan-Kongress would be the counter-weight to the HA, the executive organ (Gerçek 1998: 108–9). Congruent with the conception of the CA as a legislature, Germany preferred a strong parliament with real decision-making and budgetary powers to a weak parliament solely endowed with control powers.[54] French scepticism about the powers of the assembly and about the 'second' federal element, the Council of Ministers, thus has to be seen (a) against the background of a lack of 'familiarity' with a federal institutional set-up, and, more importantly, (b) in the context of their strong preference for a largely unconstrained HA.

In the earlier discussion, I have attempted to show that the motives held by Monnet and his German colleagues to incorporate an institutional element to ascertain parliamentary democratic control in the constitutional structure of the ECSC suggests that the inclusion of such a parliamentary assembly *cannot* be deduced from the exigencies of seeking a means to effectively circumscribe the powers of the HA. In contrast, the Benelux countries considered the creation of effective control mechanisms vis-à-vis the HA paramount so as to limit the risk that the HA would adopt decisions that could turn out to have detrimental effects on domestic socio-economic policy objectives. Furthermore, the issue of procedural legitimacy was touched upon by the Benelux governments only in so far as it provided arguments for limiting the role of institutional mechanisms that would potentially rein in cherished domains of national sovereignty. A parliamentary assembly was viewed to be incapable of safeguarding important aspects of national sovereignty. A body representing the different national governments with the power to issue directives, to amend or block decisions by the HA would be more destined to achieve this goal.[55]

The Belgian and Dutch heads of delegation to the Schuman Plan negotiations, Max Suétens and Dirk Spierenburg, made explicit the link between economic interests, 'lower level' institutions and the concomitant interpretation of the accountability and legitimacy problem. The HA had to be held at bay by those who were affected by its decisions, that is, national governments and their policies. Their position is reflected in the following two citations from diplomatic documents:

[T]he Dutch government agrees, in principle, with the High Authority. Certain national prerogatives must be delegated. Yet to make the apparatus effective, one must not renounce the role of national governments. The High Authority strongly touches upon national economic policies, which are primarily conducted by governments... Governments should, in a second reading, debate the High Authority's proposals and take decisions with a two-thirds majority.[56]

As far as the institutions are concerned, the Belgian delegation supported and later expanded the Dutch proposal for the institution of a Council of Ministers as a counter-weight to the High Authority controlling its activities. The synopsis of the Treaty articles... clearly indicates that the Council of Ministers intervenes in all important questions. With regard to the Common Assembly, the Belgian delegation has challenged the German proposal, supported by the French delegation up to a certain point, to develop the assembly into a distinctively federal organ, embryo of a federal European Assembly.[57]

The dominance of socio-economic interests in informing the Benelux countries' preferences for cooperation made the search for a favourable distribution of decision-making powers among the envisaged Community institutions one of the most important questions of the early phases of the Schuman Plan negotiations. Any talk about creating a *federal state* suffered outright rejection.[58] The Benelux countries cared about 'higher level' institutional issues only in so far as these did not conflict with 'lower level' issues, a distribution of decision-making powers among the different institutions that was not likely to threaten the realization of domestic policy objectives. Furthermore, concerns for procedural legitimacy did not feature strongly and were only employed to back arguments that national governments, as elected representatives of domestic electorates and the principal carriers of democratic legitimacy, had to play *the* prominent role. A strong parliamentary institution with legislative powers, as preferred by the German government, was absolutely unacceptable to the Benelux governments because it would have implied the existence of another actor with substantial policy-making powers whose decisions could produce unpredictable and potentially detrimental effects for domestic policy objectives. However, the Benelux countries accepted the CA as an essential element of the institutional structure, but only under the condition that it did not have any legislative and budgetary powers. Why was this the case? First, the Benelux countries accepted the argument employed by France and Germany that the partial delegation of sovereignty which was embodied in the new supranational HA needed to be controlled by a supranational parliamentary body. In a discussion with Monnet, Max Suétens said: 'Given that the High Authority is not accountable to governments, yet given that it has to be accountable to some institution, the only body to realise this accountability was a representation of the sovereignty of the people.'[59] Despite acceptance of the principle of democratic (parliamentary) control of the 'executive' HA, the Benelux delegations noted their satisfaction with the fact that the CA was to play only a negligible role in the Community's institutional set-up.[60] Second, a parliamentary body that possessed 'executive' control powers (censure motion) was considered unproblematic or even beneficial because it provided an additional 'check' on the HA's activities and thus did not negatively affect the 'division of gains' problem about which the Benelux states cared so much more than France and Germany.

In this section I have demonstrated that different motivations for co-operation correlated with different logics of institution-building. Whenever 'higher level' institutional issues were a key concern for a negotiating party, as was the case for the French and German delegations, the legitimacy deficit was perceived as a serious problem that had to be tackled. Conversely, where negotiating parties were driven by socio-economic concerns and hence had a clear idea about how 'lower level' institutions were to be designed—so as to provide the best safeguards and instruments for the achievement of cherished policy goals—the legitimacy deficit was perceived as much less problematic, as was the case for the Benelux governments. I have also demonstrated that even though the national delegations agreed on the creation of a parliamentary body, this did not stop them from being at odds about the precise role and powers of this body within the Community's institutional structure. Thus, actors may share a particular definition of a situation (here, the HA has to be held to account), they may nevertheless disagree about the exact institutional design implications. These differences can be traced back to different legitimating beliefs which, in the case of the *federal state* legitimating belief, so forcibly advanced by the German delegation, carried a very compelling institutional design logic for which the previous paragraphs have provided ample evidence.[61] In contrast, the French delegation—although contemplating the creation of a federally-organized Europe as a long-term goal—did not carry a similar set of ideas, and, instead, chose to defend, wherever it could, the central position of the HA, while ensuring that key principles of democratic accountability were respected.[62] The Benelux countries, for whom the economic benefits of cooperation were the prime mover to join the ECSC negotiations, did not agree to any institutional solutions which could potentially hamper or interfere with their national economic objectives. Their 'approach' towards the design of 'higher' as well as 'lower level' institutions was thus in line with behavioural prescriptions of the *economic community* legitimating belief. A parliamentary assembly was considered an acceptable part of the Community's institutional architecture as long as it did not cause any form of interference with domestic economic objectives.

3.3 The creation of a representative parliamentary institution and logic of social action

How can we characterize the interaction between the different national delegations during the negotiations leading to the adoption of the Treaty of Paris? What evidence do we possess to assess whether the delegations engaged in hard-nosed bargaining ('null hypothesis'), strategically applied norm-based arguments to realize their existing preferences (rhetorical action hypothesis), or whether they engaged in an exchange of arguments with a view to reach a reasoned consensus about the issue of democratic control and parliamentary involvement (communicative action hypothesis)?

> *Hypothesis 3: The 'null hypothesis'*
> Decision-making is characterized by bargaining about the powers of the EP and the outcome reflects the constellation of preferences and relative bargaining power of member state governments.

> *Hypothesis 4: Communicative action*
> Decision-making is characterized by a truth-seeking discourse on the appropriate role of the EP in the Community polity as a result of which member state governments reach a reasoned consensus.

> *Hypothesis 5: Rhetorical action*
> Decision-making is characterized by the strategic use of arguments through which member state governments seek to justify and realize their own preferences regarding the powers of the EP. Proponents of the *Federal State* legitimating belief—appealing to community values—exercise social pressure on recalcitrant states with the aim to shame them into acquiescing to the EP's empowerment. Recalcitrant member states will downplay the outcomes, question their relevance or reinterpret them to their advantage in the light of domestic opposition.

The process leading to inclusion of the CA in the ECSC can be separated into two stages: an arguing stage and a bargaining stage. During the first stage, all national delegations reached consensus over the question whether or not to include a parliamentary assembly in the institutional structure of the ECSC. The evidence presented hitherto has demonstrated that the decision by the national delegations to include the CA in the institutional set-up of the ECSC was not the result of a bargain in which pre-defined preferences had to be balanced and concessions made. The perceived necessity to institute a (democratic) accountability mechanism for the supranational HA triggered a discussion among the delegations about 'appropriate' control mechanisms. The lack of pre-defined policy positions also implied that national delegations had not made pre-commitment to their domestic 'stakeholders' on the Assembly question. Instead, policy positions had to be defined before and during the negotiations as a response to what, in particular the German and French delegations came to perceive as a legitimacy deficit. The Benelux acceptance of the parliamentary assembly was a 'triumph' for proponents of the *federal state* legitimating belief. But why did the Benelux delegations accept it? I have already shown that from the outset of the negotiations, the question about control mechanisms vis-à-vis the HA was vigorously debated. Given the supranational character of the ECSC, France and Germany were expressly in favour of a parliamentary organ to control the supranational HA. Furthermore, the French and, more pronouncedly, the German delegation made it known that a parliamentary assembly was an essential part of what should, in the long term, amount to a federal European polity. Conversely, the Belgian and Dutch governments, in particular, wanted national governments to retain an important function within the institutional structure, primarily to hold the HA at bay. Despite being much more reserved towards the *federal state* conception, its analogy opened an avenue to justify the inclusion of an intergovernmental organ, the Council: during the first couple of weeks of the Schuman Plan negotiations, the Belgian and Dutch delegations argued that part and parcel of the *federal state* conception is its dualistic character. A member of the Dutch delegation expressed this point lucidly, by arguing that '[e]ven in a federation...there is such a thing as state's right.'[63] Thus, in early July 1950, the national delegations had agreed on the creation of the CA and an intergovernmental organ. The *federal state* legitimating belief was hence a useful ideational resource for the Belgian and Dutch governments to justify their preference for an intergovernmental organ. During a meeting with the heads of delegation, Spierenburg, head of the Dutch delegation, argued that if the creation of the HA was conceived of as the 'beginning of a federation, a federation also presupposes a federal government, and consequently a ministerial committee.'[64] As I have shown in the preceding sections, the French and German delegations readily accepted the validity of this argument. Yet, while some members of the German delegation expressed their outright enthusiasm,[65] Monnet was somewhat more reserved since he did not want to have to compromise on the prominent role he had foreseen for the HA. Did the Dutch and Belgian government employ the *federal state* argument expediently to strategically further their preference for an intergovernmental organ, or is there evidence that they were convinced by the validity of the argument and only brought it to its logical conclusion, that is, a federation implies state representation (Council) as well as popular representation (CA)? On the basis of the available evidence, it is difficult to discriminate between communicative or rhetorical action as the main modes of action. In either case, the outcome, that is, the inclusion of the CA in the Community's institutional architecture would have been the same.

Once we move from the first to the second stage, the question about the CA's scope of power and hence, distributive or 'lower level' issues gained prominence. The Benelux countries accepted the principle of parliamentary accountability of the HA but only under the condition that the CA would not be able to exercise any form of legislative or policy-influencing powers (which, as stated earlier, were viewed to be detrimental for the achievement of domestic socio-economic policy objectives). 'Democracy' was accepted in the form of the CA, but it should not make a difference. The second stage was thus characterized by bargaining over the scope of the CA's powers. Even though the German delegation continued to appeal to the supranational character of the Community and its nascent federal character in order to justify the delegation of legislative powers to the CA, the other delegations rejected this idea either as premature (France) or politically unacceptable (Belgium and the Netherlands). The German delegation learned soon that the other delegations were not willing to grant concessions on the question of the scope of the CA's powers. Legislative powers, as demanded by the German delegation, were out of question.[66] As mentioned above, the Benelux countries held the view that in an IGC—where every member state was supposed to have equal weight— they could pursue or protect their preferences more effectively than in a representative parliamentary body.[67] Thus, even though the Benelux countries supported the inclusion of a parliamentary body as a mechanism to ensure the democratic accountability of the HA's decisions, they opposed any moves that could lead to further redistribution of powers to supranational actors. In the Benelux countries, but also in France and partly in Germany, there was mounting domestic opposition to the idea of endowing the CA with legislative powers: which national parliament, asks Küsters (1988: 90) rhetorically, would happily renounce its prerogatives for the benefit of a European level assembly? Since the German delegation did not want to jeopardize the negotiations over the scope of the CAs' powers, the CA's role remained, as of yet, rather marginal, or as the French delegation phrased it, 'incomplete', pointing at the potential for acquiring new competencies as the Community developed.

Notes

1. The founding members of the ECSC were France, the Federal Republic of Germany (henceforth Germany), Italy, and the Benelux countries (Belgium, the Netherlands and Luxembourg).

2. The example cited by the OED of the use of the word 'supranational' in the context of interstate cooperation refers to a contribution by Winston Churchill during a debate in the House of Commons: on 27 June 1950: 'I would add, to make my answer quite clear to the right hon. and learned Gentleman, that if he asked me, "Would you agree to a supranational authority which has the power to tell Great Britain not to cut any more coal or make any more steel, but to grow tomatoes instead?" I should say, without hesitation, the answer is "No".'

3. See Gillingham (2003: 27–8) on the supranational principle.

4. Note that the following represents only a limited selection of the ample literature on the Schuman Plan and the founding of the ECSC. See, for example, Racine (1954); Diebold (1959); Mosler (1966); Milward (1984); Schwabe (1988); Gillingham (1991, 2003); Duchêne (1994); Featherstone (1994); Lappenküper (1994); Spierenburg and Poidevin (1994); Thiemeyer (1998); Bitsch (1999). See also Adenauer's and Monnet's memoirs (Adenauer 1965; Monnet 1978).

5. See Spaak (1971: 199–206) for a similar assessment.

6. Reynaud held several cabinet posts of successive Third Republic governments in the 1930s and was a delegate to the Council of Europe from 1949–55.

7. 'I [Monnet] congratulated him, but he answered: "To tell the truth, it's already no longer an "authority". To get the text voted, the word had to be removed. Now it's to be an "organization" answerable to Governments: its task will be to suggest general guidelines." "Will it have the power of decision?" "No. But it won't even see the light of the day. The Committee of Ministers will bury it" ' (Monnet 1978: 282).

8. Duchêne (1994: 202) later noted about the Schuman Plan: 'The Schuman Plan . . . had the practical advantage of being relatively focused. The Council of Europe, in its political approach, and the customs union, in its economic one, had been too broad too soon and aroused the maximum opposition. Coal and steel were more manageable.'

9. See Möller and Hildebrand (1997: 227, Document No 53, 'Unterredung zwischen Bundeskanzler Adenauer und Generalkommissar für den Plan Monnet vom 23/05/1950, Aufzeichnung (Auszug)').

10. Monnet's (1978: 292) analysis of the issue reads as follows: 'France's continued recovery will come to a halt unless we rapidly solve the problem of German industrial production and its competitive capacity. The basis of the superiority which French industrialists traditionally recognize in Germany is her ability to produce steel at a price that France cannot match. From this they conclude that the whole French production is...handicapped. Already, Germany is seeking to increase her production from eleven to fourteen million metric tons...At the same time, French production is levelling off or even falling. Merely to state these facts makes it unnecessary to describe what the results will be: Germany expanding; German dumping on export markets; a call for protection of French industry; an end to trade liberalization; [...] and France back in the old rut of limited protected production.... If only the French could lose their fear of German industrial domination, then the greatest obstacle to a united Europe would be removed.'

11. Lynch (1988: 124) stresses, however, that besides the economic importance of Monnet's plan, the political and even moral aspects of the plan were rather more crucial: 'Economic details were of secondary importance. It is true that [Monnet] did not commission a detailed examination of the relative costs in the French and German coal and steel industries...before making the proposal.'

12. See Küsters (1988: 74–5) and Lappenküper (1994: 406–7).

13. Schuman began his declaration of 9 May 1950 with a few introductory sentences: 'It is no longer a time for vain words, but for a *bold, constructive act.* France has acted, and the consequences of her action may be immense. We hope they will. She has acted essentially in the cause of peace. For peace to have a chance, there must first be a Europe. Nearly five years to the day after the unconditional surrender of Germany, France is now taking the first decisive step towards the construction of Europe and is associating Germany in this venture. It is something which must completely change things in Europe and permit other joint actions which were hitherto impossible. Out of all this will come forth Europe, a solid and united Europe. A Europe in which the standard of living will rise thanks to the grouping of production and the expansion of markets, which will bring down prices' (Schuman quoted in Fontaine 2000: 13, emphasis added). Chapter 12 in Jean Monnet's memoirs carries the heading 'A Bold Constructive Act, 1949–1950' (Monnet 1978).

14. See Möller and Hildebrand (1997: 226, Document No 52, 'Minister für Auswärtige Angelegenheiten Schuman, Regierungserklärung, 09/05/1951), emphasis in the original.

15. HAEC, MAEF—Délégation française, PS: Déclarations à la Presse anglo-américaine, 08/06/1950 (author's translation).

16. HAEC, AA/PA.SFSP—53: Kurzprotokoll der Sitzung im französischen Außenministerium vom 21/06/1950.

17. In a protocol of the conversation between Monnet and the German delegation to the Schuman Plan negotiations, it reads: 'Given that the High Authority pools sovereign prerogatives of the different states and that, from a democratic point of view, the High Authority could not work without ensuring its control, the initiators of the French plan envisaged the creation of a control body consisting of members of national parliaments.' (HAEC, AA/PA.SFSP—53: Kurzprotokoll über die Aussprache,

die zwischen Herrn Monnet und den Mitgliedern der deutschen Delegation am Mittwoch, den 22/06/1950, abends, stattfand), author's translation.

18. Robert Schuman stated: 'Auf diese Weise würde zum ersten Mal eine Versammlung, die aus den Vertretern verschiedener Länder zusammengesetzt ist, mit entscheidenden Rechten begleitet werden, und die einzelnen Parlamente, welche Vertreter in diese Versammlung entsandt haben, würden dort gemeinsam den Teil der Souveränität ausüben, den sie abgetreten haben' (HAEC, AA/PA.SFSP—53: Auszüge aus der Debatte über den Schuman-Plan in der Nationalversammlung [deutsche Übersetzung], 25-26/06/1950).

19. HAEC, AA/PA.SFSP—53: Résumé du document de travail présenté par les experts français, 27/06/1950.

20. HAEC, MAEF—Délégation française, PS: conversations sur le Plan Schuman, séance restreinte, lundi après-midi, 03/07/1950, p. 3 (author's translation).

21. HAEC, MAEF—Délégation française, PS: conversations sur le Plan Schuman, séance restreinte, lundi après-midi, 03/07/1950, p. 4 (author's translation).

22. An internal document ascribes the following comments to Jean Monnet: 'M. Monnet rappelle l'importance, dans l'opinion publique, en Europe et Amérique, de la notion même d'Autorité supranationale. Une telle autorité n'est pas seulement l'organisme le mieux en mesure de résoudre certaines taches techniques; il est l'amorce d'une fédération. La forme de l'institution, et notamment l'existence d'une assemblée de parlementaires, par opposition à un comité des ministres, a donc un intérêt en soi. Il s'agit de préparer l'avenir, de créer et de renforcer l'Europe en éliminant les anciennes divisions.' (HAEC, MAEF—Délégation française, PS: conversations sur le Plan Schuman, séance restreinte, lundi après-midi, 03/07/1950, p. 10)

23. This section draws from B. Rittberger (2001).

24. 'Classical' Waltzian autonomy-oriented realist theory cannot be squared with this view. However, influence-seeking variants of neorealism have been explored to better explain 'state behaviour' in international politics including the delegation of powers to international and supranational institutions (see, for example, Grieco [1995]; V. Rittberger [2001]; see Bates [1998] for an interesting application of neorealist thinking to explaining the creation of the International Coffee Organization).

25. The reader may notice that Italy has not been included in the ensuing analysis. This omission is mainly due to the lack of adequate archival and secondary source material. However, it will be evident from the analysis that variation in the 'independent variable' (underlying preferences for cooperation, i.e. status/security-induced or economic) is ascertained even though Italy is left out.

26. In a memorandum by the Quai d'Orsay from 3 January 1950, the core problems of the Franco–German relationship are summarized as follows (mirroring both economic and geopolitical concerns): 'La politique française à l'égard de l'Allemagne est essentiellement inspirée par un souci de sécurité. . . . A côté de [. . .] sécurité militaire qui actuellement ne paraît pas pouvoir être mise en danger, existe une *sécurité économique* à laquelle notre pays aspire et qu'il cherche à assurer également. C'est celle-ci qui constitue *le problème actuel français en matière de sécurité*. Nos compatriotes craignent la concurrence allemande; ils la craignent sur le marche extérieur où l'Allemagne réapparaît peu à peu, souvent au détriment de nos exportateurs; ils la craignent

encore bien d'avantage en France même, à la simple pensée d'une libéralisation trop poussée des échanges qui permettrait aux Allemands d'inonder le marché français ; un tel afflux de produits moins chers que les marchandises françaises aurait, estiment-ils, pour conséquence des bouleversements économiques...et par suite sociaux dont les répercussions politiques seraient imprévisibles' (Möller and Hildebrand 1997: 208, emphasis in original).

27. See Möller and Hildebrand (1997: 220–1, author's translation).

28. See also Gillingham (2003) and Lynch (1988).

29. See Lappenküper (1994: 410).

30. According to Alan Milward, 'French anxieties were more about the tendency of American policies to eliminate the bargaining advantages France still had over Germany. The Americans had given no support to France in the Ruhr Authority' (Milward 1984: 386).

31. See Milward (1984: 419) and Mioche (1988).

32. According to Gillingham (1991: 236), 'Monnet negotiated on behalf of France without the active support of any organized interests in the private sector and in the face of bitter opposition from virtually all of it.'

33. The often bitter opposition to the Constitution of the Fourth Republic by the Communists (PC) and the Gaullists (RPF) forced the 'centre' parties to form so-called *troisième force* governing coalitions between 1947 and 1951 comprising, *inter alia*, the Socialists (SFIO), the Christian Democrats (MRP) as well as other parties on the Republican left.

34. Craig Parsons has argued that the French government chose the ECSC project 'over defending the [International Ruhr Authority] or the OEEC or Council of Europe not because a spontaneous majority demanded the former, but because leaders asserted their own views in a divisive debate. Because party positions largely dissolved, Robert Schuman had the autonomy...to take a "leap in the dark" toward his interpretation of French interests' (Parsons 2003: 65–6, 2002).

35. See, for example, *Konrad Adenauer und der Schuman-Plan—Ein Quellenzeugnis* (1988).

36. AAPD—1949/50, No 47, 8 May 1950 (author's translation).

37. Milward (1984: 399) argues that the 'Korean war and the rumour of West German rearmament had raised the possibility that the Federal Republic might not have to accept the Schuman proposals as a way of getting rid of the limitations on its sovereignty.'

38. See Lappenküper (1994: 424–5) on the impact of external factors on the German negotiating position.

39. See Griffiths (1988: 38) and *Konrad Adenauer und der Schuman-Plan—Ein Quellenzeugnis* (1988: 135).

40. Adenauer was quoted in Monnet's (1978: 303) *Memoirs*: 'Schuman wrote [to me] that the aim of his proposal was not economic but highly political. There was still a fear in France that when Germany recovered she would attack France...If an organization such as Schuman envisaged were set up, enabling both countries to discern the first signs of...rearmament, this new possibility would bring great relief for France.'

41. According to Duchêne, the deliberations between Monnet and the British Foreign Office from mid-May to early June 1950 indicated that the 'British refused to commit

themselves to a supranational HA—to "buy a pig in the poke", "sign a blank cheque" or "commit ourselves in the dark"—but wanted to join the talks' (Duchêne 1994: 207–8).

42. HAEC, JMDS.A-07.02-000073, 24 May 1950 (author's translation, emphasis added).

43. Ibid.

44. HAEC, JMDS.A-07.02-000074 (US National Archives: US-NA, RG 59, State Department, 850.33, Schuman Plan); Department of State, Incoming Telegram, No 26, 6 July 1950.

45. During the negotiations, a French diplomat asked Spierenburg whether the proposed two-thirds majority in the ministerial committee would be to validate or to invalidate decisions by the HA: ' "To validate them", Spierenburg answered. The Benelux countries were clearly thinking in terms of a blocking minority' (Monnet 1978: 327).

46. AAPD (1949/50: No 89).

47. HAEC, AA/PA.SFSP—62, 11 July 1950 (author's translation).

48. HAEC, JMDS.A-07.02-000073, 24 May 1950.

49. HAEC, AA/PA.SFSP—53, 22 June 1950 (author's translation).

50. HAEC, AA/PA.SFSP—62, 27 July 1950 (author's translation).

51. See, for example, HAEC, AA/PA.SFSP—102, 26 July 1950 where it reads (in the original): 'Der Vorsitzende (Monnet, Frankreich) betonte, dass das politische Leitbild die Schaffung von föderalen Organen sei.'

52. HAEC, AA/PA.SFSP—102, 10 August 1950 (author's translation, emphasis added).

53. The following alternatives of a Montan-Kongress were considered. The first included a Council of Ministers as 'first chamber' and an EP as 'second chamber' (*dualistic solution*). The second was conceived as a one-chamber assembly in which one half would be composed of members of parliament elected from the ranks of national parliamentarians and the other half of delegates of the different governments (*monistic solution*) (Gerçek 1998: 108–9).

54. See, for example, HAEC, AA/PA.SFSP—102, 10 August 1950, HAEC, AA/PA.SFSP—103, 20 July 1950.

55. AAPD (1949/50: No. 73).

56. AAPD (1949/50: No. 84, author's translation). See also HAEC, AA/PA.SFSP—62, 11 July 1950.

57. HAEC, JMDS.A-07.02-000073: Schuman Plan and the Belgian Response, Ministère des Affaires Étrangères, Fonds van der Meulen 5216, Négociations Schuman Plan 1451, no date (Principales thèses défendues par la délégation Belge).

58. See, for example, HAEC, JMDS.A-07.02-000073: Schuman Plan and the Belgian Response, Ministère des Affaires Étrangères, Fonds van der Meulen 5216, Jan–Juin 1950, Schuman Plan; Lettre de la Ministère des Affaires Étrangèrs et du Commerce Extérieur, Direction Générale B, Bruxelles, 18 September 1950 (Note pour Monsieur le Ministre). In this document, Paul van Zeeland is reported to have expressed his stark opposition to the idea that the principles of the Schuman Plan had anything to do with an emergent 'federal state': 'Il est absolument faux de prétendre, comme certains membres de la délégation allemande, que le Plan Schuman n'est réalisable que si on institue un Etat supranational ou si on tend vers la création d'un pareil Etat.'

59. AAPD (1949/50: No 89, author's translation).

60. 'Tout en doutant de son opportunité quant aux garanties qu'elle pourrait offrir dans la réalité, on peut penser que sa création dans les conditions prévues au projet ne comporterait pas d'inconvénients majeurs.' (HAEC, JMDS.A-07.02-000073: Schuman Plan and the Belgian Response, Ministère des Affaires Étrangères, Fonds van der Meulen 5216, Jan–Juin 1950, Schuman Plan; Cabinet du Jurisconsulte [Note de J. Mûuls concernant le projet de traité relative au charbon et à l'acier, rédaction du Plan Schuman du 8 novembre 1950]).

61. The following section of an exposé of Germany's 'motives' in the Schuman Plan negotiations summarizes the institutional design implications of the *federal state* legitimating belief: 'Pour l' exécution de ce plan, la Communauté... est intentionnellement conçue d'une manière analogue à celle d'un un Etat Fédérale. La proposition initiale française avait prévu un ensemble d'institutions sans lien interne, parmi lesquelles une Haute Autorité, conçue comme un pouvoir supranational. Cependant, au cours des discussions, il fut évident que les buts proposés ne pouvaient être atteints que par la création d'une seule entité supérieure ayant des droits et des obligations; cette entité doit avoir, de même qu'un Etat Fédéral, des institutions qui lui sont attachées.... (a) La Haute Autorité... correspond au Gouvernement ou au Cabinet de l'Etat Fédéral. (b) L'Assemblée Commune... correspond au Parlement Fédéral. (c) Le Conseil Spécial des Ministres... correspond au Conseil Fédéral. (d) La Cour de Justice—a les obligations d'une Cour de Justice constitutionnelle et administrative supérieur' (HAEC, MAEF—Délégation française, PS: Exposé des motifs allemand [premier version], 31 May 1951).

62. While the autonomy of the supranational HA was at the core of French interests, it became evident 'très vite la nécessite de créer un système équilibré, conforme aux principes démocratiques, où l'autorité nécessaire serait balancée par des garanties destinées à remplacer celles que les intéresses rencontrent dans leurs institutions nationales et, en même temps, à sauvegarder les droits conservés par les Etats, qui demeurent responsables de la partie de leur économie qui ne concerne pas le charbon et l'acier.' (HAEC, MAEF—Délégation française, PS: Exposé des motifs français [provisoire], 17 June 1951).

63. The US Department of State, Incoming Telegram No 1160, 27. June 1950, for the Ambassador: William T. Nunley (The Hague).

64. MAEF.DECE: Délégation française—conversations sur le Plan Schuman, réunion du Comité de Chefs de délégation sur les questions institutionnelles, 5/7/1950.

65. 'Ferner kündigt sich im Ministerrat bereits ein Organ, das für die allgemeine Verfassung des vereinigten Europas unentbehrlich sein wird, nämlich das Staatenhaus, die Vertretung der einzelstaatlichen Interessen, also ein föderatives Organ (im kontinentalen Sinn). Deshalb sollte man den Gedanken verfolgen, mindestens für den künftigen Ausbau zu einer supranationalen Gesamtverfassung Ministerrat und Assemblée Commune in gewisser Analogie zu dem Kongress der Vereinigten Staaten, zu einem getrennt beschliessenden Organ, aber auf gegenseitige Kooperation angewiesenen bundesstaatlichen Gesamtorgan zusammenzufassen. Denn, wie auch die künftige Verfassung Europas aussehen wird, es wird in jedem Falle eine föderale, d.h. bundes-

staatliche sein' (HAEC, AA/PA.SFSP—53: Notizen für Herrn von Brentano von Hallstein, 8/10/1950).

66. In an internal German diplomatic document, the federal trajectory of the ECSC is mentioned. The German government furthermore expresses its firm support for going beyond mere supervisory powers for the CA. The document, however, acknowledges that, at present, the other governments are not ready to make far-reaching concessions in this regard: 'Es war das Bestreben der deutschen Delegation, unter einem anderen Gesichtspunkt die Stellung der parlamentarischen Versammlung zu stärken. Wir denken daran, dass der Abschluss dieses Vertrages den Anfang für die Entwicklung eines europäischen Staatswesens darstellt. Im Rahmen dieser Absicht wird es von grosser Bedeutung sein, gesetzgeberische Funktion bei einer europäischen parlamentarischen Versammlung zu vereinigen. Deshalb ist eine Stärkung der parlamentarischen Versammlung wünschenswert. Gegenüber der zurückhaltenden Darstellung anderer Delegationen waren hier aber nur geringe Gewinne zu erzielen' (HAEC, AA/PA.SFSP—54: Bericht vor Ausschuss für Besatzungsstatut und Auswärtige Angelegenheiten und vor interministeriellem Ausschuss, 31/10/1950).

67. A German diplomtic document reports on the Benelux countries' attitude towards a strengthening of the Common Assembly: 'Auf seiten der kleineren Staaten bestehen ein Widerstreben, weil ihnen der Gedanke eines europäischen Parlaments nicht sympathisch sei. Deshalb liege der Akzent ihrer Wünsche auf dem Ministerrat. Jedes der beteiligten Länder sollte durch einen Minister vertreten sein. Auf deutscher Seite gehe das Bestreben dahin, diesem Ministerrat nicht zu grosse Befugnis zu geben. Die kleinen Staaten würden im Ministerrat ebenso stark sein wie die grossen Länder' (HAEC, AA/PA.SFSP—63: Protokoll über die Sitzung der Vertreter der Deutschen delegation zum Europarat in Strassbourg mit den Vertretern der deutschen Delegation für den Schumanplan in Paris, 13/10/1950).

4

Budgetary Powers and the Treaty of Luxembourg

Budgetary politics in the EU has—for long—been a largely under-researched area.[1] Although the size of the EU budget is very small in relative terms (only 0.98% of EU Gross National Income in 2004),[2] spending for agriculture, structural, regional, and social policies nevertheless provides concentrated as well as diffuse benefits for a considerable range of stakeholders. In this context, it is important to ask which of the different Community actors are able to influence spending decisions since different actors are likely to have different spending preferences. Changes in the procedural arrangements of budgetary decision-making are thus likely to have considerable welfare implications for the groups affected. This chapter explains the creation of one of the EP's 'stepping stones' towards a parliamentary institution with 'traditional' competencies: the adoption of the Luxembourg Treaty in 1970 enabled the EP to play an increasingly influential role in the Community's budgetary process. After the creation of the CA and the delegation of certain supervisory powers vis-à-vis the HA, the Luxembourg Treaty marks another watershed in the institutional development of the EP. Far-sightedly, the Dutch government recognized the potentially sweeping implications of the Luxembourg Treaty provisions for their effects on the balance of power among the Community institutions. In an explanatory statement which the Dutch government attached to the ratification legislation, it reads:

On the basis of the new provisions, the European Parliament will have the opportunity to make life difficult for the Commission and the Council because it can deny the funds for administrative expenses and hence make talks with the Parliament unavoidable. . . . Throughout history the rights of parliaments resulted less from the adoption of certain precise texts but rather through contestation with the governments. The present text [the Luxembourg Treaty] offers . . . ample opportunities for such contestation.[3]

What was viewed in rather positive terms for some was considered a bleak prospect for others. During the ratification debate in the French National Assembly, the Euro-sceptic Gaullist MP Jacques Vendroux issued a metaphoric warning:

It will...be possible for the Parliament in the future to amend the Council's proposals by imposing a slight augmentation of administrative expenses...potentially against the will of the governments...It has been underlined...that this power applies only to amounts judged insignificant...But surely, this signifies the tiny origin of a minuscule embryo, but there are only few examples where these embryos have not grown and sometimes even turned into monsters.[4]

However dramatic these visions may sound, they both point to the same trajectory: the EP, once it is being given a taste of more power, will seek to exploit these powers as fully as possible.[5] The objective of this chapter is, however, to go back and ask why the six Community member state governments agreed on endowing the EP with powers to influence the outcomes of budgetary decision-making. In section 4.1, the hypothesized link advanced in *hypothesis 1a* between the delegation and pooling of sovereignty and political elites' perception of a legitimacy deficit will be subjected to scrutiny. Section 4.2 portrays the legitimating beliefs held by the different actors and, concomitantly, the proposals advanced for the alleviation of the legitimacy deficit. In Section 4.3, I ask how the normative constraints imposed by the perceived legitimacy deficit and domestically held legitimating beliefs affected governments' behaviour and interactions during negotiations leading to the adoption of the Luxembourg Treaty.

4.1 Member states' delegation of sovereignty and the legitimacy deficit

In the ensuing paragraphs I offer a brief historical overview of the run up to the IGC leading to the Luxembourg Treaty of 1970. In this context I also assess the value of the independent variable (*pooling/delegation* or *no pooling/no delegation*) in order to explore whether the expectation laid down in hypothesis 1a holds:

Hypothesis 1a: Legitimacy deficit
Delegation and pooling of national sovereignty will produce an asymmetry between consequentialist and procedural legitimacy (legitimacy deficit).

4.1.1 The creation of a system of own resources

It can be considered an irony in the evolution of the European Community that the one member state which pressed most strongly for the completion of a common market for agricultural products, France, was the most reluctant to accept the institutional consequences of creating such a common market. Whereas the French government accepted the creation of a system of own financial resources as an unavoidable corollary of the creation of a common market for agricultural products, another corollary that was equally considered unavoidable by the other five member states was contested vehemently by the French government: the conferral of certain budgetary powers to the EP.

The documents signed to establish the EEC and the EAEC or 'Euratom' did not endow these two communities with financial autonomy. It is common for international organizations that their budgets depend on annual contributions from their member states. This was also the case for the EEC and EAEC. Given the nature of the financial resources—they had to be approved in the annual budgetary procedures in the NPs of every member state—it was undisputed that the national governments in the Council were to determine the distribution of the Community budget (European Parliament 1970: 14). However, the Treaty of Rome did not exclude the possibility of the creation of a Community financing system where financial resources would directly accrue to the Community budget and not via the approval of NPs. Considering the Community's trajectory—the creation of a common market with a common customs tariff on goods coming from outside the Community was hotly discussed—a reform of the system of Community financing was not a too distant possibility. From this point of view, the wording of Article 201 EEC is all but surprising:

> The Commission shall study the conditions under which the financial contributions of Member States . . . may be replaced by other resources available to the Community itself, in particular by revenue accruing from the common customs tariff when finally introduced.

EEC Council Regulation No. 25 adopted in January 1962, which set up the European Agricultural Guidance and Guarantee Fund (EAGGF), laid down that levies on agricultural imports from third countries would accrue directly to the Community by the end of a transitional period (Coombes 1972: 23).[6] The regulation also called upon the Commission to examine proposals to alter the Community's financing system as foreseen in the

Treaty in accordance with Article 201 EEC. According to Coombes, Regulation 25 resulted from an initiative which 'arose principally from the practical need for new arrangements to finance the [Common Agricultural Policy, CAP]' (Coombes 1972: 24). Regulation 25 provided for an 'interim method of financing the [EAGGF] through June 30, 1965, after which a new financial regulation...would be needed' (Newhouse, 1967: 57).[7] Consequently, at the end of 1964, the Council called upon the Commission to submit a proposal to cover the following years. This proposal was to include measures providing for the levies to accrue directly to the Community in the single market stage. The 'Commission maintained, with the support of the French representatives on the Council, that this stage would be reached when common prices for agricultural products came into effect within the Community' (Coombes 1972: 24). France was the main engine behind the creation of a common agricultural market: 'France regarded secure financing for the CAP as a vital interest and sought to establish a system that would not require annual renegotiations' (Moravcsik 2000: 34). Despite all the public rhetoric about retaining France's 'grandeur', one of Charles de Gaulle's primary policy objectives was to secure a financial advantage for French agriculture within a common European market for agricultural products. This was sparked by the consideration that French agricultural products were only competitive within Europe but not on world market scale (see Moravcsik 1998: 179).

Following the Council's request, the Commission presented its proposals on the creation of a system of own resources to the Council in communications dated 31 March and 13 April 1965.[8] The Commission made it clear that the creation of a system of own resources would render a re-examination of the budgetary procedure as laid down in Article 203, of the EEC necessary, in particular those provisions affecting the EP's role in the budgetary procedure.[9] Under its federally-minded Commission President, Walter Hallstein, the Commission considered an increase in the EP's budgetary powers indispensable, arguing that the EP should be entitled to influence the deployment of the Community's own resources once these expenditures escaped the control of NPs (see European Parliament 1970: 75). However, the Commission proposals for reforming the budgetary procedure did not only envisage the empowerment of the EP, the Commission equally sought to enhance its own influence over the allocation of funds in the budgetary procedure (see European Parliament 1970: 81–2 and Newhouse 1967: 60–1). Yet, when the Council met in late June 1965 to discuss the Commission's proposal on a new financial package and on institutional reform, it failed to reach an agreement. In the night of 30

June–1 July 1965, the French delegation left the negotiating table, prompting what became known as the 'empty chair crisis'. Newhouse asserts that
it was the Commission's proposal on institutional reform which upset the
French and triggered the Community crisis.[10] According to Coombes, the
empty chair crisis 'marked the end of a period in which progress in the EEC
depended on a coalition between the French representatives in the Council and the Commission. The French had sought to get a common agricultural policy established along the lines of Regulation 25 and to get a firm
commitment from the other member states' governments to support this
policy in the future. To this end they had sought agreement once and for
all on a general system of financing the policy rather than individual
agreement on different products at different times' (Coombes 1972: 25).
The other member states were not overly enthusiastic about a system
which would mainly benefit French farming:

Aware that other Member States' governments were reluctant to commit themselves to
an expensive agricultural policy, the Commission tried to compensate them by establishing an independent system of financing belonging to the Community, and therefore
above national interests, and by giving the European Parliament greater powers.
(Coombes 1972: 25)

At this stage, it is not necessary to re-capitulate the causes that finally
produced the 'empty chair crisis'.[11] It is important to bear in mind that
attempts to create a system of own resources which bypassed national
budgetary procedures were under way in the early 1960s, and that they
would, almost inevitably, re-surface sooner rather than later, given that—
with the empty chair crisis—the problem was not resolved, only post-
poned. Conflicts about procedural questions, such as the institutional
arrangement of the budgetary procedure and the degree to which supranational actors such as the Commission and the EP should be empowered,
would thus recur.

Consequently, the creation of the common market for agricultural
products and the question of own resources were not something that the
subsequent French governments could easily put aside. This is indicated
by abundant 'behind-the-scenes' wrangling over how to ensure the financial continuation of the CAP in the aftermath of the empty chair crisis.[12]
Coombes writes that the 'CAP was kept intact by an agreement on financing lasting until 1968. A timetable was fixed, setting the introduction of
free circulation of agricultural and industrial products in the Community
on 1 July 1968...It was agreed that from 1 July 1967 the EAGGF would take
over full responsibility for paying out compensation to exporters and for

interventions to support internal common market prices' (Coombes 1972: 25–6).

Following de Gaulle's resignation in the summer of 1969, France launched a new initiative to achieve a permanent financial settlement for the CAP. On 16 July 1969, the Commission submitted a new proposal to replace member states' national contributions with a system of own resources. And again, this proposal included suggestions to alter the budgetary procedure as laid down in the EEC Treaty. At their meeting in The Hague on 1–2 December 1969, the governments of the six Community member states agreed on a reform agenda characterized by the 'triptych' of *achèvement* (of the Common Market by instituting a common financing scheme with a view to 'lock-in' the CAP), *approfondissement* (of Community relations of the 'Six' by (re)considering political cooperation in foreign policy matters, furthering economic and monetary integration), and *élargissement* (most notably with regard to the UK). French President Georges Pompidou's agreement to open accession talks with the UK— pressed for most energetically by the Netherlands and Germany—was based on the condition that a definitive arrangement would have to be achieved for the agricultural market given that the temporary financing scheme for the CAP was running out by the end of 1969.[13] Under the category of *achèvement* the member state governments dealt with the creation of a system of own resources (pursuant Article 201, EEC Treaty) and a concomitant reform of the budgetary procedure (laid down in Article 203, EEC Treaty). Final agreement on the Community's system of own resources was not reached until April 1970; most difficulties centred around the question of common markets for wine and tobacco and the question of the budgetary powers of the EP.[14] A Council Decision adopted on 21 April 1970 foresaw the gradual replacement of financial contributions from the member states by the Community's own resources in two phases, a 'provisional period' until the end of 1974 during which 'member states' contributions will be replaced gradually by income from agricultural levies on imports from third countries and customs revenue from the common customs tariff' and a 'normal period' starting on 1 January 1975. From this date onwards, the rule applied that 'all agricultural levies and customs duties will be paid directly to the Communities' budget' (Coombes 1972: 27). The Luxembourg Treaty, signed on 22 April 1970, amended the original Treaty providing for a reformed budgetary procedure ('new' Article 203, EEC).[15]

In the above discussion, I demonstrated that much of the Community's activities in the 1960s revolved around the issue of the creation of a system of own resources replacing national budgetary contributions in the context of the introduction of common customs tariffs for agricultural and industrial products. About eight years after the adoption of Regulation 25 introducing the EAGGF, the Council Decision of 21 April 1970 finally paved the way for the introduction of a system of own resources. This move implied that, after a transition period which was to end in 1975, the Community budget would not rely on annual contributions approved by NPs of the member states any longer. From the perspective of the theory laid out in Chapter 2, the creation of a Community system of own resources constituted an instance of delegation: member states transferred authority for the levying of financial resources for the Community budget to the Community level, whereby the resources henceforth levied escaped domestic parliamentary approval. Following *hypothesis 1a*, we would expect that the creation of a system of own resources on the Community level posed a challenge to procedural legitimacy on the level of the domestic polity unless the creation of a system of own resources was accompanied by mechanisms to ensure that some form of parliamentary input and control was exercised over the deployment of the Community's own resources.

4.1.2 *The nature of the perceived legitimacy deficit*

This section is divided into two parts. The first part focuses on the pre-'empty chair crisis' period, while the second concentrates on the subsequent attempt to create a new financing system based on own resources which culminated in the adoption of the Luxembourg Treaty (1970). In order to find support for *hypothesis 1a* we need to observe that during both periods, prior to the 'empty chair crisis' and the adoption of the Treaty of Luxembourg, political elites in the member states expressed concerns about the consequences of transferring sovereignty by creating a Community's own resources system based on domestic democratic processes (thereby challenging procedural legitimacy).

4.1.2.1 France against the 'rest': the first attempt to empower the EP

As soon as the discussion about the creation of the own resources system surfaced, calls for an extension of the EP's budgetary powers intensified. The Commission, the EP, many national governments and NPs claimed that a link had to be established between the creation of a Community system of own resources and the empowerment of the EP in the budgetary process. Following the adoption of Council Regulation 25, the EP issued a number of reports and resolutions between 1963 and 1965 in which it demanded the extension of its budgetary powers as a logical corollary of the introduction of a Community system of own resources. In the Furler Report of 1963,[16] it was stated unmistakably 'that the moment a system of own resources is instituted on behalf of the Community, [the EP's] own budgetary powers must be reinforced according to the provisions laid down in Article 201, EEC. Since NPs can only exercise control over member state contributions, it is up to the EP to control the Community's financial resources' (European Parliament 1970: 56, author's translation). The same argument was advanced in two additional reports (the Vals I and Vals II Reports published in 1964 and 1965).[17] The first of the two reports discussed several national proposals (from the governments of Luxembourg, Germany, and the Netherlands) which univocally called for an extension of the EP's budgetary powers.

When the Council called upon the Commission to present proposals for a reform of the Treaty's budgetary provisions by referring to Regulation 25 and the introduction of own resources to fund the EAGGF after the end of the transition period in 1965, the Commission affirmed that the changes envisaged by reforming the CAP and the creation of own resources must lead to a re-examination of the budgetary procedure as laid down in Article 203, EEC and, in particular, those provisions affecting the EP.[18] According to the Commission '[a]n extension of the European Parliament's powers appears indispensable to guarantee that, on the European level, parliamentary control can be exercised as concerns the Community's own resources whose deployment escapes the control of national parliaments' (European Parliament 1970: 75, author's translation). Overall, the Commission's proposals to reform the budgetary procedure anticipated a strengthening of the EP's influence over the allocation of funds in the draft budget (while it did not 'forget' to propose an extension of its own powers).[19]

While the vast majority of MEPs and the Commission perceived a direct link between the creation of the common agricultural market, the creation of a Community system of own resources, and the need to empower the EP, did political elites in the member states follow suit? Given the overlapping membership of MEPs and national MPs, there is a good reason to assume that MEPs pushed vigorously for an extension of their own powers in their respective domestic parliamentary arenas. As a result of the prospects of the completion of the common agricultural market and a Community system of own resources, many NPs passed resolutions in which they called for an extension of the EP's budgetary powers. These calls were most pronounced in the German and Dutch parliaments. The respective governments undoubtedly accepted the argument of the 'logical' link between the financing of the CAP, own resources, and the EP's budgetary powers.[20]

With transfers of sovereignty imminent, the time seemed ripe for the launch of a concerted endeavour to extend the EP's powers. The Dutch permanent representative to the European Communities made it clear that with the creation of the EAGGF, the NPs would lose control of a considerable sum of expenditure. It was therefore necessary, he argued, to establish an appropriate institutional mechanism to control the use of these funds on the supranational level, a role to be exercised preferably by the EP.[21] In France, on the other hand, the Commission's proposal to link the creation of an own resources system with a reform of the budgetary procedure received a cool reception. The Gaullist government accused the Commission of feigning a problem where, in fact, none existed. The French government underlined that the Council solely would be responsible for the levying of resources for the Community. They accused the Commission of using the pretext of making the Community more democratic to give way to what was likely to become irresponsible spending and a waste of resources, especially if the EP was to be endowed with more powers in the budgetary procedure.[22]

Whereas one national government after the other accepted the 'logical link' between the establishment of a new financing arrangement for the CAP and the extension of the budgetary powers of the EP, the French government continuously disputed that such a link existed.[23] Interestingly, although it was not (yet) admitted publicly, internal government documents provide evidence that the argument about the fading of NP's budgetary powers was taken seriously by the French government. One internal document from the ministry of foreign affairs enumerates various provisions on NPs' influence in their respective budgetary procedures. The document concludes that—given the limited influence of NPs to amend draft budgets in their domestic arenas—the EP could not be given any powers that exceeded those of NPs.[24] This argument, as I show below, was used again five years later, becoming an important argumentative device for the French government in negotiating the Luxembourg Treaty.

The initial reactions to the prospect of delegation of budgetary powers to the Community level provide support for *hypothesis 1a*: political elites were aware of the detrimental consequences of a partial delegation of sovereignty (here, by creating a Community financing system of own resources) for domestic parliamentary participation and accountability in budgetary matters. After the issue of delegation itself was shelved as was, consequently, the issue about the extension of the EP's budgetary powers as a result of the 'empty chair crisis', it took almost four years until the issue resurfaced. Following our theory, the episode culminating in the adoption of the Luxembourg Treaty in April of 1970 should coincide with another display of proposals to delegate budgetary powers to the Community level and, at the same time, fuel worries about democratic control and accountability if the Community's budgetary procedure was not amended (thereby taking account of the procedural legitimacy problem).

4.1.2.2 Turning back the wheel: the summit in The Hague

After President de Gaulle's resignation, Georges Pompidou and the new Gaullist government pushed for resuming the talks on the completion of the common market for agricultural products and on the establishment of a permanent financing arrangement. This move was considered urgent since a further transition period for the financing of the CAP came to a close at the end of 1969.[25] Consequently, in mid-July 1969 the Commission presented the Council with a communication which contained proposals for the replacement of member states' financial contributions with a system of own resources. In comparison to the proposals which the Commission had issued in the mid-1960s, this time the Commission remained virtually silent on potential changes to the power of the EP.[26] Following the Commission's communication, the EP published a report which, unsurprisingly, heavily criticized the Commission for failing to make 'concrete proposals regarding the establishment of genuine budgetary powers' for the EP (European Parliament 1970: 128, author's translation).[27] Parliament called upon the Commission to remedy this situation and in a further communication, the Commission evoked the same principle that had been advanced half a decade before. The Commission argued that as long as the income of the Community mainly originated through states' contributions the member states should decide on the overall amount of expenditure. Consequently, the Council should have the final say over the budget. On the other hand, once the Community's income is financed from own resources accruing directly to the Community, the final say over the adoption of the Community budget should lie with the EP.[28] This argument was supported by those member states who had already fervently supported this logic some five years before. The French government, this time, though not declaring open dissent, remained mute on the issue: at the summit meeting in The Hague, the French delegation was all but keen to discuss the institutional questions that were associated with the completion of the common market for agriculture and the creation of a system of own resources (see Bitsch 2001: 548). President Pompidou did not even mention the issue of the EP's powers during his address at the first summit reunion.[29] However, there continued to be broad agreement among the other 'Five' on the validity of the general principle, that the creation of a system of own Community resources necessitated an enhanced role for the EP in the budgetary procedure. The communiqué which was published after the summit meeting in The Hague indicated that even France was willing to go along with an extension of the EP's role in the Community's budgetary procedure. The communiqué reads that the member states 'agree to replace gradually ... the contributions of the member countries by the Community's own resources... with the object of achieving, in due course, the integral financing of the Communities' budgets in accordance with the procedure provided for in Article 201 of the Treaty establishing the EEC and of *strengthening the budgetary powers of the European Parliament.*'[30] In the aftermath of the summit meeting in The Hague, the discussion about the EP's budgetary powers ceased to centre on the question *whether* there should be an extension of its powers at all; the 'new' discussion was about 'degree-ism': France had accepted the 'logic' pressed for by the Commission, the EP and the 'Five', yet the exact institutional implications remained disputed. What exact role should the EP play in the budgetary procedure? In sum, political elites in the Community member states thus shared the perception that the partial delegation of sovereignty posed a challenge to existing democratic practices in the member states' domestic polities. There was, hence, widespread agreement that something had to be done to alleviate the looming legitimacy deficit. But what should be done?

4.2 Political parties' legitimating beliefs

In this section, the legitimating beliefs held by the political parties in government in the run up to the Luxembourg Treaty negotiations will be assessed. The following hypothesis will be subject to scrutiny in the ensuing paragraphs.[31]

Hypothesis 2: Legitimating beliefs

Alternative proposals to create and reform institutions with a view to reducing the asymmetry between procedural and consequentialist legitimacy (the legitimacy deficit) are likely to reflect differences in legitimating beliefs held by different political elites.

4.2.1 *France: an intergovernmental Europe*

The foreign policy debates in the French National Assembly which preceded the summit meeting in The Hague and the signing of the Luxembourg Treaty were marked by the absence of any explicit government commitment to a specific course of action regarding the reform of the Community's institutions. Implicitly, however, statements by members of the government indicated that de Gaulle's 'heritage' which stressed *equality among nations* and the pursuit of *national independence* within a European framework of political (i.e. foreign policy cooperation) and economic cooperation was still the focal point of 'Gaullist' foreign policy.[32] In his speech before the National Assembly on 4 November 1969, Minister for Foreign Affairs, Maurice Schuman, referred to the government's commitment to advance Community affairs by dealing with the triple objectives of *achèvement*, *renforcement*, and *élargissement* at the forthcoming summit in The Hague. He pointed to the centrality of the CAP and the establishment of a permanent financing arrangement before accession negotiations could kick-off with the UK. Schuman did not mention the potential institutional consequences of creating a new Community financing arrangement: no reference was made to the proposals about enhancing the EP's budgetary powers.

Jacques Vendroux, MP and member of the governing Gaullist UDR (Union des Démocrates pour la République), was more explicit: he claimed that the Community activities prior to The Hague summit reflected an 'active approach towards integration and supranationality... [S]upranational aspirations presently experience a virulent resurgence in the context of the end of the transition period on 31 December... Professor Hallstein's [the Commission President] re-launch which is taken up today by certain adversaries of national independence is founded on the development of the Community institutions' financial autonomy.'[33] Vendroux then accused the Commission of having used its powers abusively in the past and that it was also likely to do so in the future. He called upon the Minister of Foreign Affairs, Maurice Schuman: 'You have already rendered your country many services.... We call upon you to render it one more:

Ensure that Europe develops in respect of the independence of nations and the authority of the state.'[34]

The French government's line under President de Gaulle's, which posited that the empowerment of supranational institutions such as the Commission and the EP, was absolutely insupportable,[35] was abandoned by Pompidou. Since the government was primarily interested to lock-in a favourable arrangement on the CAP, it hence relegated institutional questions to 'second rank': institutional questions should not be addressed in The Hague in order not to jeopardize agreement on substantive issues.[36] However, this did not mean that the government completely renounced the core principles of its conception about Europe, the preservation of 'national independence',[37] and the maintenance of a Europe of *intergovernmental cooperation*. However, the pursuit of commercial interests in conjunction with the CAP was considered to justify the partial delegation of sovereignty. Hence, the fact that institutional questions were evaluated by their effects on the realisation of economic objectives suggests that the government was less 'dogmatic' about institutional question to which a number of Gaullists MPs attached a high symbolic value: the issue about the EP's budgetary powers was one of such questions. The government's approach to the EP question thus displayed elements

Table 4.1 Legitimating belief of the Union des Démocrates pour la République

France—Union des Démocrates pour la République (UDR)	
Legitimating belief	Intergovernmental cooperation, economic community (government)
Source of legitimacy	National sovereignty, support for sectoral integration if it is in the national (economic) interest
Democracy at the international level?	Democracy vested in national democratic institutions; Council to remain the most important organ of Community decision-making
Nature of and remedies for the legitimacy deficit	Institutional provisions are legitimate as long as they advance economic interests; indifferent to EP empowerment as long as it does not hamper realisation of policy goals (government)

which are compatible with both an *intergovernmental cooperation* and *economic community* legitimating belief.

4.2.2 'The Rest': democratising community governance

The question about the empowerment of the EP assumed a much more prominent role in the domestic arena in the other five member states and most of the five national governments firmly committed themselves to press for an extension of the EP's powers before their domestic parliaments. In this section, I will focus on the discussions in the Netherlands and Germany to illustrate the differences in legitimating beliefs held by these member states and France. Belgium, Luxembourg, and Italy expressed views similar to those held by the German and Dutch parties in government. Therefore, they do not add substantial value to the elaboration of the dominant legitimating belief of this group of member state governments.

In Germany, all political parties represented in the Bundestag, Christian Democrats (CDU/CSU), Social Democrats (SPD), and Liberals (FDP), agreed on the trajectory of German policy towards Europe and its ultimate goal, the creation of a federal Europe. The adoption of resolutions either proposed by individual party groups or by the whole of the Bundestag calling for more 'parliamentary democracy' at the European level was a distinct feature throughout the 1960s, and their number even multiplied in the run-up to the Community crisis of mid-1965.[38] When the Bundestag debated the Commission's proposal to reform the Community's financing system—on the same day which marked the beginning of the 'empty chair crisis'—Carl Carstens, State Secretary in the Ministry of Foreign Affairs, expressed that it was the opinion of the government that the proposal for the creation of a system of Community's own resources presented an opportunity to strengthen the EP's powers. According to Niblok (1971: 87), '[t]his line was consistent with the position taken by the Bundestag itself...The Bundestag was content to restate the principle of no independent resources without parliamentary control and to call upon the Government to give its support to the [Commission's] proposals.' Following the debacle of 30 June 1965, the Bundestag was taking stock of the 'empty chair crisis', and MPs from all political groupings indicated their continuing support for an extension of the EP's powers. Käte Strobel, MP and MEP from the Social Democrats, reminded all political party groups that the 'Bundestag has always held the view that the influence of the European Parliament has to be enhanced; and the more significant

Community decisions turn out to be and the more decisions are taken by majority vote, the more influential the European Parliament has to become.'[39] In his address to the Bundestag Social Democratic MP Hans Apel pointed to the trade-off between the introduction of majority voting (which had been put aside since the breaking out of the 'empty chair crisis') and the potential weakening of the EP if majority voting in the Council was introduced. He hinted at the danger of a creeping 'de-parliamentarisation' ('Entparlamentarisierung') of national political systems and consequently called for supranational remedies to offset domestic de-parliamentarisation by strengthening the EP:

> It will be ever more difficult for [the Bundestag] to call upon the responsible minister who has been outvoted on a particular question and ask: 'How could this have happened?' With the introduction of qualified majority voting in the Council we have to think about changing the entire structure of the Community if we do not want to run into danger of an increasing de-parliamentarisation of the Community.[40]

When the question of Community reform re-surfaced in the second half of 1969, both the opposition (CDU/CSU) and the government coalition (SPD and FDP) continued to support institutional reform destined at an extension of the EP's powers. Walter Hallstein, the former Commission President, and Carl-Ludwig Wagner, both MPs from the CDU/CSU, asked Walter Scheel, the Minister for Foreign Affairs, whether the (then) new government would press for the application of qualified majority voting (QMV), and whether he would champion the extension of the powers of the EP in the wake of the creation of a Community financing system based on own resources. Scheel responded to these questions in the affirmative.[41] After the summit meeting in The Hague, Chancellor Willy Brandt made reference to the planned reform of the Community financing system before the Bundestag. He indicated support for the argument that there was a direct link between the creation of own resources and reform of the budgetary procedure, and the extension of the EP's budgetary powers: 'The new provisions regarding Community finance will promote the Community's budgetary independence and this...leads inevitably to an increase in the powers of the European Parliament.'[42]

Walter Scheel played the same tune affirming that the government would spare no efforts to press for an extension of the EP's powers and affirmed that the logic which links the strengthening of the EP to the creation of a system of Community's own resources had gained widespread acceptance among the member state governments:

[A]ll delegations have underlined the importance to extend the competencies of the European Parliament, because it is requisite that once we decide to walk down the path of a system of own resources it cannot be that parliamentary control would not be continuously adjusted from extended to fully-fledged budgetary powers.[43]

Support for an extension of the EP's budgetary powers was not only voiced by the party spectrum in Germany. The major political parties in the Netherlands were among the most outspoken supporters of a 'democratization' of European governance in this period. Joseph Luns of the Catholic People's Party (KVP)[44] and Minister of Foreign Affairs between 1956 and 1971 committed his government to a far-reaching extension of the EP's competencies, not only in the budgetary but equally in the legislative domain. Already in 1964 when both the introduction of QMV (following the end of the transition period foreseen in the EEC Treaty) and the reform of the Community's financing system were on the agenda, he mentioned, during a Council meeting, that a key issue facing the Community has, thus far, not been addressed adequately: the future development of the Community's democratic credentials. Contrary to the Gaullist view on how Europe should be governed, he argued that there was a deeply entrenched institutional imbalance in the Community:

The legislative and executive powers in the Community are presently exercised principally by the Council and the Commission. On the European level we do not see the balance [of powers] which exists in our national constitutions... In the legislative domain as well as with regard to the adoption of the budget and the control of Council acts, the Community lacks a genuine parliamentary authority.[45]

With the Community system of agricultural financing on the agenda for re-negotiation in mid-1965, supporters of a more influential EP saw a good opportunity to emphasize their case. Also in December 1964, the Foreign Affairs (Budget) Committee adopted a resolution which passed unanimously in the Dutch Second Chamber stressing the EP's role in a reformed Community budgetary decision-making procedure:

[T]here can be no question... upon the next review of the financial regulation of the Agricultural Fund, of replacing... the direct financial contributions of the Member States by resources available to the Community itself, and at the same time provide the European Parliament with a distinctive role in the budgetary procedure of the EEC.[46]

Before 'high noon' (Newhouse 1967: 94), in the Council on 30 June 1965, the Foreign Affairs (Budget) Committee sought a firm commitment from Jospeh Luns to press the Dutch government to 'do all in its power to see that the powers of the European Parliament are strengthened... The

creation of independent revenues for the Community must go hand in
hand with a corresponding increase in the powers of the European Parliament' (Newhouse 1967: 95). Luns was asked to stand by and defend the
Commission's point of view as long as the Commission stuck to it 'however unpromising that may have appeared' (Newhouse 1967: 95).[47] When
the question of a reform of the Community's budgetary procedure was
taken up again in the late 1960s, the Dutch position remained unchanged.
In a speech delivered in Milan on 28 February 1968, Foreign Minister
Joseph Luns stated that '[e]very week a large number of important decisions is taken [on the Community level] on which the representatives of
the peoples of Europe cannot exercise reasonable weight. For several years,
the Agricultural Fund alone absorbs at least five-hundred million dollars
without there being any parliamentary control of the kind we are subject
to in our national polities' (European Parliament 1970: 209, author's translation).[48] During a debate in the Dutch Second Chamber on 21 November
1968, Luns confirmed the government's stance that an approval to the
creation of a Community system of own resources would be made conditional upon an increase in the EP's budgetary powers (see European Parliament 1970: 210). In its sitting of 9–10 September 1969, the Second
Chamber of the Dutch Parliament adopted a resolution in which it called
'upon the government to give its accord to a final decision on the financing of the Community's agricultural policy... only under the condition
that the role of the European Parliament is reinforced satisfactorily' (European Parliament 1970: 211, author's translation).

Summarizing the above discussion, this section has shown that the
German and Dutch governments and major political parties shared a
view about the desirability and possibility to 'democratize' the Community system of governance that was different from that of the French
Gaullists. Most importantly, the proponents of the *federal state* legitimating belief, such as the German and Dutch governments, held that the
source of democratically legitimate governance was not vested exclusively
in each individual domestic polity. They argued that the delegation of
budgetary powers to the Community level through the creation of a
system of own resources required mechanisms of democratic control and
accountability at the European level. Consequently, the legitimacy deficit,
which was perceived to result from the 'de-parliamentarization' of national political systems, had to be alleviated at the Community level by
strengthening the role of the EP. While the French Gaullists equally considered the delegation of sovereignty to create a challenge for procedural
legitimacy at the domestic level, the 'solutions' to alleviate the legitimacy

Table 4.2 Legitimating belief of political parties in government of the 'Five'

'The Five'	
Legitimating belief	Federal state
Source of legitimacy	Popular sovereignty
Democracy at the international level?	Sovereignty can be shared across levels of governance
Nature of and remedies for the legitimacy deficit	Decline of NPs as a result of transfers of sovereignty can be compensated by empowering the EP

deficit were of rather different nature. The Gaullists either shied away from addressing the issue (the government in particular) or argued that Community reforms must not be to the detriment of the role of national parliaments.

4.3 Social action and institutional reform outcomes

In the preceding sections it has been demonstrated that the French government and the other five member state governments held different legitimating beliefs and hence opted for different interpretations of the challenge posed by the delegation of sovereignty for procedural legitimacy. Furthermore, it has been shown that the different governments displayed varying degrees of commitment to 'uphold' the dominant legitimating belief in their respective polities. While the German and Dutch governments, in particular, were firmly committed by their domestic parliamentary audience to pursue a course destined at strengthening the EP's budgetary powers, the French government showed a rather low degree of commitment to conform to the behavioural implications of the legitimating belief advanced by its parliamentary majority. In this section, I analyse how and to what degree the interaction between the different national governments in the run-up to the adoption of the Luxembourg Treaty was affected by their respective legitimating beliefs and the perception of a legitimacy deficit. Furthermore, I ask how these constraints affected the institutional reform outcome. The following hypotheses will be examined in the course of answering the above questions:

Hypothesis 3: The 'null hypothesis'
Decision-making is characterized by bargaining about the powers of the EP and the outcome reflects the constellation of preferences and relative bargaining power of member state governments.

Hypothesis 4: Communicative action
Decision-making is characterized by a truth-seeking discourse on the appropriate role of the EP in the Community polity as a result of which member state governments reach a reasoned consensus.

Hypothesis 5: Rhetorical action
Decision-making is characterized by the strategic use of arguments through which member state governments seek to justify and realize their own preferences regarding the powers of the EP. Proponents of the *federal state* legitimating belief—appealing to community values—exercise social pressure on recalcitrant states with the aim of shaming them into acquiescing to the EP's empowerment. Recalcitrant member states will downplay the outcomes, question their relevance or reinterpret them to their advantage in the light of domestic opposition.

4.3.1 Rhetorical action and social influence

During the 1960s, the Community member states knew that the completion of the common agricultural market required a new system of Community financing. It was shown in the preceding sections that most member states supported the idea that in the context of reforming the Community's budgetary provisions the EP should play a role in the allocation of the Community budget. Among the six member states only the French government—even though not in open dispute—avoided the EP question. In the run up to the adoption of the Treaty of Luxembourg, the French government, under Prime Minister Jacques Chaban-Delmas and Minister for Foreign Affairs Maurice Schuman, tried to refrain from any form of pre-commitment on questions of institutional reform when they were brought up by other member states. For the French government, the main objective was to achieve the locking-in of a permanent financing arrangement for the much-cherished CAP.[49] During the summit meeting in The Hague in early December of 1969, President Pompidou remained mute on the question of the EP's role in a reformed budgetary procedure. Between the summit in The Hague and the Council meeting of 19–22 December 1969, the French government, however, had come to embrace the 'logic' which linked the creation of a system of own resources to the extension of the EP's budgetary powers. During the subsequent Council meeting on 19–20 January 1970, the question of the EP's budgetary powers was subject to an extensive debate. Even though the French government was proposing a tight circumscription of the EP's role, it had become apparent that the French government was not opposing the notion that the role of the EP had to be newly defined once the system of own resources was in operation.

In the light of the prospective delegation of powers, all member states had come to share the view that the creation of an own resources system would undermine domestic channels for parliamentary participation. The French government thus bought into the argument that there existed a 'problem' for domestic procedural legitimacy—what I have termed the legitimacy deficit. This, however, did not imply that a solution to the legitimacy deficit was imminent. The French acceptance of the link between delegation and re-considering the EP's role in budgetary decision-making had two implications. First, proponents of the *federal state* legitimating belief had achieved a partial victory. Once the French government had accepted the validity of the argument that the delegation of sovereignty induced a legitimacy deficit, any appeals by the French government to oppose the empowerment of the EP by referring to status-related self-interest would from now on undermine the consistency and legitimacy of the French position and would also expose the French government to shaming activities by the proponents of the *federal state* legitimating belief. The observation that the French government was shying away from making arguments that pointed to status-related self-interest is an indicator for the presence of social influence and the effectiveness of rhetorical action.

Second, even though the French government was rhetorically entrapped, it was now in a position to expose potential weaknesses and inconsistencies in the arguments advanced by the proponents of the *federal state* legitimating belief. The French government sought to reinforce its position not by issuing threats, making commitments or, alternatively, through truth-seeking behaviour. Instead, it employed norm-based arguments strategically to further its own preferences: once the French government had come to acknowledge that the consequences of 'accepting' the existence of the legitimacy deficit implied serious pondering over the role of the EP, the French delegation countered demands for more parliamentary budgetary powers, not by appealing to the other governments' self-interest to keep the power in the Council, but by adopting and employing the democratic legitimacy discourse for its own ends. During the Council meeting on 20 January 1970, Minister of Foreign Affairs Maurice Schuman attempted to counter calls for making the EP the budgetary co-authority by taking recourse to domestic constitutional provisions which, so his argument runs, allowed the NPs less influence in budgetary decision-making than some of the 'maximalist' member state governments, the Dutch government in particular, envisaged for the EP. During the Council meeting of 20 January, Maurice Schuman cited a Standing Order adopted by the House of Commons in 1713 which stated that '[t]his House will receive no petition for any sum of money relating to public service but what is recommended from the Crown'.[50] Schuman thus criticized the fact that some of the member state governments attempted to give the EP competencies that opened pathways to spending excesses which NPs were constitutionally prevented from exercising. He also mentioned Article 113 of the German Basic Law and constitutional provisions from France and Italy to emphasize that national constitutions contained detailed provisions for limiting expenditure excesses.[51] Prior to the Council meeting, Schuman had already 'tested' this argument with his German counterpart, Walter Scheel. Schuman affirmed that the EP could not be endowed with competencies that exceeded those of NPs. In particular, he disagreed with the proposal that the EP should be given the power to create new budget lines and increase the expenditure for certain items without providing for equivalent reductions elsewhere in the budget.[52] Although Scheel disputed that the domestic constitutional provisions cited by Schuman could be applied one-to-one to the Community, he bowed to the argument that provisions had to be in place that did not allow the EP to unilaterally increase expenditure. Similar exchanges occurred between the chiefs of government, Prime Minister Jacques Chaban-Delmas and Chancellor Willy Brandt. In order to prevent 'financial demagogy', Chaban-Delmas argued that the EP's role had to be carefully circumscribed and affirmed that the 'Strasbourg Assembly' could not demand powers that exceeded those of NPs.[53] The French government furthermore demanded that the EP be prohibited from using its prospective budgetary powers to 'reign' into domains from which it was excluded by the Treaties. The French delegation expressed its concern that the EP could potentially legislate 'through the backdoor' if the member states did not make it explicit that under no circumstances would the EP be able to modify expenditure in areas which fell into the exclusive competencies of the Council (such as the CAP). This crucial qualification gave birth to the distinction—introduced by the French—between *compulsory* expenditure, that is expenditure that flows directly from the application of Community legislation and *non-compulsory* expenditure (all other expenditure).

Chancellor Willy Brandt and his Minister for Foreign Affairs, Walter Scheel, sympathized with the French proposal to circumscribe the role of the EP and introduce firm spending limits.[54] Despite the German government's tacit support for the French position, Chancellor Brandt, however, was under social pressure from his domestic parliamentary audience to honour his commitment to make every effort to obtain a more potent role of the EP in budgetary decision-making. In a conversation with the French Prime Minister he stated that the question of the EP's powers must not be oversimplified by pointing out that he could 'run into trouble' vis-à-vis his own parliament if he did not devote sufficient attention to the issue.[55] Yet, even though the German government was committed domestically to honour the *federal state* legitimating belief by pressing for more powers for the EP, its tacit support for the French position points to its role as a bystander. In the case of the Dutch government both domestic pre-commitment and intrinsic motivation to empower the EP account for its much more pronounced and uncompromising stance on the role of the EP. While rhetorical action helps us to understand why the French government accepted that the EP play a role in budgetary decision-making, the question of why the 'maximalist' Dutch government gave in to the key tenet of the French position—the distinction between compulsory and non-compulsory expenditure—remains unanswered. Do rhetorical action and the power of social influence explain why the Dutch government accepted the, all in all, relatively moderate increase in the EP's budgetary powers?

4.3.2 Bargaining over the final provisions

In their meeting of 5–7 February 1970, the Community member states came to agree on the question of the EP's involvement in budgetary decision-making. The broad outline of the Council decision of 22 December 1970 was retained while substantial tribute was paid to French concerns: the distinction between compulsory and non-compulsory expenditure was accepted. The procedural provisions adopted by the Council on 22 December 1969—which would have enabled the EP to propose modifications for all expenditure items—applied now only to the non-compulsory.[56] This also implied that the EP had the 'last word' only with regard to non-compulsory expenditure which, at the time, made up roughly 3.5% of the total budget. Furthermore, it could not propose expenditure beyond a rate of maximum increase (for non-compulsory expenditure) which was defined by the Commission (and was based on criteria such as GNP, growth of national budgets, etc.). This annual rate of increase was tightly circumscribed, again mostly upon French insistence. As for compulsory expenditure, parliamentary influence was not significantly enhanced and the Council only made a 'moral commitment' vis-à-vis the EP to improve its participation in domains falling under compulsory expenditures. This commitment included the provision of 'giving reasons' for rejecting parliamentary amendments. The compromise provisions were signed in Luxembourg on 22 April 1970.

How can we account for this rather moderate increase in the EP's budgetary powers? Why did French government largely succeed in achieving its key aim to limit the potential influence of the EP in the budgetary decision-making process? Why did the Dutch government, which so vehemently pressed for full co-decision rights in budgetary matters, make significant concessions? Shortly before the February agreement, German diplomats still conceived of the Dutch position as 'very rigid' on the matter of the extension of the EP's budgetary powers (AAPD 1970: No 31: 138). The Dutch government continued to demand that the distinction introduced by the French negotiators between compulsory and non-compulsory expenditure be dropped. It also asked for the overly rigid expenditure ceilings to be abandoned. However, in order to push the outcome further towards its most preferred position, the Dutch government did not have a credible threat at hand—the French government was very confident that the Dutch government did not wish to delay accession negotiations with the UK which would only commence once the financial settlement was agreed and the CAP 'locked-in'. In the final phases of the negotiations, linking the question about the EP's powers with the question of British accession offered a bargaining advantage to the French government.[57]

4.4 Conclusion

This chapter set out to find an answer to the question of why the Community member states endowed the EP with budgetary powers in 1970. The first part of this chapter addressed a crucial challenge that the political elites in the member states saw themselves confronted with at the time.

I argued that the creation of a system of own resources to establish a permanent financing arrangement for the CAP represented an instance of delegation whereby budgetary competencies were partially transferred from the national to the Community level. Once the prospect of the own resource system became imminent, concerns were voiced that there had to be a compensatory mechanism for the decline in NPs' budgetary prerogatives which undermined the procedural legitimacy of the domestic member state polities. The perception of this legitimacy deficit induced political elites to advance different proposals as to how this legitimacy deficit could be addressed. I also demonstrated that political elites in the member states advanced different proposals for how to alleviate the legitimacy deficit. It was illustrated that the different proposals for tackling the legitimacy deficit were derived from different legitimating beliefs and it was shown that the *intergovernmental cooperation* and *economic community* legitimating beliefs which informed the Gaullists' response to the legitimacy deficit contrasted strongly with those resulting from the *federal state* legitimating belief adhered to by the other national governments. In the final section, I have addressed the question how the interaction between the Community member states during the negotiations leading towards the adoption of the Luxembourg Treaty can be accounted for and how the institutional reform outcome can be explained. I have argued that once the French government had accepted the existence of the legitimacy deficit as a consequence of the creation of the own resources system, arguments based on self-interest, that is: opposition to the empowerment of the EP for status-related reasons, were no longer viewed as legitimate. The French government—though motivated by status-related concerns—played the rhetorical-action game. The French delegation thus sought to counter arguments calling for the EP as a budgetary co-authority by employing arguments about the constitutional limitations of NPs in budgetary decision-making. Normative constraints thus played a double role: on the one hand, accepting the existence of the legitimacy deficit implied that the French government had to accept that the EP's role would be enhanced. On the other hand, it also enabled the French government to moderate the 'maximalist' claims by pointing out flaws in their arguments. The German government was quite happy to accept the French proposals, since it privately sympathized with the French position and could still sell the achievements to a federally-minded domestic parliamentary audience as a success. The Dutch government, in contrast, was hostile towards the distinction between compulsory and non-compulsory expenditure and the effect this distinction had for the role they envisaged the EP would play. For the Dutch government, which was firmly pre-committed domestically to enhance the EP's budgetary powers, the distinction between compulsory and non-compulsory expenditure was much harder to swallow. However, it did accept the proposal, albeit grudgingly, since it did not wish to see the negotiations in jeopardy. The Dutch government's interest in starting accession negotiations with the UK led to concessions that were reflected in the final outcome which was closer to the French than to the Dutch position.

Notes

1. See Shackleton (1990), Brehon (1997), Laffan (1997, 2000), Laffan and Shackleton (2000), Lindner (2003a, 2003b), Laffan and Lindner (2005) for existing works on EU budgetary politics.
2. See <http://europa.eu.int/comm/commissioners/schreyer/Presse/241103_eu-budget 2004_en.pdf> (accessed 15 August 2004).
3. See European Parliament (1971: 175, author's translation).
4. Journal Officiel, Assemblée Nationale, debate of 23 June 1970: 2935 (author's translation).
5. Lindner and Rittberger (2003) show that the above assessments were almost 'prophetic' since they accurately echo the subsequent interaction dynamics between the EP and the Council. See also Pollack (1994) and Lindner (2003a, 2003b).
6. Article 2, first intent of the Regulation reads as follows: '1. Revenue from levies on imports from third countries shall accrue to the Community and shall be used for Community expenditure so that the budget resources of the Community comprise those revenues together with all other revenues decided in accordance with the rules of the Treaty... The Council shall, at the appropriate time, initiate the procedure laid down in Article 201 of the Treaty in order to implement the above-mentioned provisions' (Official Journal B 030, 20/04/1962: 0991–0993).
7. See also Coombes (1972: 24).
8. Extracts from these communications are reprinted in European Parliament (1970: 71–82).
9. The relevant sections of the non-amended Article 203 EEC read as follows: '3. The Council shall, by a qualified majority vote, draw up the draft budget and then transmit it to the Assembly.... The Assembly shall be entitled to propose to the Council amendments to the draft budget. 4. If, within the period of one month from the receipt of the draft budget, the Assembly has given its approval, or has not made its opinion known to the Council, the draft budget shall be considered as finally adopted. If, within this period, the Assembly has proposed any amendments, the draft budget so amended shall be transmitted to the Council. The Council shall then discuss it with the Commission and, where appropriate, with the other institutions concerned and shall finally adopt the budget by qualified majority vote.'

10. According to Newhouse, de Gaulle asked as early as January 1965 'for an opinion from within the Government on whether the coming into effect of majority voting on numerous substantive matters might create any difficulties for France. He was told that this was most unlikely. But he could not have been reassured by proposals clearly intended to coax from him an institutional price for the financial regulation, which he regarded, or would choose to regard, as a solemn Community obligation unrelated to other matters. In any case, neither de Gaulle *nor* the French Administration could have been expected to swallow so large an expansion of the Commission's power, the dominant element of the package' (Newhouse, 1967: 67, emphasis in the original).

11. See, for example, Lambert (1966), Newhouse (1967), Moravcsik (2000), and AAPD (1965: No. 248, 265, 266, 267, 272).

12. See, for example, AAPD (1966: No. 12), Moravcsik (1998: chapter 3).

13. See Bitsch (2001), Moravcsik (1998), and Pollack (n.d.). Mark Pollack, for instance, argues succinctly that the 'calling of the Hague summit . . . should be understood in the context of Pompidou's plans for a grand bargain or package deal, which would guarantee France the Community financing which it sought, in return for French assent to British membership' (Pollack n.d.: 153).

14. See Lambert (1966), Newhouse (1967), and Coombes (1972: 27).

15. Extracts from both documents can be found in Coombes (1972: 91–102).

16. European Parliament, Doc. 31/63, extracts in European Parliament (1970: 55–6).

17. European Parliament, Doc. 28/64 and Doc. 34/65 (extracts in European Parliament 1970: 57–66 and 82–4 respectively).

18. See the Communications of 31 March and 13 April 1965 (extracts in European Parliament 1970: 71–82).

19. Conditional on the Commission's approval, the EP should be allowed to propose amendments which the Council can accept by a majority of its members. However, to change the EP's amendments, the Council needs to muster a five-sixth majority (European Parliament 1970: 81–82).

20. See AAPD (1964: No 266). In July 1963, the German government, for instance, called upon the Committee of permanent representatives of the member states of the EU (COREPER) to study proposals about the strengthening the EP's powers. The government demanded improved mechanisms for consultation between the Community organs. A proposal from the Luxembourg government played to a similar tune by calling for an extension of the consultation procedure to areas where no such consultations were yet foreseen (HAEC, MAEF.DECE-05.02, MAEF 1124, 18 December 1963).

21. See HAEC, MAEF.DECE-05.02, MAEF 1124, 18 December 1963; see also AAPD, 1965 [No 243] for a reference to a resolution adopted by the Dutch Second Chamber calling for the extension of the EP's budgetary powers once a system of own resources was introduced.

22. The main lines of criticsm against the Commission advanced by French diplomats read as follows: '[I]l s'agirait d'étendre les prérogatives de l'Assemblée sous prétexte que le budget comprendrait désormais des ressources propres et non plus seulement des contributions financières des Etats membres. Mais il faut bien voir que le droit

d'initiative en matière de recettes appartient seulement au Conseil. En effet, c'est lui qui fixe le montant des prélèvements et le niveau du tarif douanier commun. Vouloir... étendre les prérogatives de l'Assemblée en matière budgétaire reviendrait en définitive à lui donner seulement plus de pouvoirs pour agir sur les dépenses de la Communauté. Sous prétexte de démocratie, l'on cèderait à la démagogie du gaspillage, dont il est superflu de rappeler qu'elle a toujours été, dans tout les pays, une tentation très forte pour les représentants du peuple. "Le budget, monstre énorme, admirable poisson auquel de tout côté on jette l'hameçon" disait Victor Hugo' (HAEC, MAEF.DECE-05.02, MAEF 1124, 10 May 1965).

23. See AAPD (1965: No 219).

24. See HAEC, MAEF.DECE-05.02, MAEF 1124, 10 May 1965.

25. During a Council meeting on 22 July 1969, French Foreign Affairs Ministers Maurice Schuman proposed to convene a summit of the member states (AAPD 1969: No 253).

26. For extracts from this Communication, see European Parliament (1970: 123–6).

27. For extracts of Doc. 102/69 (Furler Report) and the adjoined European Parliament resolution, see European Parliament (1970: 126–9).

28. See European Parliament (1970: 129–32).

29. Katharina Focke, Secretary of State in the German Ministry for Foreign Affairs, reports on the summit meeting in The Hague: 'As far as institutional issues were concerned the questions of the European Parliament's budgetary powers and direct elections were addressed... (Pompidou remained silent on these issues)' (AAPD 1969: No 385, author's translation).

30. See Bulletin of the European Communities, 1–1970 (emphasis added).

31. The following indicators will be employed to assess political parties' legitimating beliefs and the concomitant institutional design implications: first, what do political parties consider to be the sources of democratic legitimacy? Second, do they have a blue-print of how democracy should be exercised at the supranational level (if it should be exercised in an international/supranational polity at all)? Third, how do political parties perceive the legitimacy deficit and what remedies do they propose?

32. In his speech before the National Assembly on 4 November 1969, Foreign Affairs Minister, Maurice Schuman referred to the immutable principles of French foreign policy: '[S]ouveraineté sans autre limitation que réciproque et volontaire, égalité des nations, respect de leur intégrité, non-recours à la force, non-ingérence dans les affaires intérieurs' (Journal Officiel, Assemblée Nationale, debate of 4 November 1969: 3301).

33. Journal Officiel, Assemblée Nationale, debate of 4 November 1969: 3307 (author's translation).

34. Journal Officiel, Assemblée Nationale, debate of 4 November 1969: 3308 (author's translation).

35. John Lambert (1966: 228) interpreted the 'empty chair crisis' 'as a constitutional clash, involving an attempt to change certain basic rules: but it was also probably part of a more long-term political conflict over the nature of the Community that in no way ceased when the immediate crisis ended on 29 January [1966]. The difference in question can be expected to persist and to be reflected continually in relations

between the member governments inside and outside the framework of the Treaties.' Moravcsik takes a more cautious stand in his assessment of the impact of different ideas about the 'nature of the Community' on the 1965-crisis: 'Confidential discussions and public speeches reveal a man [i.e. de Gaulle] obsessed with the possibility that QMV might be exploited to undermine the carefully negotiated arrangements for net EEC financial transfers to French farmers.... Although he admitted to a close associate in July 1965 that the boycott might endanger the CAP financial settlement, which was then nearing agreement, he sensed that it might equally heighten French pressure for a favorable resolution. He predicted that within a year, if QMV remained in place, Erhard and other West German politicians were sure to "call everything into question" by calling for a majority vote on the CAP' (Moravcsik 2000: 39).

36. See Bitsch (2001) and AAPD (1969: No 319).

37. See the notes by a German diplomat in AAPD (1969: No 319).

38. See, for example, the Bundestag resolutions (Drucksachen) 4/1104 of 15 May 1964, 4/1660 of 23 November 1963, 4/2211 and 4/2212 of 28 April 1964.

39. Deutscher Bundestag, debate of 27 January 1966: 678 (author's translation).

40. Deutscher Bundestag, debate of 27 January 1966: 690 (author's translation).

41. Deutscher Bundestag, questions of 6 November 1969: 279 and 283.

42. Deutscher Bundestag, debate of 3 December 1969: 593.

43. Deutscher Bundestag, debate of 3 December 1969: 600.

44. The KVP was founded in 1922 as Roman Catholic State Party (RKSP) and changed its name to Catholic People's Party (KVP) in 1945. In 1980 it was a founding component of the Christian Democratic Appeal (CDA).

45. HAEC, MAEF.DECE-05.02, MAEF 1124, 3 December 1964 (author's translation).

46. Quoted in Niblock (1971: 84).

47. Newhouse argues that the 'supranational aspects of the Commission proposal reflected much of the thinking of Dutch parliamentarians. For them, the key element was the expanded authority of the European Parliament in budgetary affairs, a historic parliamentary prerogative.' (Newhouse 1967: 72–3)

48. See European Parliament (1970: 209, author's translation).

49. See AAPD (1969: No 253, 279, 319); see also Moravcsik (2000). In diplomatic circles, it was shared knowledge that the primary objective of the French government was the completion of the agricultural common market, in particular through the establishment of an ultimate financing arrangement for the CAP. The French government made the solution to this issue a precondition for assuming accession negotiations with the UK whereas the other 'Five' did not support such a linkage (AAPD 1969: No 253).

50. HAEC, EN 112, p. 2.

51. The relevant provision of Article 113 [Consent of the Federal Government to increases in expenditures or decreases in revenue] reads as follows: '(1) Laws that increase the budget expenditures proposed by the Federal Government, or entail or will bring about new expenditures, shall require the consent of the Federal Government. This requirement shall also apply to laws that entail or will bring about decreases in revenue. The Federal Government may demand that the Bundestag postpone its

vote on bills to this effect. In this event the Federal Government shall submit its comments to the Bundestag within six weeks.'

52. See AAPD (1970: No 11).

53. See AAPD (1970: No 30).

54. See AAPD (1970: No 31).

55. AAPD (1970: No 30, p. 134).

56. For the conclusions of the Council summit meeting on 19–22 December 1970, see Bulletin der EG, 1/1970: 20–24. Initially, the '22 December' decision envisaged that the EP could modify the draft budget, and even if the Council would alter or reject parliamentary amendments by qualified majority, the EP could—in the last instance—decide on the Council's changes with a three-fifth majority and ultimately adopt the budget. At the 19–22 December Council meeting, no distinction was yet made between compulsory and non-compulsory expenditure.

57. See AAPD (1970: No 41, p. 138).

5

Legislative Powers and the Single European Act

Calls from member states and, unsurprisingly, the vast majority of the MEPs to enhance the EP's influence in the Community's legislative process had been floating around for a long time. Despite the agreement to directly elect the EP for the first time in 1979, it was only with the adoption of the SEA in February 1986 that the EP was to become a significant player in the sphere of legislative politics. The introduction of the *assent procedure* gave the EP effectively a veto over association and accession agreements. But, much more importantly, in the realm of day-to-day policy-making, the newly introduced *cooperation procedure*, which was to be applied in most areas of single-market legislation, supplemented the—from the EP's perspective—rather inconsequential *consultation procedure*. The move from consultation to cooperation effectively endowed the EP with what Tsebelis has termed 'conditional agenda-setting power', the right for the EP to propose amendments in a second reading of the legislative procedure which, if supported by the Commission, could only be overturned by a Council unanimous, but could be accepted by the Council by a qualified majority (Tsebelis 1994). Legislation amended by the EP, so the argument runs, is thus easier for the Council to accept (it can do so by qualified majority) than to reject or amend (for which it needs unanimity). A strategically acting EP will thus propose amendments which the Commission and the pivotal Council member will prefer to a unanimous Council decision.[1] There is broad agreement that the introduction of the cooperation procedure represented a *quantitative* and *qualitative* leap for the EP as regards the *scope* and *impact* of its actions on Community legislation.[2] Empirical evidence demonstrates that the EP was able to exercise considerable influence on the substance of important pieces of Community legislation which it most likely would have not been able to exercise under the consultation procedure.[3] Following the Maastricht Treaty and the introduction of the new *co-decision procedure*, the academic debate about the relative influence of the different Community legislators under different legislative procedures equally shows that the EP was able to significantly influence legislation under both cooperation and co-decision procedures.[4]

The SEA thus ranks alongside the Treaty of Paris which created the CA and the Luxembourg Treaty which endowed the EP with budgetary powers. The introduction of legislative powers through the cooperation procedure marks the final element in the EP's power *trias*. In order to shed light on the question why the Community member state governments decided to endow the EP with legislative powers, I proceed as in the preceding chapters. First, I ask whether or not the political elites in the member states perceived a legitimacy deficit as a result of the prospective pooling of sovereignty, the introduction of QMV in the Council. If this is the case, I ask, in a second step, what remedies the different member state governments proposed with a view to alleviating the perceived legitimacy deficit. In the third section I ask how the normative constraints imposed by the perceived legitimacy deficit and domestically held legitimating beliefs affected the different governments' behaviour and interactions during negotiations leading to the SEA.

5.1 The pooling of sovereignty and the legitimacy deficit

In the ensuing paragraphs, I provide a brief historical overview of the run-up to the IGC leading to the SEA and assess the value of the independent variable (*pooling* or *no pooling*). I then move on to evaluate whether the expectation laid down in *hypothesis 1a* holds:

> *Hypothesis 1a: Legitimacy deficit*
> Delegation and pooling of national sovereignty will produce an asymmetry between consequentialist and procedural legitimacy (legitimacy deficit).

5.1.1 *What is being pooled?*

'Eurosclerosis' or 'Europessimism' have been among the most widely used terms to characterize the state of the Community in the early 1980s. Despite the introduction of the European Monetary System (EMS) and the first direct elections of the EP in 1979, the integration process appeared paralysed for much of the first half of the 1980s. Despite some declaratory attempts to deepen integration and reform Community institutions, there was a definitive shortage of concrete results. The Genscher-Colombo initiative of 1981, proposed by the German Minister for Foreign Affairs and his Italian counterpart, called for increased European unity in the light of widespread economic recession and the European Community's ongoing 'institutional malaise' (Moravcsik 1991: 33). The initiative, however, encountered stark opposition in a number of member states, France and Britain most notably.

The 'Solemn Declaration on European Union' which was signed at the Stuttgart European Council meeting in June 1983, proposed an even wider array of policy areas in which cooperation should occur, yet, similar to the Genscher-Colombo initiative, the document had a very limited impact given its non-binding nature. On the issue of institutional reform, the 'Solemn Declaration' called for the *de facto* application of the provisions foreseen in the founding EEC Treaty (which demands that, after a transition period, QMV be applied for certain Treaty articles, mainly those affecting the completion of the internal market) and for member states to abstain from decision-making instead of invoking the unilateral veto in order to reduce decision-making blockage. However, some of the 'usual suspects' did not hesitate to ensure that the Luxembourg Compromise would still be in force (Moravcsik 1991: 34). The Danish Foreign Minister, Kjeld Olesen, referred to the declaration as a 'substanceless' paper that could be 'archived' (Gaddum 1994: 237). Malcolm Rifkind, Minister of State in the British Foreign and Commonwealth Office, declared that the emphasis on institutional reform without linking it to substantive policy issues was something he and his government were highly sceptical of: 'To us, institutions must be subservient to policies. . . . Substance and reality must come before form' (Malcolm Rifkind quoted in George 1990: 177). In a similar vein, the French Minister for European Affairs, André Chandernagor, told the National Assembly that the Stuttgart Declaration represented an effort to build Europe from the roof downwards and exclaimed that the government was opposed to this enterprise (see Gaddum 1994: 237).

On the 'policy front', nitty-gritty bargaining, mainly about the British contribution to the Community budget, dominated the European Council meetings for much of the first half of the 1980s and practically delayed any other business (see De Ruyt 1989; Moravcsik 1991, 1998). Besides the disputes that came to the fore in the context of the Genscher-Colombo initiative and the Stuttgart Declaration, there were other issues of contention such as the squabbles over southern enlargement (Portugal and Spain), bickering over milk quotas as part of the CAP and, as already mentioned, the British contribution to the Community budget. In the aftermath of the Athens and Brussels European Council summit meetings of December 1983 and March 1984 respectively, disillusionment was almost complete: although some advances had been made on issues relating to the CAP and milk quotas, the British budgetary question was still stalling most other Community affairs.[5]

When France took over the Presidency in the first half of 1984, President François Mitterrand and his close ally, Chancellor Helmut Kohl of Germany, seemed determined to launch an initiative to re-launch Europe once the question of the British budget contribution was resolved. In an address to the plenary of the EP on 24 May 1984, Mitterrand made it known that he intended to head for Treaty reform.[6] Although Mitterrand advocated a deepening of Community competencies, in his speech he did not prioritize the completion of the internal market but instead focused on issues such as cooperation in environmental matters, culture, space, transport, foreign policy, and defence.[7] Shortly after his appearance before the EP, the Community appeared to escape the gridlock caused by the 'British Question'. At the European Council summit meeting in Fontainebleau in June 1984, a solution was finally found. Furthermore, the summit decided to institute two *ad hoc committees* composed of personalities appointed by the governments of the member states. One of the committees was to address issues related to citizenship and identity (the *Adonnino Committee*, named after its Italian chairman); the other was to discuss the issues of deeper cooperation and institutional reform (the *Dooge Committee*, named after its Irish chairman). Although the Dooge Committee was often referred to as *Spaak II Committee*, connoting hopes that a breakthrough similar to the one produced by the original *Spaak Committee* leading to the adoption of Treaties of Rome could be achieved, the committee's mandate was very prudent and much more ambiguous than the one chaired by Paul-Henri Spaak in the mid-1950s. The Dooge Committee which met between June 1984 and March 1985 was authorized to make 'recommendations' concerning possible ways to improve the 'functioning of European cooperation' (De Ruyt, 1989: 52). The Dooge Committee submitted its final report to the Brussels European Council meeting in late March 1985. The report advocated the creation of a 'fully integrated internal market', the promotion of 'common values of civilisation' (environmental protection, social area, judicial and cultural cooperation) as well as a search for an 'external identity' with regard to foreign and security policy issues.[8] The final part of the report addressed the question of institutional reform. A plea was made for the provisions of more 'efficient' and 'democratic' institutions. The Dooge Report differed from usual Community documents since its contents did not enjoy unanimous support but instead represented the majority opinion of the participating committee members; minority opinions were footnoted or annexed. The report thus offered a 'maximalist' view with the majority opinion supporting calls for enhanced pooling of sovereignty by instituting majority voting in the Council. Although unanimous decision-making would still be required for a vast number of Treaty provisions, a list of these cases should be drawn up in a 'restrictive' fashion. However, the committee members from Denmark, Greece, and the UK expressed their reservations about the proposed weakening of the possibility of invoking the national veto. Similarly, while a majority of member states argued for more 'democratic' decision-making by endowing the EP with powers to participate more effectively in the legislative process, the delegates from Denmark, Greece, and the UK were critical of this proposal.[9] In sum, the 'majority opinion' called for a revision of the existing Treaty provisions to deepen integration in the selected policy areas and concomitantly reform the decision-making procedures through increased pooling. Budden argues that the establishment of the link between 'deepening' and institutional reform was 'the key to the Committee's contribution to the making of the SEA' (Budden 1994: 228).

In the aftermath of the publication of the Dooge Committee's report, the supporters of Treaty reform gained momentum. Among the large member states, France, Germany, and Italy (which held the Presidency in the first half of 1985) there was agreement that an IGC should be convened to tackle the issues addressed in the report. Although the UK expressed its opposition to a formal revision of the Treaty, it vehemently supported the drive for the completion of the internal market, an ambition that also found its way into the Dooge Report and into a Commission White Paper (CWP) issued shortly before the Milan European Council Meeting of June 1985. During the same period, diplomatic efforts to prepare for a re-launch reached new heights. While Mitterrand and Kohl met frequently to discuss the substance and scope of Treaty revision—expressing a clear preference for increased pooling of decision-making powers and a tightly circumscribed scope for applying the national veto[10]—Geoffrey Howe, Minister for Foreign and Commonwealth Affairs, detailed the UK's position on the occasion of a preparatory Council meeting in Stresa in early June 1985.[11] Not only did Howe issue a plea for the completion of the internal market by 1990, he also called upon the Milan European Council meeting, which was scheduled for late June 1985, to discuss possible improvements in the decision-making processes. Howe's proposal differed from what most other member states had suggested or hoped to see. To speed up the process of market integration, the British government expressed its willingness to make more frequent use of QMV and to develop specific procedures to limit the use of the national unilateral veto. He suggested that member states should make greater use of abstention and abandonment of calls for unanimity when the matter in question is an already agreed objective.[12] For the UK it was important to stress that the proposed changes did not and should not require a formal revision of the Treaty but could be achieved more 'pragmatically' within the existing framework and by employing 'soft law' instruments such as 'gentleman's agreements' (see De Ruyt 1989: 57).

In the run-up to the Milan European Council meeting and despite continuing disagreement over the method of the re-launch—by means of formal Treaty amendment or 'within-the-Treaty' reform—it became increasingly apparent that member states' positions on institutional reform (majority voting), and on substantive policy cooperation (internal market) moved inside a still very broadly perceived 'zone of possible agreement'. This development was possible in spite of persisting differences in priorities as far as the scope and substance of policy cooperation, the decision-making mechanisms and the different reform paths were concerned.[13] In Milan, however, only the latter issue, the reform method, was resolved. The Italian Presidency proposed to convene an IGC later during the year and called for a vote on whether or not this IGC should be convened. Although prime ministers Margaret Thatcher (UK), Poul Schlüter (Denmark) and Andreas Papandreou (Greece) considered the Italian presidency's step to call a vote on this matter a 'coup d'état' (De Ruyt 1989: 62) since it was considered common practice to seek a consensus on the question whether or not to convene an IGC, none of the three wanted to be excluded from the negotiations leading to a revision of the Treaty. In the end, they grudgingly accepted the convening of the IGC which was to commence in September 1985. In order not to give a false impression, the Milan summit meeting was not only occupied with the question of whether or not to turn to formal Treaty revision, the Community member states also laid out a trajectory for the reform of the Community. The communiqué issued after the Milan European Council meeting stressed that institutional reform and 'deepening' would be the focus of the member states' endeavours during the coming months. It was made clear that a solution to the question of institutional reform was linked to the achievement of policy objectives, most notably to the internal market and technology cooperation.[14]

With institutional reform and commitment to deeper cooperation firmly on the agenda, the Commission made every effort to rapidly press forward the internal market programme. Taking account of the widely differing views among the member states on enhanced monetary integration, the creation of an 'external identity' (the deepening of foreign policy cooperation), the internal market idea moved in the spotlight. Commission President Jacques Delors and Commissioner Lord Cockfield, the 'brain' behind the CWP on the completion of the internal market, 'picked the Big Idea whose time was ripe.' (Grant 1988: 66) Furthermore, as far as the three large member states were concerned, 'Margaret Thatcher was at the height of her powers and eager for the EEC to take on a practical and liberal objective. West Germany's coalition of Christian Democrats and Free Democrats was committed to the principle, if not the practice, of freer markets. France's socialists had veered towards pro-business policies and financial deregulation. Right-of-centre coalitions held power in Holland, Belgium, Italy, and Denmark. Privatization, tax cuts and competition were in the air' (Grant, 1988: 66). In the period following the Milan European Council meeting, it became increasingly obvious that the realization of the internal market programme and institutional reform were inexorably linked: to ensure the passage of the 297 pieces of Community legislation the CWP had proposed for the harmonization of different national legislations on internal market matters, more speedy and efficient decision-making procedures had to be adopted. For some of the member state governments, most notably the British government, which had hitherto resisted proposals for institutional reform, the issue of institutional reform lost its 'doctrinaire' element, given that the move to more QMV, as far as it affected the completion of the internal market, had a solid economic justification (see De Ruyt 1989: 71).

The application of QMV to matters relating to the abolition of barriers impeding the free flow of goods, services, persons, and capital was one of the quintessential features of what was to become the SEA, signed by the member states in two rounds on 17 and 28 February 1986. All national governments came to the conclusion that pooling (with or without a formal Treaty amendment) was acceptable, given the objective to pass the large number of pieces of Community legislation until 1992 to complete the internal market. Pooling was thus expected to partially fulfil the function of speeding up decision-making by making it more demanding to muster a blocking minority and to equally demonstrate the member states' commitment to advance the internal market programme (see Moravcsik 1998: Chapter 5).

In this section, I have emphasized that the prospect of pooling sovereignty had become a crucial underpinning of the Community's re-launch in the mid-1980s. *Hypothesis 1a* leads us to expect that pooling 'does not come alone'. Where member state governments pool sovereignty to enhance the problem-solving capacity of a polity (by abolishing barriers to the free flow of goods, services, capital, and persons) and to improve the efficiency of decision-making, *hypothesis 1a* expects political elites to be concerned about the implications of transfers of national sovereignty for procedural legitimacy. How and to what degree does the pooling of decision-making power impact on the role of NPs and the accountability of national decision-makers? How and to what degree are national democratic institutions and channels of representation affected by pooling in the eyes of political elites?

5.1.2 The nature of the perceived legitimacy deficit

Although several governments, MPs from various NPs and MEPs have consistently maintained that the Community suffered from a democratic deficit throughout the 1980s (Corbett 1998), proposals to remedy this 'deficit' by, for example, increasing the powers of the EP, never came to fruition before the breakthrough achieved by the SEA. Every time the democratic deficit issue was brought to the fore—the EP's Draft Treaty establishing the European Union of 1984 providing a particularly shining example—national governments disagreed vividly on whether such a democratic deficit actually existed. Yet, it was with the concrete prospect of the pooling of sovereignty—especially since the Milan European Council meeting of June 1985 which set Treaty revision *en route*—that the potential impact of pooling on domestic democratic institutions and processes, such as the accountability of government ministers before NPs or the potential disempowerment of NPs, became an item on the European Council's agenda.

In the member states, parliamentary debates indicated that MPs established a direct link between the proposals for partially pooling sovereignty and challenges to procedural legitimacy. In the French National Assembly, Charles Josselin of the (then) governing Socialist Party (PS) stated during a foreign policy debate prior to the Milan European Council that 'the process embarked upon will lead...to a considerable reduction of the competencies of national parliaments in almost all domains', and directly addressing the plenary, he asked the rhetorical question: 'Do you think that a Europe of ministers and civil servants would be viable? Do you think that, in the long term, it could command legitimacy?'[15] In a similar vein, the centre-right politician Adrien Zeller from the UDF (Union pour la Démocratie Française), emphasized that an increase in decision-making efficiency had to go hand-in-hand with the empowerment of the EP because 'national parliaments are not able to sufficiently control Community decisions.' And with a view to remedying this problem, he argued that 'the only means to re-establish democratic control of such decisions [which evade national parliamentary control] is to endow the European Parliament with the means not just to *influence* Community decisions but also to *legitimise* them by its votes.'[16] In the UK, the House of Lords Select Committee on the European Communities published a detailed report on the impact of proposals for Community reform (such as the EP's Draft Treaty and the Dooge Committee's report) on Britain's political institutions. Malcolm Rifkind, Minister of State in the Foreign and Commonwealth Office, who represented the UK on the Dooge Committee, was asked to give evidence on the developments in the Community before the House of Lords Select Committee. He was queried at length on the government's position on institutional reform and the proposals advanced by the EP and the Dooge Committee's report. Rifkind made it clear that for the completion of the internal market—the government's top priority—it was desirable to speed up decision-making and render it more effective. In the eyes of his government, domestic procedural legitimacy was not under threat as long as governments kept the ultimate right to veto decisions:

As long as there is the ultimate safeguard of the right of veto in very special circumstances, then there is every reason to encourage more majority voting on the vast number of issues where questions of vital national interest need not...apply....Given that we are dealing not with a federation or a confederation, but with a community of nation states who have pooled a certain proportion of their sovereignty, but which essentially still do remain national governments responsible to their own national parliaments, then I think that at this stage in the Community's development it is *not* practical to contemplate the non-existence of an ultimate right of veto.[17]

In Germany, the Bundestag debated the state of European integration on 27 June 1985, prior to the Milan European Council meeting. The governing Christian Democrats (CDU/CSU) and Liberal Democrats (FDP) as well as the Social Democrats (SPD) from the opposition benches were explicit about the challenges further pooling implied for procedural legitimacy. SPD party leader Hans-Jochen Vogel stated that, as a consequence of pooling, sovereignty would be taken away from NPs. He warned that sovereignty transferred to the European level must not be steered into 'a parliament-free space'. In the long-run, he claimed, 'Europe cannot live with a Parliament whose competencies are less than those of nineteenth-century representative institutions.'[18] Renate Hellwig of the CDU/CSU and chairwoman of the Bundestag's EC Committee criticized the executive dominance in the Community's decision-making processes and concluded that it was necessary to enhance the legislative powers of the EP to alleviate the legitimacy deficit.[19] Parliamentary debates and resolutions in many of the other NPs equally reflected the awareness that increased pooling would exacerbate the legitimacy deficit.[20] Awareness of the existence of a legitimacy deficit was also raised in other political arenas. In June 1985, leaders of European Christian democratic parties met in Rome to propose an agenda for the Milan European Council meeting. Among those present were the German Chancellor Kohl, the Irish Prime Minister Fitz-Gerald, the Italian Deputy Prime Minister Forlani, and Minister for Foreign Affairs Giulio Andreotti. A resolution was adopted which made explicit the link between pooling and the institutional reforms to bolster procedural legitimacy as a response to the decline of the competencies of NPs: it was requested that the EP be given legislative co-decision powers in all those policy fields where the Community exercised competence.[21]

The evidence presented here permits the following preliminary conclusions. First, in the run up to the IGC it became evermore apparent that the Community member states intended to pool sovereignty by extending the *de facto* use of QMV, especially in the areas affecting the completion of the internal market. Second, we have seen that even prior to the IGC (in the run-up to the European Council meeting in Milan in June 1985), there was considerable awareness among political elites that the pooling of sovereignty could not go unaccompanied in terms of institutional reform.[22] For instance, parliamentary reports and resolutions which were passed in France, Germany, Italy, Ireland, and the Benelux countries invoked the need to compensate national parliamentary institutions for the expected loss of competencies by strengthening the powers of the EP.[23] While the evidence presented here provides support for *hypothesis 1a*, it also points at two other phenomena. First, political elites differed in their perceptions of the degree to which the challenge to procedural legitimacy was considered a serious threat to their domestic democratic process; second, political elites also disagreed about the solutions to alleviate the perceived legitimacy deficit. In this context, the preceding section briefly pointed at the British case where the ruling Conservative government considered that selective pooling did not pose a serious threat to procedural legitimacy *as long as* economic effectiveness and decision-making efficiency were enhanced and *as long as* the national veto was retained as the *ultima ratio*. In Section 5.2, I will demonstrate that political elites 'activated' different legitimating beliefs which affected their responses to the question of how to reform the Community polity in the light of the increased pooling of sovereignty.

5.2 Political parties' legitimating beliefs

Before turning to the analysis of the different legitimating beliefs held by the French, German and British parties in government, it is worthwhile to recall *hypothesis 2*.

Hypothesis 2: Legitimating beliefs
Alternative proposals to create and reform institutions with a view to reducing the asymmetry between procedural and consequentialist legitimacy (the legitimacy deficit) are likely to reflect differences in legitimating beliefs held by different political elites.

5.2.1 France: lukewarm commitment to more parliamentary powers

Before the parliamentary elections in 1986, government and presidency were firmly in the hands of the PS (which commanded an absolute majority of seats in the National Assembly). At the time the SEA was submitted for ratification to the Assemblée Nationale, the PS-led government suffered an outright defeat and handed power over to a centre-right governing coalition comprising the Neo-Gaullist Rassemblement pour la République (RPR), as well as centrists and liberal parties united in the Union pour la Démocratie Française (UDF). Jacques Chirac (RPR) succeeded Socialist Laurent Fabius as Prime Minister. In this section, I analyse the legitimating belief held by the governing PS. However, I also sketch the legitimating beliefs held by the RPR and UDF since their approval was crucial for the ratification of the SEA.

It has already been mentioned that President Mitterrand sought to generate momentum for the integration process when France assumed the Council Presidency in the first half of 1984. In his address to the EP on 24 May 1984 he picked up the notion of building a 'European Union' and committed himself to the convening of an IGC. Mitterrand continued to emphasize the 'independence of fatherlands' and remained sufficiently vague on the question of the 'democratization' of the European Community, claiming that he was in favour of improved 'coordination' between the Council and the EP (Gaddum 1994: 239). However, Mitterrand expressed his willingness before the EP to examine the EP's Draft Treaty, claiming that he would 'examine and defend your [the MEPs] project, the inspiration behind which [France] approves.'[24] Despite the allegedly positive reception of the EP's efforts to 'democratize' Community policy-making, President Mitterrand and members of the PS-led government avoided committing themselves explicitly to bestowing the EP with legislative powers. Vague and rather lukewarm support for the democratization of Community decision-making was expressed, for example, by Cathérine Lalumière, Secretary of State responsible for European Affairs. Addressing the National Assembly on 11 June 1985, she said that it was desirable to have the EP 'intervene' in Community decision-making, but she affirmed at the same time that this should not be to the detriment of decision-making efficiency: the prospect of slower decision-making by empowering the EP was considered undesirable.[25]

Despite the noncommittal nature of the French government's support for enhancing the procedural legitimacy of the Community polity, the French PS supported its democratization. Unlike the Gaullists, for the PS national sovereignty was not considered *indivisible*: it was conceivable that sovereignty could be *shared* across different levels of governance, whereby the EP could assume an important role. During the foreign policy debate of 11 June 1985 in the National Assembly, statements by both Socialist MPs and government officials highlighted that democratic accountability could not be safeguarded exclusively at the national level but had to be provided at the European level. Among the members of government, Minister of Foreign Affairs, Roland Dumas, made a commitment stating that '[a]t the Milan Council, the Community will manifest ... a willingness to reform institutional practices by making use of ... the democratic legitimacy provided by the EP.'[26] During the same debate, Socialist MP, Charles Josselin, pointed out that the government's focus on improving Community decision-making inevitably had to go hand-in-hand with enhancing the legislative powers of the EP. This issue was even more pressing, since NPs' power to influence Community decision-making and to control its outcomes increasingly faded with the prospect of pooling sovereignty at the Community level:

Against the background of the weakening of national parliaments' powers, the European Parliament ... has, for long, embodied an opportunity, and maybe still does: to control the proliferation of Community legislation. . . . All in all, we as national parliamentarians will have to seek consolation for our decline in the thought that a substitute [for our loss in competencies] lies in Strasbourg, by reminding us of what John the Baptist had to say: "Il faut qu'il croisse et que je diminue".[27]

These were, however, not the only statements expressing support for the empowerment of the EP. Following the publication of the Dooge Committee's report in March 1985, the majority of the National Assembly adopted a report in May 1985 which affirmed that an increase in the EP's legislative powers was 'inevitable'. Although the report mainly reflected one of the dominant concerns expressed by all member state representatives in the Dooge Committee, namely that of enhancing the efficiency of the Community's decision-making process, it considered the *democratization* of the decision-making process no less vital (see Corbett 1998: 188). Despite the PS' support for enhanced powers for the EP, the French government and President Mitterrand did not intend to commit themselves too keenly to the empowerment of the EP. Whereas some member state governments, most notably Italy, demanded comprehensive powers for the EP, the French government was refusing to back the proposals going as far as pure legislative co-decision. In the run-up to the Milan European Council, the French government issued a memorandum entitled 'For the progress of the construction of Europe' in which it accepted the 'orientations' put forth in the Dooge Report. Under the sub-heading 'Improving the efficiency of the existing institutions', the memorandum expressed its support for more QMV, enhanced administrative powers for the Commission and improved 'participation' of the EP in the legislative process. However, the memorandum stated unambiguously that, in case of disagreement over legislation, the Council must always have the final word.[28] Despite the call of the PS to provide for a substantial increase of the EP's legislative powers, the government and President Mitterrand refused to give a firm commitment in that direction.

On the centre-right of the political spectrum, the Neo-Gaullist RPR and the UDF held a positive attitude towards the internal market programme and hence considered the adoption and ratification of the SEA a desirable venture. With regard to the question of the EP's legislative powers, however, differences in opinion became visible between the PS and the RPR and UDF. Whereas the trajectory of the Neo-Gaullists' European policy was dictated by economic 'pragmatism'[29] the Neo-Gaullists' foreign policy agenda emphasized that the ultimate right to veto was to be retained in areas where individual member states claimed a *vital* national interest. At the time of ratification, the SEA package was considered to pay

Table 5.1 Legitimating belief of the French Socialist Party

France—Parti Socialiste	
Legitimating belief	Federal state
Source of legitimacy	Popular sovereignty
Democracy at the international level?	Sovereignty can be shared across levels of governance
Nature of and remedies for the legitimacy deficit	Decline of national parliaments as a consequence of pooling can be compensated by empowering the European Parliament

sufficient respect to these principles.[30] However, in the run-up to the IGC, while still in opposition, some prominent voices in the RPR called for a policy that should pay tribute to firmly upholding national sovereignty and fending off supranational incursions. Ex-foreign minister Maurice Couve de Murville was one of the most outspoken adherents of the *intergovernmental cooperation* legitimating belief, calling for the preservation of the 'Luxembourg Compromise', resistance to attempts destined at the empowerment of the EP and the Commission, while, at the same time, propagating enhanced involvement of national parliaments in Community matters.[31] In contrast to the RPR, the UDF was more at ease with the notion of strengthening of the EP. Prior to the SEA, Adrien Zeller, MP and member of the UDF, claimed that there existed a fundamental 'institutional incoherence' in the Community which originated from the 'inadequate contribution of the European Parliament' in Community decision-making.[32] He affirmed, furthermore, that increasing decision-making efficiency must not necessarily be to the detriment of democratic decision-making at the Community level.[33] While the RPR thus remained sceptical about enhanced participation of the EP in Community decision-making as a legitimate 'substitute' for the loss of NPs' influence over Community matters, the UDF, prior to the adoption of the SEA, seemed to be closer to the position of the PS on the question of parliamentary powers.

5.2.2 Germany: 'democratizing' Europe

Hans-Jochen Vogel, leader of the opposition SPD, remarked during a Bundestag debate that one of the defining features of German policy towards European integration was the existence of a multiparty consensus.[34] One indicator of the said consensus is the vast number of resolutions on European policy introduced by the governing CDU/CSU–FDP coalition and the SPD which made the same demands on the government: while the CDU/CSU–FDP coalition called upon the government, *inter alia*, to 'take irrevocable decisions towards the creation of European Union, ... enhance the legislative powers of the EP... apply the Rome Treaties and enhance the scope of majority decision-making'[35], the SPD called for far-reaching institutional reforms, in particular with regard to the voting procedures in the Council. The SPD also called for the augmentation of the decision-making competencies of 'the directly elected representatives', demanding that 'the EP has to be given legislative powers.'[36] During the Bundestag debate of 27 June 1985, Renate Hellwig (CDU), chairwoman of the EC Committee, pointed out that as a result of pooling, NPs are even further deprived in the capacity to influence and control Community decisions and decision-making. To counter this development, she argued that legislative decision-making at the Community level had to be democratized and the EP's legislative role strengthened.[37] She also compared the present state of the European level decision-making to that of 'cabinet politics' ('Kabinettspolitik') under absolutist leaders. She asked rhetorically:

Do we want a Europe of the type of eighteenth- and nineteenth-century cabinet-politics? A Europe resembling the Congress of Vienna where the heads of government and crowned leaders took 'European' decisions... with the peoples having no input and being the victims of these decisions? Has the Congress of Vienna been resurrected disguised in form of the summit meetings in Brussels, Athens and Milan?... We thus welcome that Chancellor Kohl has set himself the core task to convince the other heads of government in Milan that the European Parliament has to become involved in the legislative process.[38]

The parliamentary statements and draft resolutions from the different parliamentary party groups reveal that the vast majority of Germany's political elite considered domestic democratic process to be negatively affected by enhanced pooling.[39] It is also obvious from the resolutions and statements presented thus far, that the challenge to domestic procedural legitimacy had to be targeted at the Community level by enhancing the legislative powers of the EP. In contrast to the rather vague statements in support for the EP by President Mitterrand and French government officials, Chancellor Kohl committed his government firmly to push for its empowerment. Addressing the Bundestag prior to the Milan European Council, Kohl declared:

In Milan, we intend to press for an empowerment of the European Parliament. . . . We are ready to make considerable advances on this issue, given that . . . in the area of Community policies there are a number of developments which are outside any form of parliamentary control . . . [I]t must be possible to institute a procedure between Parliament and Council which will . . . give Parliament considerably more competencies.[40]

In sum, it can be argued confidently that the Bundestag expressed broad support for the proposals to render European decision-making processes more democratic. The government also openly committed to this course of action. Horst Teltschick, Chancellor Kohl's principal advisor on foreign policy, wrote to the House of Lords Select Committee on the European Communities about the prospect of Community reform and stated that 'the German Government . . . remains committed to strengthening the European Parliament. We have already seen how the turnout slumped for the second direct elections in 1984. The third direct elections will be a fiasco unless Parliament is given a greater say in shaping Community policy and is allowed . . . to develop into a genuine legislative body.'[41]

5.2.3 United Kingdom: completing the internal market

In contrast to the German governing parties, the British Conservative party had a different picture of what it considered desirable and appropriate with regard to the reform of the European polity. In her memoirs, Margaret Thatcher summarized her 'ideal' of Europe as a 'free enterprise Europe des patries'.[42] Although she viewed the term 'European Union' with suspicion, a more 'unified' Europe was considered acceptable as long as this implied the creation of an internal market for goods and services. This view was outlined in a memorandum issued by the Foreign and Common-

Table 5.2 Legitimating belief of political parties in Germany

Germany—CDU/CSU and FDP (and the SPD opposition)	
Legitimating belief	Federal state
Source of legitimacy	Popular sovereignty
Democracy at the international level?	Sovereignty can be shared across levels of governance
Nature of and remedies for the legitimacy deficit	Decline of national parliaments as a consequence of pooling can be compensated by empowering the European Parliament

wealth Office. In the memorandum, the 'submerging' of sovereignties under the label of a 'United States of Europe' was rejected, yet support was expressed for 'greater unity' as long as this implied 'Europe united as a single market'. Furthermore, the government was willing to accept QMV where its application was expected to further the creation and smooth operation of the internal market.[43] The majority in the Conservative Party was willing to 'relegate' institutional issues to the realm of the 'practical' domain ('which procedures are most likely to help realize the internal market?') rather than treat them in the sphere of dogmatism ('the national veto must be kept at all costs'). However, a considerable number of back-benchers rejected the (even selective and by no means enthusiastic) support for more QMV on issues relating to the completion of the internal market. Consequently, the government repeatedly gave assurances that the Luxembourg Compromise would remain unscathed.[44] Yet, as mentioned earlier, the government did not rule out pooling on an *a priori* basis which reflected the overarching priority to create and complete the internal market. Buller states that '[a]s early as the start of 1983, Francis Pym, the then British Foreign Secretary, was reported as saying that the Thatcher government was not dogmatically opposed to the extension of majority voting' (Buller 2000: 98).[45]

While the majority position in the Conservative Party and the government supported the selective use of QMV, there was open rejection of the view that the EP had to be empowered as a corollary of decisions to pool sovereignty. As far as decision-making was concerned, the Conservative Party's position was that decision-making procedures had to be made more 'efficient' in order to promote the completion of the internal market; in turn, an increase of the legislative making powers of the EP was not considered to enhance decision-making efficiency (rather the contrary). Opposition to the legislative empowerment of the EP was, however, not only motivated by the potentially harmful effects on decision-making efficiency, but also by the belief in the sovereignty of the Westminster Parliament, a belief which emphasized the procedural dimension of legitimacy: the widespread demand, not only among backbenchers, that national parliamentary sovereignty had to emerge unscathed from any attempts to Treaty reform was difficult to meet in reality by the government if it took the application of QMV seriously. Rhetorical assurances that Westminster retained the ultimate source of sovereignty were repeatedly pronounced by members of the government. A memorandum published by the Foreign and Commonwealth Office unmistakably stated that government ministers were first and foremost accountable to their NPs:

Strengthening the powers of the European Parliament would increase the probability that Member States would find themselves under pressure to accept proposals which they judged to be against their national interest. Moreover, the present balance of power reflects the role and importance of national parliaments to whom members of the Council, as representatives of the governments of Member States, are answerable. Any change in the balance of power between the Council and the European Parliament would diminish the ability of national Parliaments to control Community policies, and their financing for which they would nonetheless remain answerable to national electorates.[46]

The notion of *national parliamentary sovereignty* posits that NPs are the ultimate sources of authority and legitimacy. This view was widely held among the ranks of both the Conservative and the Labour Party. Prior to the Luxembourg summit in December 1985, before the SEA negotiations entered their final round, Foreign Secretary, Geoffrey Howe, assured the House of Commons that 'all the proposals made so far for enlarging the power of the Parliament do not involve the transfer of democratic power from any national Parliament to the European Parliament. . . . Our concern is to see that the powers of the European institutions are adjusted to enable them to work effectively and continue to take decisions in a sensible fashion.'[47] These statements demonstrate that efficiency concerns and the support for selective pooling collided with the notion of *national* parliamentary sovereignty. The drive for more efficiency would inevitably result in a change of the prevailing *de facto* application of the provisions of the Treaty of Rome. The actual application of QMV in the Council would then ultimately lead to the possibility that individual governments could be outvoted. This, in turn, would result in a situation where ministerial responsibility vis-à-vis NPs could break down, a scenario that clashes fundamentally with the notion of national parliamentary sovereignty. As will be shown in more detail in the following section, the possibility of such a scenario was loathed by many Conservative MPs. The government in particular alleged that national parliamentary sovereignty was not at all affected by the proposed institutional changes. It argued, furthermore, that the institutional changes improved decision-making efficiency and the promotion of a true European *Economic* Community, and that national parliamentary sovereignty was respected because the Council kept the ultimate right to veto. Margaret Thatcher's personal views support this assessment. She stated that she 'was prepared to go along with some modest increase in the powers of the European Assembly, which would shortly and somewhat inaccurately be described as a Parliament: but the Council of Ministers, representing governments answerable to national parliaments, must always have the final say' (Thatcher 1993: 554).

The British government's position on the EP question was somewhat ambiguous: on the one hand, as an actor in Community decision-making, the EP was considered negligible as long as it did not compromise the efficiency of decision-making and the bringing about of the internal market (which reflects elements of the *economic community* legitimating belief). On the other hand, any potential increase in its legislative powers was viewed with hostility not just from an efficiency perspective but also from the belief in the sovereignty of the Westminster Parliament: no Community level representative institution could offer surrogate democratic legitimacy (which reflects elements of the *intergovernmental cooperation* legitimating belief). Malcolm Rifkind had already provided a taste of the position the British government was going to adopt during the IGC by entering a reservation on the relevant section in the report issued by Dooge Committee. Furthermore, Margaret Thatcher and Geoffrey Howe had remarked repeatedly that institutional reform was acceptable as long as it helped to bring about the completion of the internal market, and would not hamper decision-making efficiency or national parliamentary sovereignty. Empowering the EP would run to the detriment of all of these goals. Contrary to the French Socialists and the CDU/CSU–FDP coalition in Germany, the Conservative Party rejected the view that democracy at the European level was desirable or even possible. As far as a legitimacy deficit was considered to exist, it could not be solved by empowering the EP, but by ensuring that NPs were sufficiently informed and able to scrutinize government policy (a position most vehemently supported by Conservative Party backbenchers and the Labour Party).

5.3 Institutional reform and social action

In Sections 5.1 and 5.2, I have shown that the French, German, and British parties in government held different legitimating beliefs which produced different interpretations of the challenge posed by pooling for the democratic legitimacy of their respective domestic polities and of the Community polity. Furthermore, the governments in power before and during the negotiations of the SEA displayed different degrees of commitment to the domestically prevailing legitimating beliefs. In this section, I concentrate on addressing the following questions: how and to what degree did national governments feel constrained by domestic legitimating beliefs and the perception of a legitimacy deficit during the IGC? How did these

Table 5.3 Legitimating belief of the Conservative Party

United Kingdom—Conservative Party	
Legitimating belief	Economic community (members of government); Intergovernmental cooperation (parts of the parliamentary party)
Source of legitimacy	Economic efficiency; national parliamentary sovereignty has to be upheld
Democracy at the international level?	Irrelevant for economic effectiveness and efficiency; sovereignty is vested in national parliaments
Nature of and remedies for the legitimacy deficit	Economic effectiveness and efficiency guarantee legitimacy; indifferent to EP empowerment as long as it does not hamper effectiveness and efficiency; opposition to EP empowerment also based on belief in sovereignty of Westminster Parliament

constraints affect the institutional reform outcome? Before answering these questions, it is worthwhile to recall the hypotheses to be examined in this section.

Hypothesis 3: The 'null hypothesis'
Decision-making is characterized by bargaining about the powers of the EP and the outcome reflects the constellation of preferences and relative bargaining power of member state governments.

Hypothesis 4: Communicative action
Decision-making is characterized by a truth-seeking discourse on the appropriate role of the EP in the Community polity as a result of which member state governments reach a reasoned consensus.

Hypothesis 5: Rhetorical action
Decision-making is characterized by the strategic use of arguments through which member state governments seek to justify and realize their own preferences regarding the powers of the EP. Proponents of the *federal state* legitimating belief—appealing to community values—exercise social pressure on recalcitrant states with the aim of shaming them

into acquiescing to the EP's empowerment. Recalcitrant member states will downplay the outcomes, question their relevance or reinterpret them to their advantage in the light of domestic opposition.

5.3.1 The power of rhetorical action and the interstate arena

During the course of the IGC, heads of government and national delegates were well aware of the possibility that empowering the EP in the Community legislative process would run to the detriment of the Council's powers, whose influence over legislative outcomes would be reduced as a result. Furthermore, all governments, having subscribed to create the internal market by improving and speeding up Community decision-making through the use of QMV, realized that a more influential EP would certainly not add to the improvement of the efficiency of the legislative decision-making process. A number of ministers from different national delegations insisted that an increase of the legislative powers of the EP would run the risk of complicating or even paralysing the legislative decision-making process and would thus counteract the overarching objective of creating the internal market (see De Ruyt 1989: 75). Unsurprisingly, the proponents of this argument were the national governments who subscribed to the *economic community* or *intergovernmental cooperation* legitimating beliefs. As the proceedings of the so-called 'Dondelinger Group' (a group of high-ranking civil servants representing their respective national governments during the IGC) show, the adherents of both the *economic community* and *intergovernmental cooperation* legitimating beliefs—most notably the delegations from the UK, Denmark, and Greece—rejected calls to empower the EP on the ground that the strengthening of the EP was hard to square with their domestically-held legitimating beliefs. For example, it was argued that the prerogatives of NPs would be put into doubt once the EP was given more powers. This, so the argument continued, could potentially induce national MPs to put Treaty ratification into jeopardy. Moreover, the efficiency norm was introduced into the debate to allude to the potential conflict that could arise between the empowerment of the EP and the realization of the efficiency goal since the enhanced participation of the EP in the legislative process was likely to introduce an element of delay rather than an improvement and speeding-up of the decision-making process.[48]

Governments opposed to the legislative empowerment of the EP advanced their preferences by pointing to domestically prevailing legitimating beliefs and competing norms, the efficiency argument, to counter calls for the empowerment of the EP. Interestingly, however, the governments opposing enhanced legislative powers for the EP used a mixed strategy to convince the supporters of the EP to refrain from advocating 'real' legislative powers. They did so by appealing to the governments' status-related self-interest ('keeping the power in the Council'), (competing) community norms and specific interpretations of domestically held legitimating beliefs. The British government sought to appeal to governments' status-related self-interest since, in private, the proponents of a more potent EP appeared much less enthusiastic than their domestic precommitment suggested. Jacques Attali, special adviser to President Mitterrand, noted that Mitterrand's personal view on the question of the empowerment of the EP was primarily conditioned by status-related concerns: 'As far as the [European] Parliament is concerned, one must not—at present—lessen the powers of the Council of Ministers to increase those of the parliamentarians.'[49] The British Foreign Secretary, Geoffrey Howe, noted in his memoirs that the discussion revolving around the powers of the EP demonstrated that the 'federal rhetoric' employed by the proponents of the *federal state* legitimating belief did not necessarily coincide with their private views:

This is an issue [the powers of the European Parliament] on which there was particularly wide gap between the national posturing of some heads of government and the positions which they were finally ready to adopt—after a certain amount of 'grandstanding' in the Council for the sake of their national press. Most of Margaret's [Margaret Thatcher] colleagues—particularly Mitterand, Kohl, Craxi and the Benelux premiers—found it popular (at least at this stage) to present themselves as champions of the European Parliament.... Yet in truth all the heads of government had a common interest in maintaining their own joint and several authority, as represented by the powers of the European Council' (Howe 1994: 455).

Margaret Thatcher, however, did not appeal only to the status-related self-interest of the other governments. She also appealed to the democratic legitimacy of national officials in Community policy-making: 'MEPs, she said, are democratic representatives. So are we. We have to take decisions for our own countries and in the Council for the Community as a whole' (Howe 1994: 455). Buller made a similar observation noting that the British government combined the use of different arguments to legitimize its opposition to strengthening the EP. Besides appeals to self-interest, the British government pointed at the contradictory effects of opting for efficiency-enhancing institutions—such as QMV—and an increase in the EP's legislative powers (see Budden 1994: 292). The British delegation also appealed to the 'democratic conscience' of the other member state governments by arguing that, *inter alia*, NPs would be sidelined as a result of giving the EP a more pronounced say in the legislative process. Buller's quotation illustrates nicely the British government's strategy to employ different arguments strategically to convince the *federal state* proponents to refrain from advocating more powers for the EP:

First, at a time when all national delegations were on record as wanting to make the Community's decision-making process simpler and more effective, the British team continually questioned how joint decision-making would contribute to this goal.... Not surprisingly, British queries concerning how [empowering the European Parliament] would make decision-making simpler and quicker commanded substantial tacit support from many quarters in the maximalist camp.... Second, British negotiators emphasized that the proposals for extending the powers of the European Parliament threatened to alter the balance of power at the Community level to the extent that all national governments would be forced in the future to accept decisions that they deemed to be against their national interest. The argument stressed that the present institutional structure of the Community rightly gave the Council of Ministers the final say on legislative matters. Ministers were responsible to national parliaments and any interference with this institutional balance would be perceived in national capitals as a challenge to the influence of democratically elected national parliaments.... Despite the public rhetoric, British officials remember receiving substantial tacit support for their arguments and some open support from the Danish delegation. (Buller 2000: 107–8)

While the British delegation, backed by the Danish and Greek delegations, engaged in rhetorical action—the strategic use of norm-based arguments—to fight off proposals for empowering the EP, there is no evidence to suggest that the governments, such as the German government, who had domestically committed themselves to the *federal state* legitimating belief, tried particularly hard to convince recalcitrant governments of the desirability and appropriateness of their 'quest' to empower the EP. If, thus, none of the governments under scrutiny felt a sincere attachment to empowering the EP, two questions pose themselves: first, why did the member state governments nevertheless endow the EP with 'conditional agenda-setting power' under the cooperation procedure? And, second, why did they not grant the EP full co-decision?

At the outset of the IGC, the British government pursued a line of argumentation stressing that the main criterion for institutional reform was the efficiency of adopting a new procedure for decision-making. Procedures should be designed with a view to improving decision-making efficiency in order not to impede the goal of creating the internal market.[50] At that stage, the British delegation did not make any 'principled' objections to enhancing the role of the EP, but assessed its prospective role

in the light of achieving substantive policy goals, a line of reasoning
reflected in the *economic community* legitimating belief. This line of reasoning and arguing, however, left a door open to 'creative maximalist
draughtsmen' (Budden 1994: 327): as long as a solution could be presented
that did not compound the efficiency of the new decision-making procedure and would meet the British government's demand that the 'balance of
power' among the Community institutions remained unscathed (the code
for this being the Council keeping the last word in any reformed decision-
making procedure), proposals to empower the EP would have a chance to
succeed. For instance, a proposal by the German delegation—acting under
pressure from domestic MPs and MEPs—which foresaw a conciliation
committee between Council and EP[51] was quickly hailed by opponents
of the EP as failing the 'efficiency test' and was soon scrapped. However, as
Budden (1994: 333) put it, the British government's strategy to play the
efficiency-card 'left the Government potentially exposed to discovery of
a . . . procedure which met the [efficiency] criterion.' And so it came. 'The
introduction of a Council "common position" and second EP reading
marked a breakthrough . . . Drawing on French ideas to link the Council's
decision-making rule to the EP's vote, the Presidency introduced a formal
procedure offering considerable influence to the EP, while protecting . . .
Council prerogatives' (Budden 1994: 338). Having fallen into the efficiency-
rhetoric trap, the British delegation had to live grudgingly with the proposal of the so-called cooperation procedure which gave the EP a substantial role in the legislative process. The government did not dare to advance
different arguments since it was shying away from paying the social cost of
being accused of acting inconsistently or hypocritically.

5.3.2 The power of rhetorical action and domestic sources of social influence

What made the privately uncommitted governments push for a more
influential role for the EP? While the French government—privately *and*
domestically uncommitted—did not show a strong interest in the matter
of the EP's legislative participation, the German government, which (as
demonstrated previously) showed strong domestic pre-commitment to
the empowerment of the EP, became an important player during the
later stages of the IGC. Even though the German government did not
have to fear a domestic threat over ratification if it 'failed' over the EP
issue, the government was keen to appear to honour its domestic pre-
commitment to the *federal state* legitimating belief. Attali, President Mit-

terrand's special adviser, remarked on this point that 'as far as the powers of the [European] Parliament are concerned, the Germans are very worried that nothing serious will be proposed, because they fear the rage of their own parliamentarians. They have it in mind to demand a prudent increase of the Parliament's power to co-decide even if they will not get their way.'[52] François Mitterrand employed equally federalist rhetoric–his address to the EP is often cited in this respect–yet he was not at all committed to empowering the EP.[53] Moreover, the weakness of the French government's domestic commitment reduced the potential for social pressure to be exercised by the domestic audience. Hence, even though non-ratification was never a real threat, member state governments sought to please their domestic audiences depending on their degree of domestic pre-commitment to a particular legitimating belief. The fact that national governments tailored their arguments in favour or against an increase in the EP's legislative powers so as to be in line with prevailing domestic legitimating beliefs strongly supports the rhetorical action hypothesis. By taking a closer look at the national parliamentary debates during the IGC and the ensuing domestic ratification debates, it is apparent that German government officials readily employed arguments to defend the institutional outcomes of the SEA in the light of the *federal state* legitimating belief, primarily by over-emphasizing the achievements. In his address to the Bundestag after the Luxembourg European Council in December 1985, Chancellor Kohl claims credit for successfully pursuing the question of the EP's powers, even though—as I showed above—his commitment during the IGC was all but enthusiastic:

[A]n intense struggle at the summit centred on the question of the empowerment of the European Parliament. We . . . have constantly pointed at that issue, and that the democratic self-understanding of the Community requires a Parliament with enhanced powers of co-decision.[54]

Chancellor Kohl felt equally compelled to defend any institutional reform outcome which fell short of full co-decision, as demanded by the parliamentary party groups. Providing reasons to explain the limited scope of the reform, Kohl pointed at the historical differences in the role of parliamentary institutions in the member states which affected the easiness or uneasiness with which different national governments were willing to delegate powers to the EP.[55] Kohl also did not shy away from over-emphasizing and overstating the Treaty outcomes with regard to the EP's new competencies; he referred to the EP as co-legislator ('Mitgesetzgeber') even though the EP fell short of actual co-decision powers.[56]

Hans-Dietrich Genscher's assessment of the Luxembourg European Council meeting echoed that of Chancellor Kohl. He emphasized that Germany's efforts to enhance the legislative powers of the EP met with obstacles which reflected the differences in parliamentary traditions in the different member states.[57] Yet, he also made clear that 'from our point of view, the European Parliament should have been given more competencies.'[58]

As in the case of Germany, ratification legislation sailed relatively smoothly through the British House of Commons, but only after a guillotine motion had been introduced to end six days of debate to silence 'the usual handful of predictable dissenters' within the Conservative party's own ranks (Howe 1994: 457). In the British case, the content of the government's commitment to their domestic audience differed markedly from that of the German government. As we have already explored at length, the British government prioritized the completion of the internal market and institutional reform to improve decision-making efficiency, but was equally committed to preserving the ultimate right to evoke the unilateral veto and national parliamentary sovereignty. Pursuing the objectives of decision-making efficiency, retaining the veto and parliamentary sovereignty posed a contradiction which was exploited by the opposition Labour Party and Conservative 'dissenters' alike and forced the government to give assurances that the Treaty reform outcomes, such as increased pooling and the (limited) empowerment of the EP, could still be squared with increased decision-making efficiency and the belief in the sovereignty of the Westminster Parliament. The government's strategy was to downplay the institutional reforms affecting the EP's legislative powers while, at the same time, interpreting the outcome to appear in line with domestic pre-commitments. In her address to the House of Commons immediately after the Luxembourg European Council in December 1985, Prime Minister Margaret Thatcher insisted that 'the last word on ... legislation will rest with the Council. There will be no transfer of power on these matters from this House to the Assembly.'[59] She also affirmed that enhanced legislative involvement by the EP would not obstruct the achievement of government's core objectives, the realization of the internal market and improved decision-making efficiency.[60]

In his address to the House of Commons during the first reading of the European Communities Amendment Bill on 23 April 1986, Foreign and Commonwealth Secretary Geoffrey Howe also launched an attempt to assure the members of the Commons that sufficient safeguards were in place to protect the 'national interest' against any encroachments by the

EP. However, Howe—deliberately or unknowingly—misrepresented the implications of the new cooperation procedure for the Council's capacity to affect legislative outcomes. He claimed that 'the [European] Parliament can in certain circumstances change the Council's voting provisions back from qualified majority to unanimity. In no circumstances can it change them the other way.'[61] Here, Howe talked into existence a 'protective' mechanism for the member states which, in fact, did not exist. The exact opposite was the case. Unanimity, as employed by Howe, meant that the Council could only *reject* or *change* amendments tabled by the EP unanimously whereas the Council 'only' needed a qualified majority to *accept* them. The 'illusion' of unanimity, which Howe refers to here, thus works to the detriment of the Council and not to its advantage.[62] The government also had to fend off accusations that the Westminster Parliament was being sidelined as a result of endowing the EP with a more prominent role in decision-making. Addressing the Commons, Margaret Thatcher stressed that the institutional reforms, under no circumstances, undermined the sovereignty of Westminster (and carefully avoided to call the EP a 'parliament'):

The European Assembly is different from our national sovereign Parliament. Any changes to the treaty are a matter for each and sovereign Parliament to which we as a Government are responsible. I think that it is reasonable to consult the European Assembly.... [I]t is the differences between the European Assembly and a national sovereign Parliament which impress me more than the similarities.'[63]

The pursuit of conflicting objectives—decision-making efficiency on the one hand and the retention of the ultimate right to veto as well as the respect for the sovereignty of Westminster on the other hand—put the government under social pressure to appear in line with its domestic pre-commitments. According to Budden, '[t]hroughout the IGC, backbenchers' suspicion would restrict the Government's room for manoeuvre' (Budden, 1994: 257).

In the preceding two sections I have demonstrated that by manoeuvring itself into the efficiency-rhetoric trap, the British government was vulnerable to national governments' proposals to enhance the powers of the EP as long as they met the 'efficiency' benchmark. It has also been shown that the German government—even though tacitly sympathizing with the arguments advanced by the British—bowed to social pressure exercised by an attentive domestic audience while the French government, domestically uncommitted, did not feel compelled to lobby for a strengthening of the EP's powers. The outcome of the IGC was a legislative procedure that allowed the British and German governments in particular to save face before their domestic audiences: for the British government, it was crucial that the Council kept the last word (even though it needed unanimity to change amendments by the Commission and EP)[64] while for the German government it was important to present the domestic audience with an outcome that represented a qualitative improvement for the EP, even though falling short of co-decision.

5.3.3 *Bargaining over the final provisions*

Although the empirical evidence presented hitherto supports the rhetorical action hypothesis, it does not explain the full picture. In the final stages of the IGC, the interactions between the national delegations displayed the characteristics of bargaining—the exchange of threats—rather than those of rhetorical action. Threats to delay or jeopardize the adoption of the SEA originated from 'maximalist' governments, the staunch proponents of the *federal state* legitimating belief, most notably the Italian government. The Italian government had committed itself to full-fledged co-decision between the Council and the EP. According to Budden (1994: 326), the goal of this maximalist 'rejection group' attempted 'to raise the negotiations' common denominator with threats to reject the whole process if it did not go far enough.' Between the Milan European Council meeting in June and the Luxembourg European Council meeting in December 1985, the Commission proposed a formula linking the use of QMV with enhanced parliamentary participation, proposing a second reading on all matters where QMV would be applied: during the second reading phase, the EP should be given the right to propose amendments, which—if adopted by the Commission—could only be rejected or amended by a unanimous Council and adopted by a qualified majority. This formula was accepted by a majority of European Council members. De Ruyt argues that, during the Luxembourg European Council meeting in December, the question of the EP's legislative powers could have been resolved quickly based on this proposal by the Commission. However, the Italian delegation staunchly fought for more extensive powers of co-decision for the EP (De Ruyt 1989: 80). In Luxembourg '[e]ight foreign ministers had already accepted the cooperation procedure, largely as it left the Council with the last word and did not seem to alter the inter-institutional balance.' It was the Italian delegation led by Prime Minister Benito Craxi who 'threw the debate into confusion by attempting to upgrade the entire institutional package with a commitment to full co-decision' (Budden 1994: 361–2).

Instead of coming to an agreement on the question of the Parliament's powers, the Italian government 'maintained "conditional acceptance" of the reforms until the [European Parliament] had passed judgement. Craxi also retained a specific reserve on [European Parliament] procedures' (Budden 1994: 364). Following the Luxembourg European Council meeting, the foreign ministers had to convene again, waiting until the EP had issued its opinion on the Luxembourg package. Based on interviews with the British and Belgian foreign ministers, Geoffrey Howe and Leo Tindemans, Budden argues that 'the foreign ministers had to take the [European Parliament]'s opinion seriously due to the commitment which the Italian Government had made on behalf of its national parliament' (Budden 1994: 365) and, consequently, took on board some of the EP's demands. The governments thus took the Italian threat seriously and incorporated some of the EP's demands into the provisions governing the new legislative procedure. The most important of these changes gave the EP an additional lever over the Council: if the EP decided to reject the Council's common position, the Council could only overturn the rejection by unanimity. According to Budden (1994: 366), 'this minor change would alter the balance within the EC's decision-making system. If the EP had one ally among the ministers... the Council—having to decide with a three-month deadline—might come under considerable parliamentary leverage over such decisions.'

5.4 Conclusion

This chapter set out to answer the question why the Community member states endowed the EP with legislative powers which had far-reaching implications for the balance of power between the EP and the member states in the Council. In the first part of the chapter, I have shown that the decision by the member state governments to transfer sovereignty through the introduction of QMV (pooling) posed a challenge for traditional channels of interest representation and accountability. In particular, political elites across the Community member states were worried about the repercussions on the role of NPs. In the second part of this chapter, I argued that despite political elites' awareness of this legitimacy deficit, they advanced different proposals for its reduction which were founded on different legitimating beliefs held by the different actors. As a third step, I argued that during the IGC leading towards the adoption of the SEA, the question of remedies for the legitimacy deficit became

acute for national governments. In this situation, most national governments found themselves confronted with a tension between their status-
related self-interest—retaining power in the Council instead of 'losing'
power by strengthening the EP—and behaviour that conformed to the
pre-commitments given to domestic audiences about pursuing the prescriptions of a particular legitimating belief. I asked why governments,
when they confronted the tension between self-interest and following the
behavioural prescriptions of a legitimating belief, tended to follow the
latter and argued that social influence played an important role as a
mechanism which not only ensured that national governments complied
with the prescriptions of a legitimating belief, but which also affected the
final outcome of institutional reform.

Notes

1. See, for example, Tsebelis (1994), Garrett and Tsebelis (1996) and Moser (1997). For a
   more recent excellent contribution, see Selck (2004).
2. See, for example, Westlake (1994), Maurer (1999), and the overview in Judge and
   Earnshaw (2003: 246–8).
3. See, for example, the studies by Judge et al. (1994), Earnshaw and Judge (1996), and
   Hubschmid and Moser (1997).
4. Tsebelis et al. (2001) offer a comprehensive analysis of amendments under the
   different legislative procedures.
5. Wilfried Martens, Prime Minsiter of Belgium at the time, summarized this state of
   affairs aptly: '[A]ll the time I have been taking part in European Councils, and that is
   for five years now, Europe has been poisoned by the problem of the British budget
   contribution. We have better things to do than waste our time with that. Let us
   rather tackle the Community's economic and social situation' (Agence Europe, 22
   March 1984).
6. 'I...suggest that preparatory consultations, perhaps leading to a conference of the
   Member States concerned, be started up. The project on European Union and the
   solemn declaration of Stuttgart will be a basis for this' (The full version of Mitterrand's address to the European Parliament on 24 May 1984 is re-printed in Gazzo 1985:
   82–5).
7. Agence Europe, 25 May 1984 and 28 May 1984.
8. Agence Europe, 16 March 1985, see also Gazzo (1985: 123–47) for the full report.
9. See Agence Europe, 16 March 1985. The report reveals that three delegates were
   manifestly marginalized by their colleagues: the Danish representative, Otto Møller
   (Under-Secretary of State for Foreign Affairs) who rejected the committee's general
   approach, as well as the Greek representative Ioannis Papantoniou, a counsellor to
   the Prime Minister and Malcolm Rifkind, Secretary of State in the Foreign and
   Commonwealth Office.

10. See Attali (1993), especially the entries made on 13 May and 28 May 1985.

11. This address is also known as Howe's *Stresa Plan*.

12. Agence Europe, 19 June 1985; see also De Ruyt (1989: 57–8).

13. See, for example, Corbett (1987), De Ruyt (1989), Garrett (1992), and Moravcsik (1991, 1998: Chapter 5).

14. Bulletin of the EC, No 6, 1985.

15. Journal Officiel, Assemblée Nationale, debate of 11 June 1985: 1599–1600 (author's translation).

16. Journal Officiel, Assemblée Nationale, debate of 11 June 1985: 1613 (author's translation, emphasis added).

17. House of Lords, Select Committee on the European Communities, 14th Report, 23 July 1985: 56 (emphasis in original).

18. Bundestag debate of 27 June 1985: 11089 (author's translation).

19. Bundestag debate of 27 June 1985: 11111.

20. See Corbett (1998: 185–94) for an analysis of the debates in NPs prior to the SEA.

21. Agence Europe, 21 June 1985.

22. The interim and final reports of the Dooge Committee stated that a 'Parliament elected by universal suffrage cannot, if the principles of democracy are logically applied, continue to be restricted to a consultative role or to having cognisance of only a minor part of the Community expenditure. That dooms it to oblivion or overstatement, and more often than not to both. An enhanced role will be sought for it in three areas: by effective participation in legislation, in form of joint-decision-making with the Council; . . . by increasing its supervision of various policies of the Union and its political control over the Commission and over cooperation in the external policy field; [and] by giving it responsibility in decisions on revenue' (Agence Europe, 2 December 1984).

23. See Corbett (1998: 185–94).

24. See Gazzo (1985: 85).

25. Journal Officiel, Assemblée Nationale, debate of 11 June 1985: 1617.

26. Journal Officiel, Assemblée Nationale, debate of 11 June 1985: 1573 (author's translation).

27. Journal Officiel, Assemblée Nationale, debate of 11 June 1985: 1600 (author's translation).

28. Agence Europe, 18 July 1985.

29. See European Parliament (1988: 42).

30. See European Parliament (1988: 43).

31. During a foreign policy debate in the National Assembly in June 1985, Maurice Couve de Murville vehemently criticized the European Parliament's Draft Treaty which he considered a 'retour de trente ans en arrière' and also accused the French government of having been 'seduced' by the Draft Treaty's proposals (see Journal Officiel, Assemblée Nationale, debate of 11 June 1985: 1588). See also Jachtenfuchs (2002: 87–9) for the relative consistency of the Gaullists attitude towards the EP.

32. Journal Officiel, Assemblée Nationale, debate of 11 June 1985: 1613 (author's translation).

33. 'The increase in decision-making efficiency...has to be accompanied by the strengthening of the European Parliament's role. In fact, the national parliaments are not in the position anymore to effectively control Community decisions....The only means to re-establish control of these decisions is to endow the European Parliament with the means not only to influence the decisions, but also to legitimize them by its votes.' (Journal Officiel, Assemblée Nationale, debate of 11 June 1985: 1613, author's translation).

34. Bundestag debate of 27 June 1985: 11089.

35. Bundestag, Drucksache 10/3569 ('Antrag der CDU/CSU und der FDP zur Europapolitik') of 26 June 1985 (author's translation).

36. Bundestag, Drucksache 10/3564 ('Antrag der SPD-Fraktion zum Europäischen Rat am 28–29 Juni in Mailand') of 26 June 1985 (author's translation).

37. Bundestag debate of 27 June 1985: 11111 (author's translation).

38. Bundestag debate of 27 June 1985: 11111 (author's translation).

39. Bundestag, Drucksache 10/3152 ('Antrag der SPD-Fraktion zur Europapolitik') of 9 April 1985; Bundestag, Drucksache 10/3564 ('Antrag der SPD-Fraktion zum Europäischen Rat am 28–29 Juni in Mailand') of 26 June 1985; Bundestag, Drucksache 10/3569 ('Antrag der CDU/CSU und der FDP zur Europapolitik') of 26 June 1985.

40. Bundestag debate of 27 June 1985: 11098 (author's translation).

41. Memorandum 'The Future of European Community', by Horst Teltschik, Foreign Affairs Adviser to Chancellor Kohl for the House of Lords Select Committee on the European Communities, in House of Lords, Select Committee on the European Communities, 14th Report, 23 July 1985: 325.

42. Thatcher (1993: 536).

43. The relevant sections in the memorandum read as follows: '15....In Britain the term [union] evokes the Act of Union which made England and Scotland a unitary state. In other Member States what most people seem to have in mind is progress towards a more united Europe. Except in the minds of a minority of federalists, the term "European Union" no longer implies the creation of a United States of Europe in which national sovereignties would be submerged; 16. The United Kingdom wants to see greater unity. Within the European Community this means Europe united as a single market....; 18. The most effective means of promoting a more united Europe would be to make a reality of the Treaty of Rome by implementing key provisions of the Treaty. Activities which generate wealth and jobs and which enhance competitiveness vis-à-vis the United States and Japan must be a top priority. We want to see practical steps to make a reality of the Treaty in relation to completion of the common market' (Foreign and Commonwealth Office, Memorandum of 26 March 1985 for the House of Lords Select Committee on The European Communities, in House of Lords, Select Committee on the European Communities, 14th Report, 23 July 1985: 4–5).

44. For instance, Labour MP George Foulkes reports that Margaret Thatcher emphasized after the Milan European Council that the internal market must be completed, 'but I think it can be completed keeping the unanimity rule' (Hansard, House of Commons, debate of 23 April 1986: 384).

45. In a statement before the House of Lords Select Committee, Malcolm Rifkind supported institutional measures that would help bring about the internal market: 'One of the main concerns of the British Government is the need to complete...the "internal market"...the main priority is to identify the practical economic and industrial issues where a common policy is desirable, and on the internal market, and then determine if it is necessary to have an institutional change to achieve these results' (House of Lords, Select Committee on the European Communities, 14th Report, 23 July 1985: 42).

46. Foreign and Commonwealth Office, Memorandum of 26 March 1985 for the House of Lords Select Committee on The European Communities, in House of Lords, Select Committee on the European Communities, 14th Report, 23 July 1985: 3.

47. Hansard, House of Commons, 20 November 1985: 1028.

48. Agence Europe, 10 October 1985.

49. See Attali (1993: 817), entry of 28 May 1985, author's translation.

50. Agence Europe, 19 June 1985.

51. Agence Europe, 27 September 1985.

52. See Attali (1993: 820), entry of 6 June 1985, author's translation.

53. Interview with Philip Budden, Cabinet Office, 23 April 2002. John Major recalls that, during the Maastricht Treaty negotiations, Mitterrand had been expressly hostile towards any attempt to delegate more powers to the EP. John Major (2000: 270) writes in his memoirs: 'His view, expressed to me privately, was that the European Parliament "has no legitimacy and will not have for a hundred years" '

54. Bundestag debate of 5 December 1985: 13766 (author's translation).

55. Kohl chose a modest form of 'scapegoating' or blame attribution by referring to historical and structural causes which rendered power delegation to the EP difficult to achieve: '[I]n particular the centrally organized states, which—beside their "central" parliament—never had parliaments of decentralized or local nature—beyond the municipal level, had a great deal of problems to accept the thought of a modern federal polity with a decentralization of legislative powers' (Bundestag debate of 5 December 1985: 13766, author's translation).

56. Bundestag debate of 5 December 1985: 13766.

57. Bundestag debate of 5 December 1985: 13785.

58. Bundestag debate of 5 December 1985: 13785 (author's translation).

59. Hansard, House of Commons, 5 December 1985: 429.

60. Hansard, House of Commons, 5 December 1985: 436–37.

61. Hansard, House of Commons, 23 April 1986: 322.

62. This manoeuvre worked all but well, as the contributions by a number of MPs illustrate. Conservative MP Teddy Taylor remarked: '[I]f the European Assembly, by a clear majority, does not like what the Council is doing, the Council can overturn the rejection only by a unanimous vote. In those circumstances, obtaining a unanimous vote will be difficult, particularly in view of the attitude that Italy has to the views of the European Parliament. So in this case a major new blocking power is provided' (Hansard, House of Commons, 23 April 1986, 368). Equally from the ranks of Conservative MPs, Sir Edward du Cann questioned the government's argument that the 'empowerment' of the EP would be as 'inconsequential' as they claimed it

was: if the 'Bill is passed in its present form, the Assembly will be able to block Council proposals, unless the Council disagrees unanimously with its views. It is obvious to anybody who knows anything about the way in which the European Community now operates that that is extremely unlikely.... If the Council wants to get legislation through there will be immense pressure on it to accommodate the views of the European Parliament. Whether we like it or not, whether people know about it or not, the European Parliament will take immense new authority' (Hansard, House of Commons, 26 June 1986: 489).

63. Hansard, House of Commons, 5 December 1985: 438.
64. In the case of the British government, I have already mentioned that—to 'save face'—the cooperation procedure was misinterpreted!

6

From Maastricht to the Constitutional Treaty: the Return of National Parliaments?

The SEA marked a watershed for the EP. With the introduction of the cooperation procedure, the EP was given real influence in the legislative decision-making process in an important area of Community legislation. The SEA, however, marked another important development. In the two previous chapters, I have argued that as a result of transfers of sovereignty, the role of national parliaments in EU decision-making—budgetary and legislative—has been challenged. During domestic debates and intergovernmental negotiations leading to the adoption of the SEA, political elites have come to ponder over the question of how to respond to the increasing marginalization of NPs and their role to exercise control and influence in EU decision-making.

The questions driving this chapter are the following: first, do the Treaty revisions of the 1990s and the Treaty changes resulting from the Post-Nice process and the adoption of the TCE in October 2004, support *hypothesis 1a* which posits that transfers of sovereignty 'trigger' a perceived legitimacy deficit among political elites which leads to proposals for its alleviation. Second, how can it be explained that proposals to strengthen the role of NPs in EU decision-making have flourished since the adoption of the Maastricht Treaty (see Table 6.1) alongside further proposals to (continue to) enhance the powers of the European Parliament (see Table 6.2).

The information conveyed in Tables 6.1 and 6.2 reflects that from the 1990s onwards, political elites across EU member states came to consider both their domestic NPs as well as the EP as possible solutions to alleviate the legitimacy deficit. Recalling *hypothesis 1a*, we would expect political elites to perceive a legitimacy deficit once the pooling and/or delegation of sovereignty is imminent. But while the empowerment of the EP continues

Table 6.1 National parliaments and EU decision-making

	Role of National Parliaments	Legal base
Maastricht Treaty (1991)	• NPs to receive Commission proposals in "good time" for information and examination	'Declaration on the Role of National Parliaments in the European Union' (No. 13)
	• Representatives from NPs and EP encouraged to discuss "main features" of the EU	'Declaration on the Conference of the Parliaments' (No. 14)
Treaty of Amsterdam (1997)	• Information for NPs: fixed six-week period between Commission proposal submitted to NPs and the Council adopting a position	'Protocol on the Role of National Parliaments in the European Union'
	• COSAC to examine legislative proposals and make "contributions" relating to fundamental rights, subsidiarity, establishment of an area of freedom, security, and justice	
Treaty of Nice (2000)	• *Inter alia*, calls upon role of NPs in the EU architecture to be debated	'Declaration on the Future of the Union' (No. 23)
Treaty Establishing a Constitution for Europe (2004)	• Information for NPs; fixed six-week period between Commission proposal submitted to NPs and the Council adopting a position	'Protocol on the Role of National Parliaments in the European Union' (No. 1)
	• 'Subsidiarity' control by NPs on Commission proposals; initiation of infringement proceedings before the ECJ (national governments on behalf of NPs)	Art. I-11 III and annexed 'Protocol on the Application of the Principles of Subsidiarity and Proportionality' (No. 2)

Table 6.2 The European Parliament and EU decision-making after Maastricht

	Role of the European Parliament and legal base
Maastricht Treaty (1991)	• Introduction of co-decision procedure (Art. 189B ECT), extension of other procedures
	• EP consulted on member states' nominee for Commission President; college of Commissioners subject to vote of approval (Art. 158 ECT)
Treaty of Amsterdam (1997)	• Reform and extension of co-decision procedure (Art. 251 ECT)
	• Nominee for Commission President has to be approved by EP plus vote of approval for the college of Commissioners (Art. 214 ECT)
Treaty of Nice (2000)	• Extension of co-decision procedure (Art. 251 ECT)
Treaty Establishing a Constitution for Europe (2004)	• Co-decision to become 'ordinary legislative procedure' (Art. I-34 I and Art. III-396)
	• Nominee for Commission President is elected by EP with member states taking into account the elections to the EP (Art. I-27 I)
	• Reform annual budgetary procedure (removal of distinction between compulsory and non-compulsory expenditure, Art. III-404); constitutionalization of multi-annual financial framework (Art. I-55 and III-402)

to be seen as an adequate institutional solution to alleviate the legitimacy deficit, how can we explain that political elites have attributed an increasing role to the NPs in the equation?

6.1 The specificity and coherence of alternative legitimation strategies

I have argued and demonstrated in the previous chapters that the perception of the legitimacy deficit does not translate automatically into institutional design proposal and cues for action: *hypothesis 2* states that legitimating beliefs provide lenses through which political elites perceive the legitimacy deficit and from which they derive prescriptions for its reduction. Member state governments who used to see the empowerment of the EP critically, such as the proponents of an *intergovernmental cooperation* legitimating belief, have long stressed the negative repercussions of European integration on NPs. How can we explain that concerns about the role of NPs have—until the 1990s—not translated into institutional reform solutions? Furthermore, once the member state governments decided to walk down the NP route, why did they only do so fairly reluctantly since, in stark contrast to the powers of the EP, the competencies of NPs in EU decision-making are of a rather limited nature? In order to answer these questions, I will turn to the discussion about the impact of norms on actor behaviour in the International Relations and Comparative Politics literature. Legitimating beliefs, akin to norms, are collectively held beliefs which prescribe the goals actors should strive towards and the behaviour associated with achieving these goals. Hence, to learn why the prescriptions of alternative legitimating beliefs have had differential success in being translated into institutional reform solutions, I have to analyse the special properties of these legitimating beliefs. The norm-literature in both International Relations theory[1] and Comparative Politics[2] can be fruitfully employed to help explain the relative success of alternative legitimating beliefs and their associated *legitimation strategies*, by which I mean the institutional reform proposals derived from alternative legitimating beliefs. In this context, I distinguish between the EP route and the NP route as alternative legitimation strategies which political elites employ to alleviate the perceived legitimacy deficit. The degree to which these two legitimation strategies 'succeed' depends on specific properties: specificity and coherence.

The *specificity* of a legitimation strategy refers to the simplicity and clarity with regard to the behavioural prescriptions (the Dos) or prohibitions (the Don'ts) offered. According to Legro (1997), specificity can be assessed by examining policy-makers' understandings of the simplicity and clarity of the prescription or prohibition inherent in a particular legitimation strategy. Hence, the more specific a legitimation strategy, the better policy-makers understand the concomitant behavioural prescriptions and prohibitions and will be able to act upon them.

The *coherence* of a legitimation strategy refers to the degree to which it fits coherently with the surrounding normative structure. According to Florini (1996: 376–7), '[a] new norm acquires legitimacy within the rule community when it is itself a reasonable behavioural response to environmental conditions facing the members of the community and when it "fits" coherently with other prevailing norms accepted by the members of the community' (Florini 1996: 376–7). Existing norms can provide a hospitable environment for a particular legitimation strategy, and a less hospitable one for another. Similarly, norm shifts can breathe new life into a 'latent' legitimation strategy increasing its standing relative to other legitimation strategies.

In the ensuing empirical analysis I will proceed as follows. First, I will ask whether—as in the previous cases—transfers of sovereignty 'triggered' a shared perception of a legitimacy deficit among political elites. Hence, I would expect political elites to react to instances of sovereignty transfers (as a result of Treaty reforms) by employing legitimating strategies which, by definition, guide the search for institutional solutions to the perceived challenges posed by transfers of sovereignty. Second, I will test the plausibility of the hypothesis that specific and coherent legitimation strategies are more likely to influence institutional reform and design decisions among political elites than legitimation strategies which are vaguely defined and which do not fit with their surrounding normative environment. What are the observable implications of this hypothesis? First, bearing the asymmetrical 'success' of both legitimation strategies in mind, we would expect the EP route to display higher degrees of specificity and coherence throughout the integration process. However, since the early 1990s we would expect the NP route to become more specific and coherent.

6.2 The relative success of the European Parliament route and the national parliament route

In the run up to the SEA, I have shown that some member state governments responded to the introduction and extension of QMV by voicing concerns about the increasing marginalization of NPs in exercising control and influence over EU decision-making since, with the introduction of QMV, ever more policy decisions would be taken at the EU level. This concern was shared by proponents of the *federal state* and the *intergovernmental cooperation* legitimating beliefs. Did member state governments in subsequent Treaty reforms equally perceive the problem of a looming legitimacy deficit which was triggered by prospective pooling of sovereignty? During the negotiations leading to the adoption of the Maastricht Treaty, the prospective extension of QMV prompted national governments and domestic political parties to activate the 'link' established in the negotiations leading to the adoption of the SEA. According to this 'link', the extension of QMV goes hand in hand with calls for legislative involvement of the EP in areas where QMV applies. All political parties in Germany unequivocally supported an extension of the EP's legislative powers. The major political parties in the Bundestag demanded that '[i]n the course of the development of the European Community towards a European Union, the democratic deficit shall be eliminated in particular by strengthening the European Parliament's legislative and control powers.'[3] Claims of a similar nature were voiced in other parts of the Community. The Belgian government complained about an increasing 'democratic shortfall' if further transfers of sovereignty were not accompanied by increasing the EP's legislative powers (see Corbett 1992: 121). The Dutch government was equally concerned about the lack of democratic 'flanking' mechanisms as the integration processes advanced. The Dutch government contended that any 'transfer of powers to a supranational authority must...be accompanied by guarantees of sufficient democratic control at this level' (Corbett 1992: 127). Even governments which, traditionally, displayed a sceptical attitude toward the democratic legitimacy leverage provided by a more resourceful EP, did not dispute the logic that transfers of sovereignty could not 'go alone'. The Danish government remarked in a memorandum which was approved by the Folketing's Common Market Committee on 4 October 1990 that '[g]reater Community integration calls for a strengthening of the democratic process' and concluded that 'the influence of both national parliaments and the European Parliament should be strengthened' (Corbett 1992: 160). The British government was somewhat more critical about the potential of the EP's capacity to alleviate the legitimacy deficit, yet with one exception: as long as the EP directed its focus on scrutinizing the Commission, the British government welcomed an enhanced role of the EP since this would constitute another institutional check on the Commission and not undermine the power of the member states in the Council.[4] Douglas Hurd, Secretary of State for Foreign and Commonwealth Affairs, was prepared to tolerate changes to EP's non-legislative roles, such as enhancing its scrutiny powers vis-à-vis the Commission 'making it the watchdog of the Community's finances' (Forster 1999: 138). However, he made equally clear that '[t]his...was not a genuine attempt to strengthen the EP, because the government did not want the EP to adopt wholesale the Westminster parliamentary model of executive scrutiny and accountability' (Forster 1999: 139). Compared to the debates prior to the SEA, Prime Minister Thatcher's public statements about the role of the EP seemed much more 'accommodating' of the very sceptical views of the majority of Conservative MPs. Forster (1999: 138) argues that '[e]nhancing the powers of the EP was seen by both parliamentarians and the government as a threat to British sovereignty and a challenge to Westminster, and ministers were acutely aware that backbenchers "had a juicy bone in their mind's eye" when they thought of EP ambitions.' During the IGC, John Major, who succeeded Margaret Thatcher as Prime Minister in November of 1990, considered proposals for the EP's involvement rather unproblematic as long as they did not affect a reduction in decision-making efficiency and provided for a closer check on the supranational Commission. Yet, it was considered unacceptable if changes in the Treaty were to impact on the distribution of powers among the Community institutions to the detriment of national governments. The British position on the question of the EP's powers thus contained elements of both the *economic community* and *intergovernmental cooperation* legitimating belief, whereby the party leadership and members of government were less doctrinal than a considerable portion of the parliamentary party which firmly adhered to the *intergovernmental cooperation* legitimating belief.

Following Maastricht, the IGCs leading to the adoption of the Amsterdam and Nice Treaties did not see serious efforts by member state governments to dispute the link between extending QMV and including the EP in the legislative process.[5] However, disagreement continued to be fierce regarding the *scope* of the EP's influence and the scope to which QMV should be extended to new policy areas. In Nice for instance, the extension of QMV to policy areas hitherto governed by the unanimity rule was sparse and so was the extension of the co-decision procedure and the EP's legislative powers.[6] In the light of the imminent enlargement, Declaration No. 23 which was attached to the Nice Treaty called for a encompassing debate about the future of the EU which should, among other things, eventually produce 'a simplification of the Treaties with a view to making them clearer and better understood without changing their meaning.'[7] Following the European Council meeting at Laeken in December 2001 and the establishment of the European Convention which was to be endowed with this task, a working group on 'Simplification' (Working Group IX) was instituted which set itself the twin objectives of making the European system of governance clearer, more comprehensible and thus more legitimate.[8] With respect to the simplification and reform of legislative procedures, the report issued by the working group stipulated that 'the logic of the codecision procedure requires qualified-majority voting in the Council in all cases'[9] and that the co-decision procedure should also 'become the general rule for the adoption of legislative acts.'[10] The ensuing IGC adopted, implemented the working group's recommendation: Article I-34 of the TCE stipulates that what was hitherto known as the co-decision procedure becomes the 'ordinary legislative procedure'. The logic inherent in the 'QMV equals European Parliament legislative involvement' formula had thus not only gained a largely uncontested status in the post-SEA era; this formula also offered a clear behavioural prescription regarding its implementation: 'If you extend QMV, you have to allow for parliamentary participation in the legislative process.' It can hence be concluded that the EP legitimation strategy thus possessed a high degree of *specificity*.[11]

The success of the EP legitimation strategy cannot only be attributed to its high degree of specificity. The *coherence* of the EP legitimation strategy with its normative environment played an equally important role in accounting for its relative success vis-à-vis the NP legitimation strategy. In the mid-1980s, however, the EP legitimation strategy did not face a particularly 'friendly' normative environment. During the IGC, leading towards the adoption of the SEA, most of the member states saw one of the key conditions to successfully implement the single-market programme in augmenting the efficiency of decision-making by introducing QMV. The call for greater parliamentary involvement in legislative decision-making, motivated by democratic legitimacy concerns, ran counter to the efficiency objective. Including another potential 'veto-point' in the legislative process could not easily be squared with the efficiency postulate. While democratic legitimacy concerns clashed with efficiency concerns in the period leading to the adoption of the SEA, the situation reversed remarkably in the mid-1990s. During the Amsterdam IGC, efficiency-based arguments were used to support the reform of the Maastricht version of the co-decision procedure, calling for a scrapping of that part of the third reading of the legislative procedure whereby the Council could reaffirm its Common Position and the EP could only vote it up or down. This simplification of the procedure, formalized in the Amsterdam Treaty, implied an increase in the EP's influence over legislation. Similarly, as already hinted at, the Convention process called for a simplification of the existing plethora of legal instruments. This development played into the hands of the EP: the decision to reduce the number of legal instruments and applying co-decison as 'ordinary legislative procedure' (Article I-34, TCE and Article III-396, TCE) for the passage of laws and framework laws did not only serve calls for efficiency but equally those for more democratic legitimacy. In sum, although the efficiency norm was 'hostile' to an increase in the EP's legislative powers at first, this situation reversed in the mid-1990s once the EP's legislative powers were firmly enshrined in the Treaties. Under such circumstances, calls for efficiency (*cum* simplification) played into the hands of the EP. Since the mid-1990s the *coherence* of the EP legitimation strategy with its normative environment became an additional factor conducive for its success.

To analyse the relative success of the NP route, I will distinguish between three phases. In the first phase, the pre-Maastricht era, the NP legitimation strategy has not left its imprint on institutional design in the Treaties. At subsequent IGCs, as shown in Table 6.1, several declarations and one protocol have been added to the Treaties primarily destined to improve the information which NPs receive with respect to EU legislative initiatives (second phase). The third phase begins with the 'Post-Nice process' and ends with the adoption of the TCE. As a result of the adoption of the TCE the information clause was included in the text of the Constitution. Moreover, the TCE endows NPs with a 'subsidiarity control' mechanism and the right to initiate infringement proceedings before the European Court of Justice which, however, national governments will have to do on behalf of their NPs.[12]

6.2.1 First phase: pre-Maastricht

How can we explain that the issue of the involvement of NPs in EU decision-making cropped up only in the early 1990s, making its way into the Maastricht Treaty as declaration No. 13 on the 'Role of National Parliaments in the European Union' and as declaration No. 14 on the 'Conference of the Parliaments'? It has been argued throughout this book that for a legitimation strategy to inform decisions for institutional reform, sovereignty has to be transferred to the European level. Although discussions about the role of NPs in legitimizing EU decision-making in the era of QMV have not materialized in terms of a Treaty declaration or even a Treaty article in the SEA, member states expressed concerns that the role of NPs in affecting EU decision-making was fading and that something had to be done about (see Chapter 5). Although countries like Denmark and the UK were firm proponents of the belief that democratic legitimacy is vested in the domestic parliament and cannot be provided by the EP, the NP legitimation strategy did not leave its mark on the SEA. Why? The explanation for its 'absence' lies in the low degree of specificity and coherence in this period. After the signing of the SEA, the member state governments had difficulties in foreseeing the impact of the introduction of QMV on the role of NPs in EU policy-making. Even though there was a sense that the pooling of sovereignty would come to the detriment of NPs, the governments who publicly expressed most concern about this development did not articulate a clear and specific strategy as to how the potential weakening of the NPs' powers could be counteracted (apart from resisting the transfer of legislative powers to the EP). Some domestic parliamentarians even viewed this as part of a strategy on behalf of their governments to further weaken the national parliaments.[13] Domestic conditions regarding the strength of NPs in scrutinizing their executives' European endeavours also vary substantially (see Auel und Benz 2004). The Danish parliament, for example, could rely on an effective parliamentary control mechanism over the government on European policy-issues which was exercised by the powerful European Affairs Committee of the Folketing.[14] Given this variation and the fact that there was no prior experience with regard to the repercussions of QMV on the workings of domestic parliaments and, consequently, no clear prescription as to how NPs should be connected to European decision-making, the *specificity* of the NP legitimation strategy assumes a low value. Additionally, even though it did not lack coherence—since there were no Community norms 'around' which could have potentially contributed to its rendering more specific and thus more successful—the impact of the NP route on institutional design decisions remained negligible.

6.2.2 Second phase: Maastricht and post-Maastricht

The entry into force of the Maastricht and Amsterdam Treaties in 1993 and 1999 respectively, was, as demonstrated, accompanied by transfers of national sovereignty through the extension of QMV (pooling). Therefore, member state governments voiced concerns about the consequences of pooling for processes of democratic accountability and interest representation. In this context, the roles of the EP and NPs in EU decision-making were mentioned as significant themes for discussion at the IGCs under the banner of 'democratic legitimacy'.[15]

While the NP route had not directly left its imprint on the SEA, the Maastricht Treaty explicitly acknowledged the role of NPs in European decision-making in two annexed declarations, one calling for improving the information received by NPs on legislative initiatives (Declaration No. 13) and the other encouraging NPs to contribute to substantive policy issues (Declaration No. 14). Furthermore, the Amsterdam Treaty annexed a protocol on the 'Role of National Parliaments in the European Union' which specified some of the provisions of the Maastricht Declaration No. 13. However, these formal Treaty changes have to be qualified as being very modest in scope. They were chiefly about improving information for NPs regarding EU legislative initiatives which they could employ to improve the scrutiny process vis-à-vis their national governments. Nevertheless, even a modest increase in the 'success' of the NP legitimation strategy has to be accounted for. The answer lies in a modest change in the specificity of the NP legitimation strategy. Analysing statements and memoranda outlining the positions of member state governments during the IGCs leading to the adoption of the Maastricht and Amsterdam Treaties, it strikes the analyst how little agreement there was among the member state governments as to how NPs should be involved in EU decision-making in order bring Europe 'closer to the citizens'. The responses offered by member states varied substantially, falling into broadly three categories:

1. Improvement of domestic scrutiny procedures vis-à-vis national governments by improving the information flow from the EU to the domestic level (unilateral action).
2. Improvement of scrutiny procedures vis-à-vis national governments by drawing on forums such a Conference of European Affairs Committees, the so-called COSAC (joint coordination).[16]
3. Instituting a (second) chamber at the European level constituted of national MPs with roles other than merely scrutiny.

With regard to the first issue—the 'upgrading' of domestic scrutiny procedures vis-à-vis national governments by improving the information flow from the EU to the domestic level—there was widespread agreement among the member state governments to improve domestic scrutiny procedures. In the run-up to Maastricht, the British Government issued a statement which stipulated that the role of NPs in scrutinizing EC legislation should be increased. It emphasized, however, that the modalities regarding the increase of their role should be 'a matter for member states, not for the Community...We would welcome if national parliaments in other states were to increase their own role in scrutinizing EC legislation.' (House of Commons 1990b: 6) A Danish government memorandum echoed the British government's position stipulating that 'a considerable part of what is known as democratic shortfall is attributable to the fact that not all national parliaments have an adequate say in the decisions taken at Community level' (Corbett 1992: 160). It was also the Danish government in the preparation for the IGC leading to the adoption of the Amsterdam

Treaty which stressed that NPs should be enabled to play a more prominent role in EU decision-making via their national governments by obtaining timely information on EU level legislative initiatives (European Parliament 1996: 24). The Spanish government equally argued that the main role of NPs 'in relation to EU decisions should concern the monitoring and control exercised by each member state parliament on the actions of its government in the Council, and that it is up to each member state, not the Union, to determine how this activity should be exercised.' (European Parliament 1996: 60) To fulfil this role properly, the Spanish government called for the European institutions, the Commission in particular, to supply NPs with all the requisite information.

As far as the second and third category of measures regarding the role of NPs in EU decision-making were concerned, both the Maastricht and Amsterdam IGCs saw selective support for closer cooperation between NPs and their MPs in weakly institutionalized forums such as COSAC and a Conference of Parliaments, modelled on the idea of the *Assizes*.[17] The question as to whether a second chamber of national parliamentarians should be instituted alongside the European Parliament was even more controversial.[18] In the run-up to Maastricht, proposals were brought forward for a *Congress* of national parliamentarians, which was later modified to being a conference of national parliamentarians and MEPs. This proposal gained initial support from the UK, Portugal, Spain, and Greece (Corbett 1992: 61). In a debate in the French National Assembly, the French Minister for European Affairs, Elisabeth Guigou, laid out the core function of such a Congress: its role should be to discuss 'themes of common interest and issue an opinion on the broad orientations of the Union.'[19] While even among the supporters of a second chamber there was no uniform view as to its exact role and competencies, other governments expressly opposed the idea. Regarding measures for cooperation between NPs which were of a less formal and institutionalized nature, such as COSAC, there was disagreement as to its exact role and status. In the run-up to Amsterdam, the Spanish government opposed a formalization of the COSAC structure arguing that 'closer links with the national parliaments should not lead to the creation of a new institution or permanent body with its own staff and premises, or of a second chamber of national MPs' (European Parliament 1996: 60). The Spanish government expressed its opposition to a regular convening of a Conference of Parliaments as laid down in Declaration No. 14 annexed to the Maastricht Treaty given their lack of success. Other member state governments, such as Austria, called for a consolidation of COSAC, yet they expressed stark opposition to any proposals establishing a second chamber. Table 6.3 illustrates that in the run up to the Amsterdam Treaty negotiations, there was a unanimous trend in favour of improving information for NPs on EU legislative initiatives and projects.[20] As already indicated above, this was the only area where the NP legitimation strategy displayed a high level of specificity. With respect to improvment in the role of joint coordination mechanisms, such as COSAC, or even the creation of a Congress or second chamber, there was partial support at most (COSAC) and almost unanimous opposition at worst (second chamber). Partial support for joint coordination mechanisms was mirrored in the relatively widespread support for improving the informal role of COSAC and in the equally widespread opposition to formalize COSAC. Only a small number of member state governments suggested a greater role, restricted to certain policy areas (such as justice and home affairs, own resources, enlargement, and general Common Foreign and Security Policy (CFSP) guidelines).

6.2.3 Third phase: the Convention process

Only a few years after the adoption of the Amsterdam Treaty, the German Minister for Foreign Affairs, Joschka Fischer, delivered a speech at the Humboldt University in May 2000 which triggered a debate among

Table 6.3 Member state positions on the role of national parliaments (Amsterdam IGC)

	A	B	D	DK	E	F	GB	GR	I	IRL	L	P	S	SF
Improving information	+	+	+	+	+	+	+	+	+	+	+	+	+	+
Joint coordination mechanisms	+/−	+/−	+/−	+/−	−	+	−	n.a.	−	−	−	+/−	n.a.	n.a.
Second chamber / Congress	−	−	−	−	−	+	−	−	−	−	−	−	−	−

'+' Supports proposed measure
'−' Opposes proposed measure
'+/−' Partial support

A = Austria	F = France	L = Luxembourg
B = Belgium	GB = Great Britain	P = Portugal
D = Germany	GR = Greece	S = Sweden
DK = Denmark	I = Italy	SF = Finland
E = Spain	IRL = Ireland	

major European political leaders. This debate featured prominent figures such as Tony Blair and Jacques Chirac. One of the recurrent issues was the question of how the role of NP in EU decision-making could be enhanced. Political leaders voiced strong support for an additional body, 'a second chamber in Brussels.' (Norman 2003: 97; House of Lords 2001) There was, however, widespread disagreement regarding the features of the said second chamber, the major being '[w]hether what is proposed is a second chamber with specific powers, or what might perhaps be better described as community or committee of parliaments, coming together to perform specific tasks, but mainly advising rather than deciding' (House of Lords 2001). During the Convention, the issue of a Congress or second chamber was taken up, expressly favoured by the President of the Convention, Giscard d'Estaing himself. Among the Convention members there was considerable disagreement not only as to its desirability but also among the proponents of the Congress idea as to how its exact role and competencies should be defined.[21] The idea of a Congress/second chamber thus displayed a low level of *specificity* since disagreement about its role remained disputed and unclear. The Convention process, however, brought about substantial change in the role exercised by NPs. By instituting an 'early warning mechanism' with respect to guarding the subsidiarity principle, NPs were attributed a substantially new role as laid down in the TCE. Although the Convention members quarrelled over the modalities of how NPs should be permitted to intervene when they objected to Commission legislative proposal on subsidiarity grounds ('yellow' or 'red card'), there was widespread agreement among the members on the general idea that NPs should not only be better informed about the legislative intentions of the EU, but that they should also be able to express their objections where legislative proposals were considered to run counter to the principle of subsidiarity.[22] To explain the introduction of the 'early warning mechanism' which can be triggered by NPs, we have to take a closer look at the *coherence* of the NP legitimation strategy. The question about the delineation of the EU's competencies—which was becoming an ever more fervently debated theme following the adoption of the Nice Treaty and the 'Declaration on the Future of the Union'—made subsidiarity a guiding principle of institutional reform. This debate proved to be extremely conducive to the success of the NP legitimation strategy. The principle of subsidiarity has been 'a fixture in the political and constitutional debate' (Sypris 2002: 13) since it was first espoused in the Maastricht Treaty and further specified at Amsterdam in the 'Protocol on the application of the principles of subsidiarity and proportionality'.[23] In

Declaration No. 23 of the Nice Treaty, the member state governments explicitly recognized 'the need to improve and to monitor the democratic legitimacy and transparency of the Union and its institutions, in order to bring them closer to the citizens of the Member States.'[24] For this purpose, they called for a broad debate about the future of the EU which should address, *inter alia*, the following questions: how can 'a more precise delimitation of powers between the European Union and the Member States, reflecting the principle of subsidiarity' be established and monitored? What role should NPs play in the 'European architecture'?[25] At its December meeting in Laeken in 2001, the European Council adopted a 'Declaration on the Future of the European Union' committing the EU to become more democratic, transparent and effective. The declaration laid down sixty questions targeting different themes concerning the future of the EU, such as the division and definition of powers, the simplification of the treaties, the EU's institutional setting, and the move towards a Constitution for Europe. It also foresaw the convening of a Convention to examine these questions and themes. It was early in the Convention-phase that two working groups were established to deal with the principle of subsidiarity (Working Group I) and the role of NPs (Working Group IV) to meet the demands of the Laeken mandate. While both themes, the role of subsidiarity and of NPs in organizing and legitimizing EU governance, had been on the member states' EU reform agendas since the early 1990s, policymakers had not established a connection between subsidiarity and NPs until the convening of the Convention.[26] The working group on subsidiarity was guided by the assumption that the application and monitoring of subsidiarity should and could be improved upon. In its final report, the group proposed to the Convention that NPs should be given an important role in monitoring the compliance of legislative initiatives with the principle of subsidiarity via an 'early warning system' (*ex ante* control). Furthermore, the working group stipulated that the Convention should adopt a provision to allow appeals to the European Court of Justice against violations of subsidiarity (*ex post* control).[27] The working group was not shy to stress 'the innovative and bold nature' of its proposals.[28] The working group on NPs 'reinforced the main findings of the subsidiarity working group by underlining that national parliaments should play a key role in monitoring the principle of subsidiarity' (Norman 2003: 98).[29] The elevation of the subsidiarity principle to a guiding norm in the discussion about delineation of the levels at which policies and competencies shall be allocated proved to be a 'hospitable' environment for the NP legitimation strategy. I have already argued that member state politicians held that NPs were a key to strengthen the democratic legitimacy of the EU by bringing it 'closer to the citizens'. It was thus seen as a logical and widely accepted argument that the political institutions that were seen to have suffered most from ever more transfers of sovereignty to the European level—NPs—should be entitled to have a say regarding the application of the principle of subsidiarity, putting—if deemed necessary—a brake on the appropriation of policy-making competencies by the Commission. Since Maastricht, the subsidiarity norm had itself undergone a process of specification, which—in the Convention process—found its expression in a concrete proposal for institutional reform, most notably in the establishment of a clearer delineation of competencies between the national and the EU level, but also in the introduction of an *ex ante* subsidiarity control mechanism to be exercised by NPs. Given its concrete mandate (to tackle the question of subsidiarity and devise a role for NPs) and broad participation, the Convention thus succeeded in increasing the specificity of the subsidiarity norm which had hitherto been too vague to have led to any concrete and mutually accepted institutional design or reform proposals. Consequently, this development had positive repercussions on the NP route by improving its *coherence* with the subsidiarity norm.

6.3 Conclusion

In this chapter I have shown that the 'trigger mechanism' which raised the salience of the legitimacy deficit among the political elites in EU member states was not only at work in the three cases studied in depth in previous chapters: transfers of sovereignty through pooling continued to be perceived by policy-makers to pose a challenge and potential threat to domestic democratic processes. Since, the scope of authoritative decision-making beyond the confines of the nation state has been extended successively throughout the 1990s, policy-makers have continued to respond by projecting domestically established procedures for democratic participation and accountability onto the European level. I have argued furthermore that these 'projections' were not uniform. It has been shown that politicians came to consider both NPs and the EP as potential reform targets when contemplating institutional solutions to alleviate the legitimacy deficit. Yet, it has also been shown that institutional reforms to alleviate the legitimacy deficit are strongly 'biased' towards the EP route as the dominant legitimation strategy. Nevertheless, it has also been shown that NPs 'have caught' up since the early 1990s and have since been

Table 6.4 Legitimation strategies and their success

	European Parliament route	National Parliament route		
		Pre-Maastricht (1st phase)	Maastricht and post-Maastricht (2nd phase)	Convention process (3rd phase)
Specificity (simplicity and clarity of prescription)	*medium/high*: the formula 'QMV=EP – legislative involvement' gains uncontested status; continuing disagreement about the degree of EP involvement (SEA, Maastricht, Amsterdam)	*low*: the post-SEA phase poses the first (and hitherto unknown) challenge to NPs' legislative prerogatives	*low/medium*: disagreement over involvement of NPs in EU decision-making due to differences in domestic traditions; agreement on improving information for and coordination between NPs	*medium*: NPs are viewed as potential guardians of the subsidiarity principle via *ex ante* and *ex post* controls; differences as to additional roles of NPs in EU decision-making persist
Coherence ('fit' with the normative environment)	*low* (SEA): efficiency norm (introduction of QMV) conflicts with EP participation in legislative process	*medium/high* (since Amsterdam): simplification of the Treaties (norms of transparency and efficiency) conducive to EP legitimation strategy	*low/medium*: emergence of subsidiarity principle, isolated proposals to link subsidiarity control with NPs: subsidiarity still a vaguely defined concept	*high*: Convention specifies application of subsidiarity principle and calls for NPs to monitor its application
Overall impact	**medium/high**		**low**	**low/medium**	**medium/high**

considered to fulfil an evermore important role in legitimizing EU governance. To explain these developments, I have argued that the *properties* of the two legitimation strategies—their individual and relative specificity and coherence—are key in determining their differential 'successes'. One of the main factors 'promoting' the NP legimitaion strategy has to be seen in the rise of the principle of subsidiarity.

Notes

1. See, for instance, Florini (1996), Legro (1997), Finnemore and Sikkink (1998), Keck and Sikkink (1998), Risse et al. (1999), and Schimmelfennig (2003).

2. See, among others, Hall (1989, 1993), Jacobson (1995), McNamara (1998), and Blyth (2002).

3. Deutscher Bundestag, Drucksache 11/7729 of 23 August 1990, author's translation.

4. Douglas Hurd, the Secretary of State of Foreign and Commonwealth Affairs, emphasized before the Select Committee on the European Communities of the House of Lords that the 'European Parliament could play a larger role . . . as a financial watchdog . . . We would like to see [the MEPs] looking more closely at anti-fraud measures, value for money, and for the financial control of the Commission to be more directly responsible to them' (House of Lords, Select Committee on the European Communities, 'Economic and Monetary Union and Political Union', Volume II—Evidence, Session 1989–90, 27th Report, HL Paper 88-II: 211). John Major also shared this view outlining the government's negotiating aims which included *inter alia*: 'More power for the European Parliament to control the Commission and investigate fraud.' (Major 2000: 274).

5. For instance, the Benelux governments issued a memorandum in which they explicitly acknowledged the link between the application of QMV and legislative co-decision for the EP (European Parliament 1996: 20). Similarly, a Spanish government document on the IGC foresaw that 'there will be considerable scope for progress through an extension of the field of application of the codecision procedure; this concept should . . . logically be viewed in close relation to majority decision-making' (European Parliament 1996: 47).

6. During the IGC leading to the adoption of the Nice Treaty, co-decision and parliamentary involvement were lesser concerns. The Treaty provided for six new cases of co-decision. Yet, among the new cases under QMV, three legislative ones remained outside the co-decision procedure: financial regulations, internal measures for the implementation of cooperation agreements, as well as the Structural Funds and the Cohesion Fund. Since these policies are particularly important issues on account of their major budgetary implications, some member states 'resisted' the call for co-decision in these areas, the EP bemoaned that 'in refusing even to consider switching matters already subject to qualified-majority voting to the codecision procedure, the [IGC] was rejecting a basic institutional principle on which significant progress had been made at Amsterdam: as a general rule, codecision should accompany qualified-majority voting in matters of a legislative nature' (European Parliament 2001: 28).

7. Treaty of Nice, 'Declaration on the Future of the Union' (No. 23, paragraph 5).

8. See European Convention, CONV 424/02.

9. See European Convention, CONV 424/02, p. 14.

10. See European Convention, CONV 424/02, p. 15.

11. Interestingly, some commentators refer to this formula as a 'technical' one, ignoring its underlying normative logic: the recommendation by the working group that QMV and co-decision should go hand in hand 'transformed the debate over the group's reports from the technical to the political and drew the plenary into discussion as to whether the EU should retain unanimity at all' (Norman 2003: 102).

12. See Raunio (2004) for an excellent discussion and assessment of the implications of the competencies conferred on NPs by the Convention.

13. For example, many British MPs argued that the introduction of QMV constituted a serious threat to national parliamentary sovereignty. To mention just one example, Michael Knowles, a pro-Europe Conservative MP, voiced disapprovingly that '[t]his House is effectively chopped off from the European Parliament, and that is no accident. The Select Committee [of the House of Commons on European Legislation] therefore cannot act effectively. Indeed, it is designed not to act effectively. Yet any suggestion that its mandate should be widened is constantly resisted by the Executive because that would shrink the powers of the Executive' (Hansard, House of Commons, 5 December 1985: 356). The government sought to downplay this concern. Only when directly confronted with a question by Robert Jackson, Conservative MP, did Foreign Secretary, Geoffrey Howe, try to give assurances that national parliamentary sovereignty would not be undermined by the outcomes of the SEA (see Hansard, House of Commons, 23 April 1986: 323).

14. Malcolm Rifkind, Minister of State in the Foreign and Commonwealth Office, stated before the House of Lords Select Committee on the European Communities: 'I think there are a number of countries, perhaps even a majority of countries, which would have the gravest of reservations about increased powers for the European Parliament and their improvement to the conciliation procedure. . . . I'm conscious that when Danish ministers are negotiating within the Council of Ministers they have to refer back to their own national parliament if they wish to change their negotiating mandate. There is a much tighter control as regards the relationship between the Danish Parliament and the Danish Minister than exists between other national parliaments and ministers in other Member States. Anything that directly or indirectly seems to affect the powers of the Danish Parliament vis-à-vis the European Parliament is treated with much more sensitivity and is much more controversial than is the case in other countries' (House of Lords 1985: 48).

15. In an exchange with Ted Rowlands, Labour MP, Douglas Hurd, Secretary of State for Foreign and Commonwealth Affairs, indicated that both legitimation strategies had supporters among the EU member states: while Rowlands argued that the 'Spaniards, French, Italians and even the Germans did not see sovereignty in terms of national parliamentary institutional powers and, in fact, there was great willingness to forsake a lot of national parliamentary power to bridge the European parliamentary deficit', Douglas Hurd replied: 'I think we do think more clearly and strongly in terms of national parliamentary sovereignty than probably any other Member States. The Danes, of course, have a sovereignty system which puts a big accent on it' (House of Commons 1990a: 13).

16. In the original, COSAC stands for Conférence des organes spécialisés dans les affaires communautaires et européennes des parlements de l'Union européenne (Conference of Community and European Affairs Committees of Parliaments of the European Union).

17. The so-called *Assizes* are based on an idea expressed by French President Mitterrand (quoted in Corbett 1998: 26) which he expressed in 1989 in a speech to the EP: 'Why should', he asked, 'the European Parliament not organize assizes on the future of the Community in which, alongside your Assembly, delegations from national parliaments, the Commission, and the governments would participate?' The EP quickly conceived of the Assizes as a possibility for a joint parliamentary preparation of the IGC leading to the Maastricht Treaty (see Corbett 1998: 296).

18. The idea of instituting a second chamber has been voiced by French politicians with Laurent Fabius (then President of the French National Assembly) and President Mitterrand advocating the creation of a second chamber in 1989 and 1990 respectively.

19. See *Le Monde*, 21 June 1991.

20. The information on the location of the member states' positions on the issues displayed in Table 6.3 was extracted from <http://www.europarl.eu.int/igc1996/fiches/fiche6_en.htm>, accessed on 20 February 2004.

21. European Convention, debate of 28 October 2002.

22. European Convention, debate of 18 March 2003.

23. The Edinburgh European Council of December 1992 defined the basic principles underlying subsidiarity and laid down guidelines for interpreting Article 5 (ex Article 3b), which enshrined subsidiarity in the EU Treaty. In Article 5 of the ECT, it reads: 'In areas which do not fall within its exclusive competence, the Community shall take action, in accordance with the principle of subsidiarity, only if and in so far as the objectives of the proposed action cannot be sufficiently achieved by the member states and can therefore, by reason of the scale or effects of the proposed action, be better achieved by the Community.' See also Große Hüttmann (1996) for an overview of the subsidiarity principle in the EU.

24. Treaty of Nice, 'Declaration on the Future of the Union' (No. 23, paragraph 6).

25. Treaty of Nice, 'Declaration on the Future of the Union' (No. 23, paragraph 5).

26. The French government tried to establish such a connection calling on NPs to monitor the appropriate application of the subsidiarity principle. Addressing the French National Assembly on 3 February 1994, then French Minister for Foreign Affairs, Alain Juppé, expressed his hope that NPs would be empowered to challenge EU legislation on the grounds that the principle of subsidiarity was violated (European Parliament 1996: 66).

27. See European Convention, CONV 286/02.

28. See European Convention, CONV 286/02, p. 5.

29. See also European Convention, CONV 353/02.

Conclusion: No Integration Without Representation?[1]

In an era when national parliamentary institutions around the world are said to be increasingly marginalized and displaced from major legislative and policy-making activities (see Burns 2000), the trend described and explained in this book marks a striking counter-point. In this concluding chapter, I argue that the *parliamentarization* of the EU can be seen at least as a partial response to the process of *de-parliamentarization* which befalls advanced industrial societies. Furthermore, I take issue with the claim—often associated with the 'de-parliamentarization thesis'—that the model of parliamentary or representative democracy, more generally, is being increasingly complemented by alternative models and instruments of democratic governance, such as direct democratic elements or participatory forms of democracy. Is the trend, described in much of the literature, towards the adoption of alternative models of democracy mirrored by developments on the EU level? This book has suggested that representative, parliamentary democracy on the EU level is all but on the wane. Last, I ask what broader lessons we can learn from the findings of this book for analysing and explaining the evolution of international institutions. Undoubtedly, the EP is 'singular' since the functions exercised and powers held are unmatched by any comparable assembly of an international organization. But does this mean that we cannot conceive of conditions under which we could expect states to create or endow parliamentary assemblies of other international organizations with powers analogous to those of the EP?

De-parliamentarization and re-parliamentarization: two sides of the same coin

It is often argued that national executives, represented in the Council of Ministers, play a (if not *the*) key role in the EU's legislative process. At the same time, NPs have only limited opportunity to scrutinize and control their executives in the day-to-day activities of EU decision-making.[2] The introduction and gradual extension of QMV has circumscribed NPs' opportunity to influence Community decision-making via their national governments as a result of the elimination of the veto option. Changes in the degree to which NPs can exercise influence over EU policy-making have not only had a *qualitative* dimension (by which I mean an effective loss of influence over outcomes) but also a *quantitative* one: the subsequent transfer of decision-making competencies from the national to the European level has affected and continues to affect an ever-increasing number of policy areas. Most *regulatory* policy decisions (affecting the movement of goods, services, capital and persons, competition rules, product standards, etc.) and *monetary* policy decisions are presently taken at the EU level. In other policy areas which can be subsumed under the label *expenditure* polices (including agriculture, regional development, research, social welfare, etc.) a high proportion of decisions is made at the EU level (agriculture); in research and social welfare the EU has assumed at least some decision-making competencies over the decades (see Hix 2005: Introduction). As a result of this trend towards the 'centralization' of policy-making, NPs' ability to shape public policies has been strongly circumscribed. Klaus von Beyme finds that about one-fifth of all legislation which passes through the German Bundestag (for the 1990–4 period) has had an 'impulse' from the EU level, that is, it was based on Community *directives* which NPs had to transpose into national law (see von Beyme 1998: 25).[3] Disaggregating this number into policy areas, it is not surprising—given the trend towards centralization—that in certain policy areas, such as environment, consumer protection, telecommunications (*regulatory* policies) or agriculture and research (*expenditure* policies)—to name only a few—NPs are occupied principally with the transposition of EU directives into national law (see von Beyme 1998: 25). This trend towards, on the one hand, an increasing centralization of competencies at the Community level and, on the other hand, a concomitant fading of NPs' influence to control and influence national executives and hence to shape public policies has been described as 'Entparlamentarisierung' or de-parliamentarisation.[4]

As I have argued in the preceding chapters, the subsequent pooling and delegation of national sovereignty has contributed to the de-parliamentarization of national polities and the short-circuiting of democratic procedures of interest representation and procedures to ensure accountability. This challenge to procedural legitimacy at the level of the domestic polity has, however, not gone unnoticed or uncontested by political elites in the member states of the EU. Although one might assume that, behind closed doors, national executives are unlikely to complain too loudly about the creeping de-parliamentarization of their domestic polities, I have shown that pressure from domestic political parties as well as the intrinsic valuation of representative, parliamentary democracy have produced behavioural responses on the part of national governments which—from a purely material interest-maximizing perspective—might seem perplexing: to remedy the perceived challenge to procedural legitimacy, political elites in the member states have proposed remedies at either the *supranational* level (by supporting the empowerment of the EP) or at the *domestic* level (by supporting closer involvement of NPs in Community affairs). Marschall (2002: 388–90) asks somewhat hesitantly whether the process of de-parliamentarization at the domestic level is being counterbalanced by a process of *re-parliamentarization* at the international or supranational level. This book has provided one answer to this question. De-parliamentarization and re-parliamentarization (the latter of which, however, comes in different forms, as 'prescribed' by alternative legitimating beliefs) are insolubly linked. Where the procedural legitimacy of a democratic polity is challenged, political elites will feel compelled to press for compensatory mechanisms, either at the domestic or supranational level. In this sense, both processes mark the two sides of the same coin.

Beyond parliamentary democracy: a democratic transformation?

This book has suggested that the model of representative, parliamentary democracy is the template which guides political elites' responses to the perceived legitimacy deficit. However, since the IGC leading to the adoption of the Maastricht Treaty, member state governments have relentlessly declared that Europe has to be 'brought closer to its citizens', a notion which implicitly points at the limits of some of the existing legitimation strategies: empowering the EP, for instance, may not be the all-encompassing solution to the legitimacy deficit. Can the ever repeated formula of 'bringing Europe closer to its citizens' be dismissed as mere legitimizing rhetoric? Or does it actually reflect EU governments' unease with dropping 'popularity ratings' of the European integration project, declining voter turnout at EP elections or the increasing popular demands to alleviate the asymmetry between the 'economic' and 'social Europe', as expressed fervently by the masses attending the European Social Forums in Florence and Paris? To put it bluntly: does the recurrent talk about 'bringing Europe closer to its citizens' and the 'democratic deficit' reflect a perceived crisis of the model of parliamentary democracy on the EU level? Do, in the eyes of the European and national political elites, both the EP and NP legitimation strategies fall short of fulfilling their part of the legitimating 'equation'?

Changes in the relative success of alternative legitimation strategies—the EP route and the NP route—do not pose a challenge to the model of representative, parliamentary democracy: the increasing relative 'success' of the NP route marks a shift in emphasis within the representative, parliamentary model of democracy. Peter Hall (1993) has dubbed this type of shift 'first order change', that is, legitimation strategies can be adjusted without challenging the model from which they are derived: representative, parliamentary democracy. But, is it conceivable that we will observe more radical and fundamental changes than the aforementioned first order change? Do alternative models of governance exist that policy-makers could employ to legitimize EU policy-making? Under what conditions would the model of parliamentary democracy itself be the object of a debate regarding its appropriateness in securing and maintaining democratic legitimacy? These questions cannot be answered in this book. Maybe, they cannot be even answered for another few decades. What can be done, however, is to ask whether we can observe any indications that policy-makers can conceive of or even propose legitimation strategies which they derive from models other than that of parliamentary democracy.

The literature in Comparative Politics has identified a trend in advanced industrial societies of a growing readiness on behalf of citizens and policy-makers 'to question whether a fundamental commitment to the principles and institutions of representative democracy is sufficient to sustain the legitimacy and effectiveness of current mechanisms of self-government' (Dalton et al. 2003b: 1). There exists a 'spreading dissatisfaction with the institutions and processes of representative democracy' (Dalton et al. 2003b: 1) mirrored, inter alia, in declining electoral participation and party membership. At the same time, modes of participation which put strong emphasis on direct citizen involvement enjoy growing popularity, such as referenda or citizen advisory committees for policy formation at the local level. Capturing this trend, Ralf Dahrendorf argues that 'representative government is no longer as compelling a proposition as it once was. Instead, a search for new institutional forms to express conflicts of interests has begun' (Dahrendorf quoted in Dalton et al., 2003b: 2). What are the characteristics of these new institutional forms or modes of democratic governance? Dalton et al. (2003b: 9–11) argue that the model of parliamentary or representative democracy is increasingly complemented by instruments of *direct democracy* and *advocacy democracy*. Both models—direct democracy[5] and advocacy democracy[6]—are distinct from representative democracy in that they represent unmediated forms of participation. Existing research suggests that democracy in advanced industrial societies is undergoing a transformation: all three models of democratic governance have undergone institutional reform in the past decades which has led to an overall expansion of citizen access and more direct participation in the political process (see Dalton et al. 2003a). This strand of research also demonstrates that different models of democratic governance are not necessarily competing but can be seen as complementary in nature. Has the democratic life of the EU has been affected by these processes of transformation?

Two more recent EU level initiatives provide an indication that the democratic transformations which leave their marks on the democratic life and institutions in modern industrialized democracies do not appear to halt before the European level. The Commission White Paper on European Governance (CWP) contains elements which strongly mirror the tenets of the model of advocacy democracy by emphasizing the prominence of non-electoral channels for citizen participation (see European Commission 2001: 11–18). To fight against peoples' 'distrust' (European Commission 2001: 3) and lack of interest vis-à-vis political institutions, the Commission advocates that the democratic institutions at both the national and European levels, 'can and must try to connect Europe with its citizens' (European Commission 2001: 3). Therefore, the 'Union must renew the Community method by following a less top–down approach and complementing its policy tools more effectively with non-legislative instruments.' (European Commission 2001: 4) To attain the objective of connecting the EU with its citizens, the Commission proposes to advance the involvement of citizens by improving information on and the transparency of EU policy-making and policy-formulating processes. Furthermore, the Commission seeks to reach out to the citizens by improving consultation and dialogue with both *territorial* and *sectoral* interests. With regard to the former, the CWP stipulates the establishment of a 'more systematic dialogue with European and national associations of regional and local government at an early stage of policy shaping' (European Commission 2001: 14). As to the latter, the CWP calls for intensifying the use of existing venues for consultation and dialogues with civil society groups representing sectoral interests (such as the social partners) through advisory committees, business test panels, venues for *ad hoc* and on-line consultation and the like (see European Commission 2001: 15).

The TCE which was adopted by the member state governments in 2004, carries explicit marks of the new modes of democratic governance mirroring the increasing prominence of unmediated channels for citizen participation. In a 'last minute operation', the European Convention inserted an element of direct democracy into the constitutional architecture of the EU providing for citizens' initiatives. Article I-47 III of the TCE stipulates that '[n]ot less than one million citizens who are nationals of a significant number of Member States may take the initiative of inviting the Commission, within the framework of its powers, to submit any appropriate proposal on matters where citizens consider that a legal act of the Union is required for the purpose of implementing the Constitution.' Next to this instrument of direct democracy, the TCE also provides for measures which are informed by the model of advocacy democracy. Title VI of the TCE contains provisions which make reference to the principles of openness, transparency, and dialogue with civil society (Article I-47 paragraphs 1–3; see also Article I-50 on transparency). Article I-47 makes explicit mention of the principle of *participatory democracy*. The purpose of this article is to provide a framework for the dialogue between civil society and EU institutions as well as for the instruments through which this can be achieved. Article I-48 of the TCE explicitly acknowledges the role of the social partners and calls for facilitating the dialogue among social partners and for promoting their role at the EU level. The TCE does not only restrict itself to 'promoting' the new models of democratic governance which assert unmediated citizen influence. In Article I-46, the model of *representative democracy* also finds explicit mention in the DTC. Article I-46, paragraph 4 emphasizes the contribution of European political parties 'to forming European political awareness and to expressing the will of citizens of the Union.' Table C.1 provides a summary view of the different models of democratic governance—representative democracy, direct democracy, and advocacy democracy—as well as of the most recent European level initiatives for far-reaching institutional reform, the CWP and the TCE.

Since neither the measures proposed in the CWP nor those laid down in the TCE have (as of yet) achieved a legally enforceable status, it is impossible to assess the actual impact and perceived effectiveness of these measures in 'bringing Europe closer to its citizens'. It may also be too premature

Table C.1 A democratic transformation at the European level?

	Representative democracy	Direct democracy	Advocacy democracy
Core characteristics	Citizen influence mediated by representatives (organized in political parties) who take decisions on behalf of citizens	Unmediated citizen influence in policy formulation and policy choice	Unmediated citizen influence in policy formulation and implementation (policy choices rest with political elites)
Decision-making institutions	Electoral institutions (affecting inter-and intra-party competition)	Electoral institutions (e.g. referenda and popular initiatives)	Non-electoral institutions (e.g. transparency enhancing measures; consultation with citizen groups)
Recent EU level initiatives: CWP* and TCE**	—	—	*CWP*: better involvement of civil society, more openness and transparency
TCE**	*TCE*: enhancing the role of NPs through 'subsidiarity' control and informational measures (Protocols 1 & 2); Art. I-46 ('The principle of representative democracy', *inter alia*, European political party statute[†])	*TCE*: Art. I-47, para. 4 (possibility of citizens' initiative)	*TCE*: Art. I-47 ('The principle of participatory democracy), Art. I-48 ('The social partners and autonomous social dialogue'), Art. I-49 ('The European Ombudsman'[††]), Art. I-50 ('Transparency of proceedings of Union Institutions')

* CWP: Commission White Paper on European Governance (European Commission 2001)

** TCE: Treaty establishing a Constitution for Europe

[†] European political parties were first recognized explicitly in the Maastricht Treaty (Art. 191 ECT, ex Art. 138a).

[††] The position of the European Ombudsman was first created by the Maastricht Treaty (Arts. 21, ex 8d and 195, ex 138e of the ECT).

to talk about a trend or a transformation of democracy on the European level. Yet, this book has given a strong indication that the model of parliamentary/representative democracy is alive and well. It still is the key reference point for policy-makers when they think about and debate mechanisms to legitimize EU governance. However, as policy-makers' perception intensifies, European citizens become ever more alienated from the project of European integration; they *may* increasingly come to consider institutional solutions which lie beyond the purview of the model of representative, parliamentary democracy. The key challenge for research on European integration in the coming decades thus lies in tracing these developments and in answering the question, how we can account for any potential moves towards alternative models of democratic governance on the European level.

The evolution of international polities and parliamentary democracy

One of the findings of this book posits that long before academics, journalists, and even some politicians have ascribed any importance to the term 'democratic deficit', political elites have created and bestowed the EP with supervisory, budgetary, and legislative powers. By the time the SEA entered into force (1987), and before the first academic articles on the 'democratic deficit' were written,[7] the decision of political elites in the different member states to create and empower a parliamentary institution as part of the Community's institutional setting stemmed from their *perception* that there already *existed* a democratic legitimacy deficit which had to be alleviated and which was triggered by decisions to pool and delegate sovereignty.

Notwithstanding the more recent debates about global (democratic) and cosmopolitan governance,[8] it is noteworthy that discussions and discourse about the 'democratic deficit' have centred most prominently on the EU. Stein (2001) shows that a correlation exists between the level of integration of an international organization (a measure which includes, *inter alia*, the degree to which sovereignty is pooled and delegated) and the public discourse (mirrored in statements by academics, practitioners, authoritative spokespersons, etc.) about the 'democratic-legitimacy deficit' (Stein 2001: 489) of the functioning and structure of international organizations. Stein finds that '[i]n an organization where the rule of consensus prevails', that is, an organization with an intergovernmental decision-making mode, 'and [where] the area of activity is essentially technical and relies on "independent" experts, the [democratic deficit] discourse does not arise or is muted. . . . At the point, however, where the member states become subject to majority vote and the organization's competence is broad enough to require the settings of priorities and mediation between conflicting interests and values, the level of discourse in democratic societies rises, and becomes linked to a more general debate on reforming the organization' (Stein 2001: 530). Comparing four different international organizations, Stein finds that the EU has the highest level of integration and displays the highest level of discourse about a 'democratic deficit'. With regard to the World Trade Organisation (WTO), where delegation of certain judicial functions has occurred, Stein (2001:530) shows that 'the discourse originated in the use of the adjudicatory power of the institution.' In contrast, international organizations such as the World Health Organisation (WHO), an essentially 'technical' agency (Stein 2001: 496), or regional economic arrangements such as North American Free Trade Agreement (NAFTA) remain essentially state-based organizations with comparatively low levels of integration and consequently, the 'democratic' or 'legitimacy deficit' discourse does not arise.

Stein's findings not only strongly correlate with some of the results presented in this book, his findings also provide ample backing for one of the main propositions advanced here: where political elites pool and delegate sovereignty, it is likely that they perceive a legitimacy deficit.[9] Yet, this book goes a step further than Eric Stein's work by emphasizing and demonstrating that there is not only a discourse among political elites about the legitimacy deficit when pooling and delegation loom. I have also demonstrated that concerns about the legitimacy deficit carry behavioural implications which affect the path of institution-building and institutional reform.

These arguments can help us to explain why, as of yet, the institutional settings of other international organizations do *not* contain strong representative, parliamentary institutions. While other institutionalized forms of interstate cooperation are some distance away from pooling or delegating major portions of their sovereignty, recent calls by globalization critics, the media, academics, and politicians to alleviate the 'democratic deficits' inherent in the functioning and the trajectory of the actions of the WTO and international financial institutions such as the World Bank and the International Monetary Fund (IMF) may, in the future, pave the way for further regional or even global parliamentary institutions (epitomized by a 'global parliament' suggested by Falk and Strauss 2001, 2002) to legitimize international governance in a world in which the production and distribution of benefits from socio-economic and security cooperation transcends the capacity of individual nation states (see, e.g. V. Rittberger 2000). The writer Michael Kurland ends his book *The Great Game* with a warning about a world of unilateralism and military threats:

'We have cut off one tentacle of the beast,' the duke said, 'but the creature still lives, and it will grow another and another—it will not be stilled until governments cease trying to establish their legitimacy by stirring up ancient hatreds and false rivalries, and join in a commonwealth of nations.'

' "Till the war-drum throbb'd no longer, and the battle-flags were furl'd in the Parliament of man, the Federation of the world" ' recited Cecily.

Moriarty nodded. 'Tennyson.'

'That will not happen in our lifetimes,' Benjamin said.

'Nor our sons, nor their sons', said the duke, 'but it must happen if we are to survive without blasting ourselves back to savagery or oblivion. For the weapons are getting more powerful and the wars are getting more absolute.'

'Tennyson goes on: "Yet I doubt not thro' the ages one increasing purpose runs, And the thoughts of men are widen'd with the process of the suns." '

'It's always good to end on a hopeful note,' the duke said.

Yet, the vision of a 'Parliament of man' or a 'global parliament' (Falk and Strauss 2001) is written off by Nye as presently unattainable owing to the absence of a 'sufficiently strong sense of community' which renders the extension of domestic and democratic voting procedures to the global level not necessarily practical nor acceptable to minorities (Nye 2002).[10] Scharpf underlines this argument, saying that *majoritarian* decision-making institutions on a global scale have their limits, particularly in the politics of *redistribution* where inter/supranational solutions do not yet command public acceptance although they may be more effective than unilateral ones. This is because the EU (and also any other international organization) is 'very far from having achieved the "thick" collective identity that we have come to take for granted in national democracies' (Scharpf 1999: 9), and only where the 'belief in a "thick" collective identity can be taken for granted, majority rule may indeed lose its threatening character, and it can also be relied upon to legitimize measures of interpersonal and interregional redistribution that would not be otherwise acceptable' (Scharpf 1999: 8–9). While thus, in Zürn's words, 'economic man', or the *bourgeois*, already thinks and acts in categories beyond the nation state, benefiting from the opportunities offered by international cooperation, 'social man', or the *citoyen*, continues to be caged in national categories, norms, and identities which partially constrain the delegation of sovereignty from the domain of domestic polities to the inter/supra-national level (see Zürn 1996: 34).

While this characterization may be true for certain policy areas, it does not preclude that political elites continue to pool and delegate parts of their sovereignty in policy areas where the 'thick' collective-identity requirement is less constraining, such as in *distributive* and *regulatory* policy areas (e.g. Majone 1996, von Beyme 1998, Scharpf 1999). Even if we accept that pooling and delegation is most likely to occur in certain designated policy areas of regulatory and distributive politics, and if we accept that this is most likely to occur in a regional rather than a global context, the argument advanced in this book still stands firm. Wherever democratically organized states pool and delegate sovereignty, questions of democratic accountability and representation are likely to loom large, and consequently, calls to alleviate the asymmetry between consequentialist and procedural legitimacy are likely to be mirrored in demands for representative, parliamentary institutions at the supra-national level.

Although I have been predominantly occupied with answering the puzzle why national governments have created and empowered the EP, I have also sought to demonstrate that the causal relationships specified in the Chapter 2 of this book are not at all restricted to the study of the EU, let alone the EP and its future development. Moravcsik (1997: 6) has argued that 'the EU provides the best laboratory for studying theoretical issues only just emerging elsewhere, such as threats of exit and exclusion, binding interstate legislative procedures, multi-level system and legal dispute resolution.' This list could also include parliamentary institutions in international polities and the conditions under which they are likely to emerge and solidify. From this perspective, institutions like the EP do not have be studied as a *sui generis* phenomenon or an instance of $N = 1$. Rather, it can be considered an 'extreme' value on the dependent variable 'power of parliamentary assemblies in international organisations': why is it that the EP—with its supervisory, budgetary, and legislative powers—is at present the most influential parliamentary assembly in the universe of inter-national organizations? Why do the parliamentary assemblies of, for instance, the Council of Europe or of the WEU merely fulfil a consultative function and lack budgetary, legislative, and supervisory powers? These differences in the strength of parliamentary assemblies in international organizations thus supply important variation that needs to be explained.[11] To account for this variation, it is the task of the social scientist to specify conditions under which we can expect national governments to opt for the creation and empowerment of parliamentary assemblies in international organizations. This book has provided one route to explain this variation: the decision of national governments to transfer portions of their sovereignty through pooling (by introducing majority voting procedures among member state governments) and delegation (by transferring decision-making powers to independent supra-national institutions) triggers a situation in which the political elites are likely to perceive a legitimacy deficit. This legitimacy deficit is character-ized by the enhanced problem-solving capacity of the international polity as a result of pooling and delegation and a challenge to domestic proced-ures for interest representation and democratic accountability.

At the dawn of the new millennium, the EP remains the most powerful parliamentary assembly in the universe of international organizations. In this sense, the EP is an 'outlier' because the EU is an outlier. But wherever democratic states will contemplate to reap the gains of socio-economic and security cooperation by pooling or delegating sovereignty and the concomitant creation of supranational institutions, the EP may well have its followers as time unfolds.

Notes

1. Frank Schimmelfennig suggested this heading. It captures the main argument of this book: transfers of sovereignty (*integration*) trigger a demand for creating mechanisms of parliamentary *representation* at the EU level.
2. See Marschall (2002: 379). See also Auel and Benz (2004) as well as Raunio and Hix (2000) for an alternative perspective.
3. Note that this number does not include Community *regulations* which are directly applicable in the member states.
4. See von Beyme (1998: 26, 1999: 540–4), Börzel (2000: 247), and Norton (1996).
5. Direct democracy bears the following features: '[C]itizens both participate in the discussion and deliberation about policies, and they make the final policy choice: it is unmediated participation in both policy formation and policy decision' (Dalton et al. 2003a: 10). For instance, referenda—as the 'classical' instrument of the model of direct democracy—are enjoying growing popularity throughout the OECD world in the past decades (see Scarrow 2003).
6. Advocacy democracy is a form of non-electoral participation 'in which citizens directly participate in the process of policy formation or administration (or partici-pate through surrogates such as environmental groups and other public interest groups), although the final decisions are still made by elites' (Dalton et al. 2003a: 10–11).
7. See, for instance, the articles by Reich (1991) and Williams (1991).

8. See, for example, the volumes by Rosenau and Czempiel (1995), Held (1995, 1997), Archibugi et al. (1998), Zürn (1998), as well as Ougaard and Higgott (2002) on the possibility of international democratic governance 'beyond the nation state'.

9. On the basis of Stein's findings and the results presented in the preceding chapters, it is reasonable to argue that the *candidate* theory presented in this book merits further application and testing. In a project supported by the Thyssen Foundation (2004–6), Frank Schimmelfennig, Alexander Bürgin, Guido Schwellnus, and the author subject the approach of this book and Schimmelfennig's rhetorical action hypothesis to further empirical scrutiny.

10. According to Keohane and Nye (2000: 33), the creation of a 'global parliament' reflects a cosmopolitan view of democracy which assumes that the globe is one big constituency. This, however, 'implies the existence of a political community in which citizens of 198 states would be willing to be continually outvoted by a billion Chinese and a billion Indians.... Most meaningful voting, and associated democratic political activities, occurs within the boundaries of nation states that have democratic constitutions and processes. Minorities are willing to acquiesce to a majority in which they may not participate directly because they feel they participate in some larger community.'

11. James Caporaso (1997) has argued that one important step to overcome the $N = 1$ problem in the study of European integration is to define classes of social phenomena (e.g. the role of interest groups in the decision making process of an organisation, the role of political elites in the development of an organisation, or, as in this book, the role and impact of parliamentary assemblies on the decision-making processes of an organization) and identify the interorganizational differences across different classes. These 'descriptive differences' thus 'provide important variation to be explained' (Caporaso 1997: 2).

Bibliography

Official publications

Bulletin of the European Communities (EC Bulletin)

Deutscher Bundestag (resolutions)

Deutscher Bundestag, 4. Wahlperiode, Drucksache 4/1104, 15/05/1964.
Deutscher Bundestag, 4. Wahlperiode, Drucksache 4/1660, 23/11/1963.
Deutscher Bundestag, 4. Wahlperiode, Drucksache 4/2211 and 4/2212, 28/04/1964.
Deutscher Bundestag, 10. Wahlperiode, Drucksache 10/3152, 09/04/1985.
Deutscher Bundestag, 10. Wahlperiode, Drucksache 10/3564, 26/06/1985.
Deutscher Bundestag, 10. Wahlperiode, Drucksache 10/3569, 26/06/1985.

Deutscher Bundestag (debates)

Deutscher Bundestag, 5. Wahlperiode, 17. Sitzung, 27/01/1966.
Deutscher Bundestag, 6. Wahlperiode, 9. Sitzung, 06/11/1969.
Deutscher Bundestag, 6. Wahlperiode, 16. Sitzung, 03/12/1969.
Deutscher Bundestag, 6. Wahlperiode, 60. Sitzung, 18/06/1970.
Deutscher Bundestag, 6. Wahlperiode, 77. Sitzung, 06/11/1970.
Deutscher Bundestag, 10. Wahlperiode, 149. Sitzung, 27/06/1985.
Deutscher Bundestag, 10. Wahlperiode, 181. Sitzung, 05/12/1985.
Deutscher Bundestag, 10. Wahlperiode, 246. Sitzung, 13/11/1986.
Deutscher Bundestag, 10. Wahlperiode, 253. Sitzung, 04/12/1986.
European Commission (1998). *The European Union: "A View from the Top", Top Decision Makers and the European Union*, <http://europa.eu.int/comm/dg10/epo/eb-top/en/top.pdf> (accessed on 20 January 2002).
European Commission (2001). *European Governance. A White Paper*, COM(2001) 428 final, <http://europe.eu.int/eur-lex/en/com/2001/com2001_428en01.pdf> (accessed 15 August 2001) .
European Parliament (1970). *Les ressources propres aux Communautés européennes et les pouvoirs budgétaires du Parlement européen: recueil de documents*, Luxembourg: Official Publications of the European Communities.
European Parliament (1971). *Die Eigenmittel der Europäischen Gemeinschaften und die Haushaltsbefugnisse des Europäischen Parlaments: Die Ratifizierungsdebatten*, Luxembourg: Official Publications of the European Communities.
European Parliament (1988). *Political Parties in the EC and European Unification*, Luxembourg: European Parliament (Directorate General for Research).
European Parliament (1996). *White Paper on the 1996 Intergovernmental Conference*, Vol. II, <http://europa.eu.int/en/agenda/igc-home/eu-doc/parlmentpeen2.htm>.

Hansard, House of Commons

Hansard Parliamentary Debates, House of Commons, Session 1985–86, Sixth Series, Vol. 87: 20/11/1985.

Hansard Parliamentary Debates, House of Commons, Session 1985–86, Sixth Series, Vol. 88: 05/12/1985.

Hansard Parliamentary Debates, House of Commons, Session 1985–86, Sixth Series, Vol. 93: 05/03/1986.

Hansard Parliamentary Debates, House of Commons, Session 1985–86, Sixth Series, Vol. 96: 23/04/1986.

Hansard Parliamentary Debates, House of Commons, Session 1985–86, Sixth Series, Vol. 100: 26/06/1986.

House of Commons—Reports

House of Commons (1990a). Second Report from the Foreign Affairs Committee, European Council, Rome 14–15 December 1990, Minutes of Evidence, Session 1990–91.

House of Commons (1990b). Second Report from the Foreign Affairs Committee, Session 1989–90, The Operation of the Single Market, Observations by the Government.

House of Lords—Reports

House of Lords (1985). Select Committee on the European Communities, 14th Report.

House of Lords (2001). Select Committee on European Union, 7th Report.

Journal Officiel de la République Française, Débats Parlementaires, Assemblée Nationale

Journal Officiel du 5 Novembre 1970, séance du 4 Novembre 1969.

Journal Officiel du 26 Juin 1970, séance du 23 Juin 1970.

Journal Officiel du 12 Juin 1985, séance du 11 Juin 1985.

Journal Officiel du 21 Novembre 1986, séance du 20 Novembre 1986.

Official Journal of the European Communities

Official Journal B 030, 20/04/1962: 0991–0993, EEC Council: Regulation No 25 on the financing of the common agricultural policy, EUR-Lex database, <http://europa.eu.int/smartapi/cgi/sga_doc?smartapi!celexapi! prod!CELEXnumdoc&lg=EN &numdoc=31962R0025&model=guicheti> (accessed 1 July 2002).

Archival documents

AAPD—Institut für Zeitgeschichte. *Akten zur Auswärtigen Politik der Bundesrepublik Deutschland*, München: Oldenbourg [1949/50, 1964, 1965, 1966, 1969, 1970].

HAEC, AA/PA.SFSP (Auswärtiges Amt, Sekretariat für Fragen des Schuman-Plans), Historical Archives of the European Communities, Florence.

HAEC, Emile Noël, EN 112, Historical Archives of the European Communities, Florence.

HAEC, Jean Monnet, Duchêne Sources—JMDS.A-07.02-000073: Schuman Plan and the Belgian Response, Historical Archives of the European Communities, Florence.

HAEC, Jean Monnet, Duchêne Sources—JMDS.A-07.02-000074: U.S. National Archives: US-NA, RG 59, State Department, 850.33, Schuman Plan, Historical Archives of the European Communities, Florence.

HAEC, MAEF—Délégation française, PS (Plan Schuman), Historical Archives of the European Communities.

HAEC, MAEF.DECE-05.02, MAEF 1124 (Ministère des Affaires Etrangères Français, Questions institutionnelles, administratives, budgétaires), Historical Archives of the European Communities.

Möller, H. and Hildebrand K. (eds.) (1997). *Die Bundesrepublik Deutschland und Frankreich: Dokumente 1949–1963*, Band 1—Außenpolitik und Diplomatie.

Press

Agence Europe

Le Monde

Oral sources

Philip Budden, Cabinet Office, 23 April 2002, London.

Richard Corbett, MEP, 22 January 2004, Brussels.

Andrew Duff, MEP, 21 January 2004.

Matthias Schauer, Permanent Representative of Germany to the EU, 11 July 2000, Brussels.

Michael Shackleton, European Parliament Secretariat, 13 March 2000, Brussels.

Dr. Joachim Wuermeling, MEP, 21 January 2004, Brussels.

References

Abelshauser, W. (1994). ' "Integration à la Carte". The Primacy of Politics and the Economic Integration of Western Europe in the 1950s', in S. Martin (ed.), *The Construction of Europe—Essays in Honour of Emile Noël*. Dordrecht: Kluwer Academic Publishers.

Abromeit, H. (1995). 'Volkssouveränität, Parlamentssouveränität, Verfassungssouveränität: Drei Realmodelle der Legitimation staatlichen Handelns'. *Politische Vierteljahresschrift* 36(1): 49–66.

—— (2000). 'Kompatbilität und Akzeptanz—Anforderungen an eine "integrierte Politie" ', in E. Grande und M. Jachtenfuchs (eds.), *Wie problemlösungsfähig ist die EU?* Baden-Baden: Nomos.

Adenauer, K. (1965). *Erinnerungen, 1945–1953*, Stuttgart: Deutscher Bücherbund.

Archibugi, D., Held, D., and Köhler, M. (eds.) (1998). *Re-imagining Political Community*. Cambridge: Polity Press.

Aspinwall, M. D. and Schneider, G. (2000). 'Same Table, Separate Menu. The Institutionalist Turn in Political Science and the Study of European Integration.' *European Journal of Political Research* 38(1):1–36.

Attali, J. (1993). *Verbatim Tome 1, Chronique des années 1981–1986*. Paris: Fayard.

Auel, K. and Benz, A. (2004). 'Expanding National Parliamentary Control: Does it Further European Democracy', unpublished manuscript.

Bates, R. H. (1998). 'The International Coffee Organization: An International Institution', in R. H. Bates, A. Greif, M. Levi, J.-L. Rosenthal, and B. R. Weingast (eds.), *Analytic Narratives*. Princeton: Princeton University Press.

Baumann, R., Rittberger, V., and Wagner, W. (1999). 'Macht und Machtpolitik. Neorealistische Auaenpolitiktheorie und Prognosen über die deutsche Auaenpolitik nach der Vereinigung'. *Zeitschrift für Internationale Beziehungen* 6(2): 245–86.

—— —— —— (2001). 'Neorealist Foreign Policy Theory', in V. Rittberger (ed.), *German Foreign Policy since Unification. Theories and Case Studies*. Manchester: Manchester University Press.

Bennett, A. and George, A. L. (1997). 'Research Design Tasks in Case Study Methods', paper presented at the MacArthur Foundation Workshop on Case Study Methods, Belfer Center for Science and International Affairs, Harvard University, 17–19 October 1997, <http://www.georgetown.edu/bennett/RESDES.htm> (accessed on 24 July 2002).

Bergman, T. and Raunio, T. (2001). 'Parliaments and policy-making in the European Union', in J. Richardson (ed.), *European Union: Power and Policy-Making*. London: Routledge.

Bitsch, M.-T. (1999). *Histoire de la construction européenne de 1945 à nos jours*. Bruxelles: Complexe.

—— (2001). 'Le sommet de la Haye. La mise en route de la relance de 1969', in W. Loth (ed.), *Crisis and Compromises: The European Project 1963–1969*. Baden-Baden: Nomos.

Blinder, A. S. (1987). 'The Rules-versus-Discretion Debate in the Light of Recent Experience'. *Weltwirtschaftliches Archiv* 123(3): 399–414.

Blyth, M. (2002). *Great Transformations: Economic Ideas and Political Change in the Twentieth Century.* Cambridge: Cambridge University Press.

Bowler, S. and Farrell, D. (1995). 'The Organizing of the European Parliament: Committees, Specialization and Co-ordination'. *British Journal of Political Science* 25(2): 219–43.

Börzel, T. A. (2000). 'Europäisierung und innerstaatlicher Wandel. Zentralisierung und Entparlamentarisierung?' *Politische Vierteljahresschrift* 41(2): 225–50.

Bräuninger, T., Cornelius, T., König, T. and Schuster, T. (2001). 'The dynamics of European integration: a constitutional analysis of the Amsterdam Treaty', in G. Schneider and M. Aspinwall (eds.), *The Rules of Integration. Institutionalist Approaches to the Study of Europe.* Manchester: Manchester University Press.

Brehon, N.-J. (1997). *Le budget de l'Europe.* Paris: L.G.D.J.

Budden, P. (1994). *The United Kingdom and the European Community, 1979–1986. The making of the Single European Act.* D.Phil. thesis. Oxford.

Buller, J. (2000). *National Statecraft and European Integration. The Conservative Government and the European Union, 1979–1997.* London: Pinter.

Burns, T. R. (2000). 'The Future of Parliamentary Democracy: Transition and Challenge in European Governance'. Green Paper prepared for the Conference of the Speakers of EU Parliaments, 22–24 September 2000, Rome.

Caporaso, J. A. (1997). 'Does the European Union Represent an *n* of 1?', <http://www.eustudies.org/N1debate.htm> (accessed on 17 October 2003).

Cederman, L.-E. (2001). 'Nationalism and Bounded Integration: What it Would Take to Construct a European Demos'. *European Journal of International Relations* 7(2): 139–74.

Coombes, D. (1972). *The Power of the Purse in the European Communities.* London: Chatham House.

Corbett, R. (1987). 'The 1985 Intergovernmental Conference and the Single European Act', in R. Price (ed.), *The Dynamics of European Union.* London: Croom Helm.

—— (1992). *The Treaty of Maastricht. From Conception to Ratification: A Comprehensive Reference Guide.* Essex: Longman.

—— (1998). *The European Parliament's Role in Closer Integration.* Basingstoke: Palgrave.

—— Jacobs, F., and Shackleton, M. (2000). *The European Parliament,* 4th edition. London: Catermill Publishing.

—— —— —— (2003). 'The European Parliament at Fifty: A View from the Inside'. *Journal of Common Market Studies* 41(2): 353–73.

Costa, O. (2001). *Le Parlement européen, assemblée délibérante.* Brussels: Editions de l'Université de Bruxelles.

Crombez, C. (1996). 'Legislative Procedures in the European Community'. *British Journal of Political Science* 26(2): 199–228.

—— (2003). 'The Democratic Deficit in the European Union. Much Ado about Nothing?' *European Union Politics* 4(1): 101–20.

Dahl, R. A. (1989). *Democracy and its Critics.* New Haven: Yale University Press.

—— (1994). 'A Democratic Dilemma: System Effectiveness versus Citizen Participation'. *Political Science Quarterly* 109(1): 23–34.

—— (1999). 'Can international organizations be democratic? A skeptic's view', in I. Shapiro and C. Hacker-Cordón (eds.), *Democracy's Edges*, Cambridge: Cambridge University Press.

—— and Tufte, E. (1973). *Size and Democracy*. Stanford: Stanford University Press.

Dalton, R. J., Cain, B. E., and Scarrow, S. E. (2003a). 'Democratic Publics and Democratic Institutions', in B. E. Cain, R. J. Dalton, and S. E. Scarrow (eds.), *Democracy Transformed? Expanding Political Opportunities in Advanced Industrial Democracies*. Oxford: Oxford University Press.

—— J., Scarrow, S. E., and Cain, B. E. (2003b). 'New Forms of Democracy? Reform and Transformations of Democratic Institutions', in B. E. Cain, R. J. Dalton, and S. E. Scarrow (eds.), *Democracy Transformed? Expanding Political Opportunities in Advanced Industrial Democracies*. Oxford: Oxford University Press.

Decker, F. (2002). 'Governance beyond the nation-state. Reflections on the democratic deficit of the European Union'. *Journal of European Public Policy* 9(2): 256–72.

De Ruyt, J. (1989). *L'Acte Unique Européen*. Brussels: Institut d'Etudes Européen.

De Vree, J. (1974). 'Parliament and the Political System: The Case of the European Parliament', Symposium on European Integration and the Future of Parliaments in Europe, Luxembourg, 2–5 May 1974 (PE 35.663).

Diebold, W. (1959). *The Schuman Plan. A Study in Economic Cooperation 1950–59*. New York: Frederick A. Praeger.

Diez, T. (1999). *Die EU lesen: Diskursive Knotenpunkte in der britischen Europadebatte*. Opladen: Leske und Budrich.

DiMaggio, P. J. and Powell, W. W. (1991). 'The Iron Cage Revisited: Institutional Isomorphism and Collective Rationality in Organizational Fields', in W. W. Powell and P. J. DiMaggio (eds.), *The New Institutionalism in Organizational Analysis*. Chicago: University of Chicago Press.

Doleys, T. J. (2000). 'Member states and the European Commission: theoretical, insights from the new economics of organization'. *Journal of European Public Policy* 7(4): 532–53.

Donahue, J. D. and Pollack, Mark (2001). 'Centralization and Its Discontents: The Rhythm of Federalism in the United States and the European Union', in K. Nicolaïdis and R. Howse (eds.), *The Federal Vision. Legitimacy and Levels of Governance in the United States and the European Union*. Oxford: Oxford University Press.

Dryzek, J. S. (2000). *Deliberative Democracy and Beyond. Liberals, Critics, Contestations*. Oxford: Oxford University Press.

Duchêne, F. (1994). *Jean Monnet. The First Statesman of Interdependence*. New York: Norton.

Earnshaw, D. and Judge, D. (1996). 'From Co-operation to Co-decision: The European Parliament's Path to Legislative Power', in J. Richardson (ed.), *European Union: Power and Policy-Making*. London: Routledge.

Eckstein, H. (1975). 'Case Study and Theory in Political Science', in F. I. Greenstein and N. W. Polsby (eds.), *Handbook of Political Science, Vol. VII: Strategies of Inquiry*. Reading, Mass.: Addison-Wesley.

Elster, J. (1994). 'Argumenter et négocier dans deux assemblées constituantes'. *Revue Française de Science Politique* 44(2): 187–256.

Elster, J. (1998) (ed.). *Deliberative Democracy*. Cambridge: Cambridge University Press.

—— (2000). 'Arguing and Bargaining in Two Constituent Assemblies'. University of Pennsylvania Journal of Constitutional Law, <http://www.law.upenn.edu/conlaw/> (accessed on 10 December 2001).

Eriksen, E. O. and Fossum, J. E. (2000). *Democracy in the European Union. Integration Through Deliberation?* London: Routledge.

—— and Neyer, J. (2003). 'Introduction: The Forging of Deliberative Supranationalism in the EU?', in Erik Oddvar Eriksen, Christian Joerges and Jürgen Neyer (eds.), *European Governance, Deliberation and the Quest for Democratisation*. Oslo: ARENA Report No. 2/2003.

Falk, R. and Strauss, A. (2001). 'Toward Global Parliament'. *Foreign Affairs* 80 (January–February): 212–20.

—— —— (2002). 'Not a Parliament of Dreams'. *Worldlink. The Magazine of the World Economic Forum*, July, <http://www.worldlink.co.uk/stories/storyReader$1152> (accessed on 3 September 2002).

Farrell, H. and Héritier, A. (2003). 'Continuous Constitution-Building in Europe: Co-Decision and Informal and Formal Institutions'. *Governance* 16(4): 577–600.

Fearon, J. and Wendt, A. (2002). 'Rationalism and Constructivism in International Relations Theory, in W. Carlsnaes, T. Risse, and B. Simmons (eds.), *Handbook of International Relations Theory*. London: Sage Publications.

Featherstone, K. (1994). 'Jean Monnet and the "democratic deficit" in the European Union'. *Journal of Common Market Studies* 32(2): 149–70.

Ferejohn, J. (1993). 'Structure and Ideology: Change in Parliament in Early Stuart England', in J. Goldstein and R. O. Keohane (eds.), *Ideas and Foreign Policy. Beliefs, Institutions, and Political Change*. Ithaca: Cornell University Press.

Finnemore, M. (1996). 'Norms, Culture, and World Politics: Insights from Sociology's Institutionalism. *International Organization* 50(2): 325–47.

—— and Sikkink, K. (1998). 'International Norm Dynamics and Political Change'. *International Organization* 52: 887–917.

Fishkin, J. S. and Laslett, P. (eds.) (2003). *Debating Deliberative Democracy*. Oxford: Blackwell Publishing.

Florini, A. (1996): 'The Evolution of International Norms', *International Studies Quarterly* 40(3): 363–89.

Fontaine, P. (2000). *A new idea for Europe. The Schuman declaration—1950–2000*, Luxembourg: Office for Official Publications of the European Communities, <http://europa.eu.int/comm/dg10/publications/brochures/docu/50ans/en.pdf> (accessed on 8 July 2002).

Forster, A. (1999). *Britain and the Maastricht Negotiations*. Oxford: Macmillan/St Antony's.

Gaddum, E. (1994). *Die deutsche Europapolitik in den 80er Jahren. Interessen, Konflikte und Entscheidungen der Regierung Kohl*. Paderborn: Schönigh.

Garman, J. and Hilditch, L. (1998). 'Behind the Scenes: An Examination of the Importance of Informal Processes at Work in Conciliation'. *Journal of European Public Policy* 5(2): 271–84.

Garrett, G. (1992). 'International Cooperation and Institutional Choice: The European Community's Internal Market'. *International Organization* 46(2): 533–60.

—— (1995). 'From The Luxembourg Compromise to Codecision: Decision Making in the European Union'. *Electoral Studies* 14(3): 289–308.

—— and Tsebelis, G. (1996). 'An Institutional Critique of Intergovernmentalism'. *International Organization* 50(2): 269–99.

Gazzo, Marina (ed.) (1985). *Towards European Union: From the "Crocodile" to the European Council in Milan (28–29 June 1985)*. Brussels: Agence Europe.

George, S. (1990). *An Awkward Partner. Britain in the European Community*. Oxford: Oxford University Press.

Gerçek, K. (1998). 'Die Europäische Gemeinschaft für Kohle und Stahl und ihr politisches Leitbild föderaler Organe', in R. Hrbek and V. Schwarz (eds.), *40 Jahre Römische Verträge: Der deutsche Beitrag*. Baden-Baden: Nomos.

Gillingham, J. (1991). *Coal, steel, and the rebirth of Europe, 1945–1955. The Germans, the French from Ruhr conflict to economic community*. Cambridge: Cambridge University Press.

—— (2003). *European Integration 1950–2003. Superstate or New Market Economy*. Cambridge: Cambridge University Press.

Goldstein, J. and Keohane, R. O. (1993). 'Ideas and Foreign Policy: An Analytical Framework', in J. Goldstein and R. O. Keohane (eds.), *Ideas and Foreign Policy. Beliefs, Institutions and Political Change*. Ithaca: Cornell University Press.

Grant, C. (1988). *Delors. Inside the House that Jacques Built*. London: Nicholas Brealey Publishing.

Grieco, J. (1995). 'The Maastricht Treaty, Economic and Monetary Union and the Neo-realist Research Program'. *Review of International Studies* 21(1): 21–40.

Griffiths, R. T. (1988). 'The Schuman Plan Negotiations: The Economic Clauses', in K. Schwabe (ed.), *Die Anfänge des Schuman Plans 1950/51—The Beginnings of the Schuman Plan*. Baden-Baden: Nomos.

—— (1990). 'Die Benelux-Staaten und die Schumanplan-Verhandlungen', in L. Herbst, W. Bührer, and H. Sowade (eds.), *Vom Marshallplan zur EWG. Die Eingliederung der Bundesrepublik Deutschland in die westliche Welt*. München: Oldenbourg.

Große Hüttmann, M. (1996). 'Das Subsidiaritätsprinzip in der Europäischen Union—eine Dokumentation'. Occasional Papers Nr. 5. Tübingen: Europäisches Zentrum für Föderalismus-Forschung.

Guggenberger, B. (1995). 'Demokratie/Demokratietheorie', in D. Nohlen und R-O. Schulze (eds.), *Lexikon der Politik, Vol. I: Politische Theorien*. München: C.H. Beck.

Hall, P. A. (1989). *The Political Power of Economic Ideas*. Princeton: Princeton University Press.

—— (1993). 'Policy paradigms, social learning, and the state'. *Comparative Politics* 25(3): 275–96.

—— and Taylor, R. C. R. (1996). 'Political Science and the Three New Institutionalisms'. *Political Studies* 44(5): 936–57.

Hasenclever, A., Mayer, P., and Rittberger, V. (1997). *Theories of International Regimes*. Cambridge: Cambridge University Press.

Held, D. (1995). *Democracy and the Global Order: From the Modern State to Cosmopolitan Governance*. Cambridge: Polity Press.

Held, D. (1997). 'Democracy: From City-states to a Cosmopolitan Order?', in R. E. Goodin and P. Pettit (eds), *Contemporary Political Philosophy. An Anthology.* Oxford: Blackwell Publishers.

Hennis, W. (1976). 'Legitimität. Zu einer Kategorie der bürgerlichen Gesellschaft', in P. G. Kielmansegg (ed.), *Legitimationsprobleme politischer Systeme*, Sonderheft 7 der Politischen Vierteljahresschrift. Opladen: Westdeutscher Verlag.

Héritier, A., Knill, C., and Mingers, S. (1996). *Ringing the Changes in Europe: Regulatory Competition and Redefinition of the State: Britain, France, Germany.* Berlin: de Gruyter.

Hix, S. (1998). 'Elections, Parties and Institutional Design: A Comparative Perspective on European Union Democracy'. *West European Politics* 21(3): 19–52.

—— (2001). 'Legislative Behaviour and Party Competition in the European Parliament: An Application of Nominate to the EU'. *Journal of Common Market Studies* 39(4): 663–88.

—— (2002). Constitutional Agenda-Setting Through Discretion in Rule Interpretation: Why the European Parliament Won At Amsterdam'. *British Journal of Political Science* 32(2): 259–80.

—— (2005). *The Political System of the European Union*, 2nd edition. London: Palgrave.

—— and Lord, C. (1997). *Political Parties in the European Union.* Basingstoke: Macmillan.

—— Raunio, T., and Scully, R. (2003). 'Fifty Years On: Research on the European Parliament', *Journal of Common Market Studies* 41(2): 191–202.

Hobsbawm, E. (1990). *Nations and Nationalism Since 1780.* Cambridge: Cambridge University Press.

Hovey, J. A. (1966). *The Superparliaments. Interparliamentary Consultation and Atlantic Cooperation.* New York: Frederick A. Praeger.

Höreth, M. (1999). 'No way out for the beast? The unsolved legitimacy problem of European governance'. *Journal of European Public Policy* 6(2): 249–68.

Howe, G. (1994). *Conflict of Loyalty.* London: Macmillan.

Hubschmid, C. and Moser, P. (1997). 'The Co-operation Procedure in the EU: Why was the EP Influential in the Decision on Car Emission Standards?' *Journal of Common Market Studies* 35(2): 225–42.

Hurd, I. (1999). 'Legitimacy and Authority in International Politics'. *International Organization* 53(2): 379–408.

Ikenberry, J. G. (1998). 'Constitutional Politics in International Relations'. *European Journal of International Relations* 4(2): 147–77.

—— (2001). *After Victory. Institutions, Strategic Restraint, and the Rebuilding of Order After Major Wars.* Princeton: Princeton University Press.

Jachtenfuchs, M. (1999). *Ideen und Integration. Verfassungsideen in Deutschland, Frankreich und Großbritannien und die Entwicklung der EU.* Habilitationsschrift: Universität Mannheim.

—— (2002). *Die Konstruktion Europas. Verfassungsideen und institutionelle Entwicklung.* Baden-Baden: Nomos.

—— Diez, T., and Jung, S. (1998). 'Which Europe? Conflicting Models of a Legitimate European Political Order'. *European Journal of International Relations* 4(4): 409–45.

Jacobson, J. K. (1995). 'Much ado about ideas: the cognitive factor in economic policy'. *World Politics* 47(2): 283–310.

Jillson, C. (1988). *Constitution Making: Conflict and Consensus in the Federal Convention of 1787*. New York: Agathon Press

—— and Eubanks, C. (1984). 'The Political Structure of Constitution-Making'. *American Journal of Political Science* 28(3): 435–58.

Johnston, A. I. (1999). 'Legitimation, Foreign Policy and the Sources of Realpolitik', <http://www.people.fas.harvard.edu/~johnston/legitimacy.pdf> (accessed on 7 January 2002).

—— (2001). 'Treating International Institutions as Social Environments'. *International Studies Quarterly* 45(3): 487–515.

Judge, D. and Earnshaw, D. (2003). *The European Parliament*. Basingstoke: Palgrave.

—— —— and Cowan, N. (1994). 'Ripples or Waves: The European Parliament in the European Community Policy Process'. *Journal of European Public Policy* 1(1): 27–52.

Jupille, J. (2004). *Procedural Politics. Issues, Influence, and Institutional Change in the European Union*. Cambridge: Cambridge University Press.

Katz, R. S. (2001). 'Models of Democracy: Elite Attitudes and the Democratic Deficit in the European Union'. *European Union Politics* 2(1): 53–80.

Katzenstein, P. J. (1993). 'Coping with Terrorism: Norms and Internal Security in Germany and Japan', in J. Goldstein and R. O. Keohane (eds.), *Ideas and Foreign Policy. Beliefs, Institutions and Political Change*. Ithaca: Cornell University Press.

Keck, M. and Sikkink, K. (1998). *Activists Beyond Borders: Advocacy Networks in International Politics*. Ithaca: Cornell University Press.

Keohane, R. O. (1984). *After Hegemony: Cooperation and Discord in the World Political Economy*. Princeton: Princeton University Press.

—— and Nye, J. (2000). 'Introduction', in Joseph Nye and John D. Donahue (eds.), *Governance in a Globalizing World*. Washington, D.C.: Brookings Institution Press.

Kersten, A. (1988). 'A Welcome Surprise? The Netherlands and the Schuman Plan Negotiations', in K. Schwabe (ed.), *Die Anfänge des Schuman Plans 1950/51—The Beginnings of the Schuman Plan*. Baden-Baden: Nomos.

Kielmansegg, P. G. (1997). 'Legitimität als analytische Kategorie', in W. Seibel, M. Medick-Krakau, H. Münkler, und M. Th. Greven (eds.), *Demokratische Politik—Analyse und Theorie*. Opladen: Westdeutscher Verlag.

—— (2003). 'Integration und Demokratie', in M. Jachtenfuchs und B. Kohler-Koch (eds.), *Europäische Integration*, 2nd edition. Opladen: Leske und Budrich.

Kluxen, K. (1983). *Geschichte und Problematik des Parlamentarismus*. Frankfurt/Main: Suhrkamp.

Knight, J. (1992). *Institutions and Social Conflict*. Cambridge: Cambridge University Press.

—— (1995). 'Models, Interpretations, and Theories: Constructing Explanations of Institutional Emergence and Change', in Jack Knight and Itai Sened (eds.), *Explaining Social Institutions*. Ann Arbor: The University of Michigan Press.

Kreppel, A. (1999). 'What Affects the European Parliament's Legislative Influence? An Analysis of the Success of EP Amendments'. *Journal of Common Market Studies* 37(3): 521–38.

—— (2002). *The European Parliament and Supranational Party System*. Cambridge: Cambridge University Press.

—— and Tsebelis, G. (1999). 'Coalition Formation in the European Parliament'. *Comparative Political Studies* 32(8): 933–66.

Küsters, H.-J. (1988). 'Die Verhandlungen über das institutionelle System zur Gründung der Europäischen Gemeinschaft für Kohl and Stahl', in K. Schwabe (ed.), *Die Anfänge des Schuman Plans 1950/51—The Beginnings of the Schuman Plan*. Baden-Baden: Nomos.

Laffan, Brigid (1997). *The Finances of the European Union*. Basingstoke: Macmillan.

—— (2000). 'The big budgetary bargains: from negotiation to authority'. *Journal of European Public Policy* 7(5): 53–71.

—— and Lindner, J. (2005). 'The Budget', in William Wallace, Helen Wallace and Mark Pollack (eds.), *Policy-Making in the European Union*, 5th edn. Oxford: Oxford University Press

—— and Shackleton, M. (2000). 'The Budget. Who gets What, When, and How', in H. Wallace and W. Wallace (eds.), *Policy-Making in the European Union*, 4th edition. Oxford: Oxford University Press.

Lambert, J. (1966). 'The Constitutional Crisis 1965–66'. *Journal of Common Market Studies* 4(3): 195–228.

Lappenküper, U. (1994). 'Der Schuman-Plan. Mühsamer Durchbruch zur deutsch–französischen Verständigung'. *Vierteljahreshefte für Zeitgeschichte* 42(3): 403–45.

Legro, J. W. (1997). 'Which norms matter? Revisiting the "failure" of internationalism'. *International Organization* 51(1): 311–63.

Lindner, J. (2003a). Conflict in EU budgetary politics: an institutionalist analysis. D.Phil. thesis. Oxford.

—— (2003b). 'Institutional stability and change: two sides of the same coin'. *Journal of European Public Policy* 10(6): 912–35.

—— and Rittberger, B. (2003). 'The Creation, Interpretation and Contestation of Institutions—Revisiting Historical Institutionalism'. *Journal of Common Market Studies* 41(3): 445–73.

Lindsay, K. (1960). *European Assemblies. The Experimental Period 1949–1959*. London: Stevens and Sons.

Lipset, S. M. (1960). *Political Man: The Social Bases of Politics*. London: Mercury Books.

Lynch, F. (1988). 'The Role of Jean Monnet in Setting up the European Coal and Steel Community', in K. Schwabe (ed.), *Die Anfänge des Schuman Plans 1950/51—The Beginnings of the Schuman Plan*. Baden-Baden: Nomos.

—— (ed.) (1996). *Regulating Europe*. London: Routledge.

—— (1998). 'Europe's 'Democratic Deficit': The Question of Standards'. *European Law Journal* 4(1): 5–28.

—— (2000). 'The Credibility Crisis of Community Regulation'. *Journal of Common Market Studies* 38(2): 273–302.

—— (2001). 'Two Logics of Delegation. Agency and Fiduciary Relations in EU Governance'. *European Union Politics* 2(1): 103–22.

Major, J. (2000). *John Major—The Autobiography*. London: HarperCollins.

Mamadouh, V. and Raunio, T. (2003). 'The Committee System: Powers, Appointments and Report Allocation'. *Journal of Common Market Studies* 41(2): 333–51.

Mankiw, G. (1990). 'A Quick Refresher Course in Macroeconomics'. *Journal of Economic Literature* 28(4): 1645–60.

March, J. G. and Olson, J. P. (1989). *Rediscovering Institutions. The Organizational Basis of Politics*. New York: Free Press.

—— —— (1998). 'The institutional dynamics of international political orders'. *International Organization* 52: 943–59.

Marschall, S. (2002). ' "Niedergang" und "Aufstieg" des Parlamentarismus im Zeitalter der Denationalisierung'. *Zeitschrift für Parlamentsfragen* 33(2): 377–90.

Maurer, A. (1999). '(Co-)Governing after Maastricht: The European Parliament's institutional performance 1994–1999. Lessons for the implementation of the Treaty of Amsterdam'. *Working Paper POLI 104*. European Parliament: DG for Research.

—— (2003). 'The Legislative Powers and Impact of the European Parliament'. *Journal of Common Market Studies* 41(2): 227–47.

—— and Wessels, W. (2003). *Das Europäische Parlament nach Amsterdam und Nizza: Akteur, Arena oder Alibi?* Baden-Baden: Nomos.

McLean, I. (2001). 'Before and after Publius: the sources and influence of Madison's political thought', paper presented at conference on James Madison's 250th Birthday, University of California, San Diego, March 2001 <http://www.nuff.ox.ac.uk/users/mclean/James%20Madison%20Jr.pdf> (accessed on 5 March 2002).

McNamara, K. (1998), *The Currency of Ideas: Monetary Politics in the European Union*. Ithaca: Cornell University Press.

Mezey, M. (1979). *Comparative Legislatures*. Durham: Duke University Press.

Milner, H. V. (1997). *Interests, Institutions, and Information*. Princeton: Princeton University Press.

Milward, A. (1984). *The Reconstruction of Western Europe 1945–1951*. London: Routledge.

Mioche, P. (1988). 'La patronat de la sidérurgie française et le Plan Schuman en 1950–1952: les apparences d'un combat et la réalité d'une mutation', in K. Schwabe (ed.), *Die Anfänge des Schuman Plans 1950/51—The Beginnings of the Schuman Plan*. Baden-Baden: Nomos.

Monnet, J. (1978). *Memoirs*. London: Collins.

Moravcsik, A. (1991). 'Negotiating the Single European Act: National Interests and Conventional Statecraft in the European Community'. *International Organization* 45(1): 19–56.

—— (1993). 'Preferences and Power in the European Community—A Liberal Intergovernmentalist Approach'. *Journal of Common Market Studies* 31(4): 473–524.

—— (1997). 'Does the European Union Represent an *n* of 1?' <http://www.eustudies.org/Nidebate.htm> (accessed on 17 October 2003).

—— (1998). *The Choice for Europe. Social Purpose and State Power from Messina to Maastricht*. Ithaca: Cornell University Press.

—— (2000). 'De Gaulle Between Grain and *Grandeur*: The Political Economy of French EC Policy, 1958–1970 (Part 2)'. *Journal of Cold War Studies* 2(3): 4–68.

—— (2002). 'In Defence of the "Democratic Deficit": Reassessing Legitimacy in the European Union'. *Journal of Common Market Studies* 40(4): 603–24.

—— and Nicolaïdis, K. (1999). 'Explaining the Treaty of Amsterdam: Interests, Influence, Institutions'. *Journal of Common Market Studies* 37(1): 59–85.

Moser, P. (1997). 'A Theory of the Conditional Influence of the European Parliament in the Cooperation Procedure'. *Public Choice* 91(3–4): 333–50.

Mosler, H. (1966). 'Die Entstehung des Modells supranationaler und gewaltenteilender Staatenverbindungen in den Verhandlungen über den Schuman-Plan', in E. von Caemmerer, H-J. Schlochauer und E. Steindorff (eds.), *Probleme des Europäischen Rechts. Festschrift für Walter Hallstein zu seinem 65. Geburtstag.* Frankfurt/Main: Vittorio Klostermann.

Newhouse, J. (1967). *Collision in Brussels. The Common Market Crisis of 30 June 1965.* London: Faber and Faber.

Niblock, M. (1971). *The EEC: National Parliaments in Community Decision-making.* London: Chatham House.

Norman, P. (2003). *The Accidental Constitution. The Story of the European Convention.* Brussels: Eurocomment.

Norton, P. (1996). 'Conclusion: Addressing the Democratic Deficit', in P. Norton (ed.), *National Parliaments and the European Union,* London: Frank Cass.

—— (ed.) (1998). *Parliaments and Governments in Western Europe.* London: Frank Cass.

Nye, J. (2002) 'Parliament of dreams. A global government is an unrealistic vision'. *Worldlink. The Magazine of the World Economic Forum,* March/April, <http://www.worldlink.co.uk/stories/storyReader$1088> (accessed on 22 July 2002).

Odell, J. S. (2000). 'Case Study Methods in International Political Economy'. *Columbia International Affairs Online,* <http://www.ciaonet.org/isa/odjo1/> (accessed on 24 July 2002).

Ougaard, M. and Richard, H. (eds.) (2002). *Towards a Global Polity.* London: Routledge.

Parsons, C. (2002). 'Showing Ideas as Causes: The Origins of the European Union'. *International Organization* 56(1): 47–84.

—— (2003). *A Certain Idea of Europe.* Ithaca: Cornell University Press.

Peters, G. (1999). *Institutional Theory in Political Science. The 'New Institutionalism'.* London: Pinter.

Pollack, M. A. (n.d.). 'Institutional Choice in the 1960s and 1970s: From The Hague to Paris', unpublished manscript.

—— (1994). 'Creeping Competence: The Expanding Agenda of the European Community'. *Journal of Public Policy* 14(2): 95–145.

—— (1997). 'Delegation, Agency, and Agenda Setting in the European Community'. *International Organization* 51(1): 99–134.

—— (1999). 'Delegation, Agency and Agenda Setting in the Treaty of Amsterdam'. *European Integration Online Papers* 3(6), <http://eiop.or.at/eiop/texte/1999–006a.htm>.

—— (2002). 'Learning from Americanists (Again): Theory and Method in the Study of Delegation'. *West European Politics* 25(1): 200–19.

—— (2003). *The Engines of Integration? Delegation, Agency and Agenda Setting in the European Union.* Oxford: Oxford University Press.

Racine, R. (1954). *Vers une Europe Nouvelle par le Plan Schuman.* Neuchâtel: Editions de la Baconnière.

Rakove, J. N. (1997). *Original Meanings. Politics and Ideas in the Making of the Constituion.* New York: Vintage Books.

—— (ed.) (2003). *The Federalist. Alexander Hamilton, James Madison, and John Joy. The Essential Essays.* Boston: Bedford/St. Martin's.

Rasmussen, A. (2000). 'Institutional Games Rational Actors Play: The Empowering of the European Parliament'. *European Integration Online Papers* 4 and 1, <http://eiop.or.at/eiop/texte/2000-001a.htm>

Raunio, T. (1997). *The European Perspective: Transnational Party Groups in the 1989–1994 European Parliament*. Aldershot: Ashgate.

—— (2004). 'Two Steps Forward, One Step Back? National Legislatures in the EU Constitution'. The Federal Trust, <http://www.fedtrust.co.uk/uploads/constitution/Raunio.pdf> (accessed on 15 July 2004).

—— and Hix, S. (2000). 'Backbenchers Learn to Fight Back: European Integration and Parliamentary Government'. *West European Politics* 23(4): 142–68.

Reich, C. (1991). 'Qu'est-ce que . . . le déficit démocratique?'. *Révue du Marché Commun* 343: 14–18.

Riker, W. H. (1982). *Liberalism against Populism*. San Francisco: W. H. Freeman.

Risse-Kappen, T. (1994). 'Ideas Do Not Float Freely. Transnational Coalitions, Domestic Structures, and the End of the Cold War'. *International Organization* 48(2): 185–214.

Risse, T. (2000). ' "Let's Argue!": Communicative Action in World Politics'. *International Organization* 54(1): 1–39.

—— Ropp, S. C., and Sikkink, K. (eds.) (1999). *The Power of Human Rights: International Norms and Domestic Change*. Cambridge: Cambridge University Press.

Rittberger, B. (2000). 'Impatient legislators and new issue-dimensions: a critique of the Garrett-Tsebelis "standard version" of legislative politics'. *Journal of European Public Policy* 7(4): 554–75.

—— (2001). 'Which institutions for post-war Europe? Explaining the institutional design of Europe's first community'. *Journal of European Public Policy* 8(5): 673–708.

Rittberger, V. (2000). 'Globalisierung und der Wandel der Staatenwelt. Die Welt regieren ohne Weltstaat', in U. Menzel (ed.), *Vom Ewigen Frieden und vom Wohlstand der Nationen. Festschrift für Dieter Senghaas zum 60. Geburtstag*. Frankfurt/Main: Suhrkamp.

—— (ed.) (2001). *German Foreign Policy Since Unification. Theories and Case Studies*. Manchester: Manchester University Press.

—— and Zangl, B. (2003). *Internationale Organisationen—Politik und Geschichte. Europäische und weltweite international Zusammenschlüsse*, 3rd edition. Opladen: Leske und Budrich.

Rosenau, J. and Czempiel, O. (eds.) (1995). *Governance without Government. Order and Change in World Politics*. Cambridge: Cambridge University Press.

Scalingi, P. (1980). *The European Parliament. The Three-decade Search for a United Europe*. London: Aldwych Press.

Scarrow, S. E. (2003). 'Making Elections More Direct? Reducing the Role of Parties in Elections', in B. E. Cain, R. J. Dalton, and S. E. Scarrow (eds.), *Democracy Transformed? Expanding Political Opportunities in Advanced Industrial Democracies*. Oxford: Oxford University Press.

Scharpf, F. W. (1970). *Demokratietheorie zwischen Utopie und Anpassung*. Konstanz: Universitätsverlag.

—— (1997). 'Economic Integration, Democracy and the Welfare State'. *Journal of European Public Policy* 4(1): 18–36.

Scharpf, F. W. (1999). *Governing in Europe. Effective and Democratic?* Oxford: Oxford University Press.

—— (2001). 'Democratic Legitimacy under Conditions of Regulatory Competition: Why Europe Differs from the United States', in K. Nicolaïdis and R. Howse (eds.), *The Federal Vision. Legitimacy and Levels of Governance in the United States and the European Union.* Oxford: Oxford University Press.

Schimmelfennig, F. (2001a). 'The Community Trap: Liberal Norms, Rhetorical Action, and the Eastern Enlargement of the European Union'. *International Organization* 55(1): 47–80.

—— (2001b). 'Strategic Action in a Community Environment. The Decision to Enlarge the European Union to the East'. European University Institute, unpublished manuscript.

—— (2003). *The EU, NATO and the Integration of Europe. Rules and Rhetoric.* Cambridge: Cambridge University Press.

Schmidt, M. G. (2000). *Demokratietheorien.* Opladen: Leske und Budrich.

Schmitter, P. C. (1996). 'Imagining the Future of the Euro-Polity with the Help of New Concepts', in G. Marks, F. W. Scharpf, P. C. Schmitter, and W. Streeck (eds.), *Governance in the European Union,* London: Sage.

—— (2001). 'What is there to legitimise in the European Union . . . and how might this be accomplished?' The Jean Monnet Working Papers, NYU School of Law, <http://www.jeanmonnetprogram.org/papers/01/011401.html> (contribution to the Jean Monnet Working Paper No 6/01, 'Symposium: Mountain or Molehill? A Critical Appraisal of the Commission White Paper on Governance').

Schneider, G. and Aspinwall, M. D. (eds.) (2001). *The Rules of Integration. Institutionalist Approaches to the Study of Europe.* Manchester: Manchester University Press.

Schneider, H. (2002). 'Gründe für die Einrichtung von "Versammlungen" bzw. "Parlamenten" in westeuropäischen Organisationen: "Staatsrechtlicher Reflex" oder "Demokratiepolitisches Feigenblatt" ', unpublished manuscript.

Schulz, H. and König, T. (2000). 'Institutional Reform and Decision-Making Efficiency in the European Union'. *American Journal of Political Science* 44(4): 653–66.

Schwabe, K. (ed.) (1988). *Die Anfänge des Schuman Plans 1950/51—The Beginnings of the Schuman Plan.* Baden-Baden: Nomos.

Scully, R. M. (2000). 'Democracy, Legitimacy and the European Parliament', in M. G. Cowles and M. Smith (eds.), *The State of the European Union, Vol. 5.* Oxford: Oxford University Press.

Selck, T. J. (2004). *The Impact of Procedure: Analyzing European Union Legislative Decision-Making.* Göttingen:Cuvillier.

—— and Steunenberg, B. (2004). 'Between Power and Luck: The European Parliament in the EU Legislative Process'. *European Union Politics* 5(1): 25–46.

Shackleton, Michael (1990). *Financing the European Community.* London: Pinter.

—— (2000). 'The Politics of Codecision'. *Journal of Common Market Studies* 38(2): 325–42.

Spaak, P. H. (1971). *The Continuing Battle. Memoirs of a European 1936–1966.* Boston: Little, Brown and Company.

Spierenburg, D. and Poidevin, R. (1994). *The History of the High Authority of the European Coal and Steel Community. Supranationality in Operation.* London: Weidenfeld and Nicolson.

Stein, E. (2001). 'International Integration and Democracy: No Love at First Sight'. *American Journal of International Law* 95(3): 489–534.

Steunenberg, B. (1994). 'Decision-making under different institutional arrangements: Legislation by the European Community'. *Journal of Institutional and Theoretical Economics* 150: 642–69.

—— and Dimitrova, A. (1999). 'Interests, Legitimacy, and Constitutional Choice: The extension of the codecision procedure in Amsterdam'. Network on Enlargement and new Membership of the European Union, Working Paper No. 99–2.

Stone Sweet, A. (2000). *Governing with Judges. Constitutional Politics in Europe.* Oxford: Oxford University Press.

—— (2002). 'Constitutional Courts and Parliamentary Democracy'. *West European Politics* 25(1): 77–100.

Sypris, P. (2002). 'Legitimising European Governance: Taking Subsidiarity Seriously within the Open Method of Coordination', unpublished manuscript.

Thatcher, Margaret (1993). *The Downing Street Years.* London: HarperCollins Publishers.

Thatcher, Mark (2002). 'Delegation to Independent Regulatory Agencies: Pressures, Functions and Contextual Mediation'. *West European Politics* 25(1): 125–47.

—— and Stone Sweet, A. (2002). 'Theory and Practice of Delegation to Non-Majoritarian Institutions', *West European Politics* 25(1): 1–22.

Thiemeyer, G. (1998). 'Supranationalität als Novum in der Geschichte der internationalen Politik der fünfziger Jahre'. *Journal of European Integration History* 4(2): 5–21.

Tsebelis, G. (1994). 'The Power of the European Parliament as a Conditional Agenda-Setter'. *American Political Science Review* 88(1): 128–42.

—— (1995). 'Decision Making in Political Systems: Veto Players in Presidentialism, Parliamentarism, Multicameralism, and Multipartyism'. *British Journal of Political Science* 25(3): 289–326.

—— (2002). *Veto Players: How Political Institutions Work.* Princeton: Princeton University Press.

—— and Garrett, G. (2000). 'Legislative Politics in the European Union'. *European Union Politics* 1(1): 9–36.

—— Jensen, C. B., Kalandrakis, A., and Kreppel, A. (2001). 'Legislative Procedures in the European Union: An Empirical Analysis'. *British Journal of Political Science* 31(4): 573–599.

Van Evera, S. (1997). *Guide to Methods for Students of Political Science.* Ithaca: Cornell University Press.

Vanberg, V. and Buchanan, J. M. (1989). 'Interests and Theories in Constitutional Choice'. *Journal of Theoretical Politics* 1(1): 49–62.

von Beyme, K. (1998). 'Niedergang der Parlamente. Internationale Politik und nationale Entscheidungshoheit'. *Internationale Politik* 53(4): 21–30.

—— (1999). *Die Parlamentarische Demokratie. Entstehung und Funktionsweise.* Opladen: Westdeutscher Verlag.

Wagner, W. (1999). 'Interessen und Ideen in der europäischen Verfassungspolitik. Ratio-nalistische und konstruktivistische Erklärungen mitgliedstaatlicher Präferenzen'. *Poli-tische Vierteljahresschrift* 40(3): 415–41.

—— (2001). 'German EU Constitutional Foreign Policy', in V. Rittberger (ed.), *German Foreign Policy Since Unification. Theories and Case Studies.* Manchester: Manchester University Press.

—— (2002). 'The Subnational Foundations of the European Parliament'. *Journal of Inter-national Relations and Development* 5(1): 24–36.

Waltz, K. N. (1979). *Theory of International Politics.* New York: Random House.

Weber, M. (1968). *Economy and Society. An Outline of Interpretative Sociology, Volume I.* New York: Bedminster Press.

—— (1992). *Politik als Beruf.* Stuttgart: Philipp Reclam.

Weiler, J. H. H., Haltern, U. R. Mayer, F. C. (1995). 'European Democracy and its Critique', in Jack Hayward (ed.), *The Crisis of Representation in Europe.* London: Frank Cass.

Wessels, B. (1999). 'Political Integration in Europe: Is it possible to square the circle?' *European Integration online Papers* (EioP), Vol. 3, No. 9, <http://eiop.or.at/eiop/texte/1999-009.htm>

—— (2002). 'Parlamentarier in Europa und Europäische Integration: Einstellungen zur zukünftigen politischen Ordnung und zum institutionellen Wandel der EU', paper prepared for the workshop 'Wahlen und politische Einstellungen' of the German Political Science Association (DVPW) Augsburg, 6–7 June 2002, <http://www.wz-berlin.de/~wessels/Lehrveran/SS02/material/bw-akw-fin1a.pdf> (accessed 28 July 2002).

Wessels, W. (1996). 'Institutions of the EU system: models of explanation', in Dietrich Rometsch and Wolfgang Wessels (eds.), *The European Union and Member States.* Man-chester: Manchester University Press.

Westlake, M. (1994). *A Modern Guide to the European Parliament.* London: Pinter.

Whitaker, R. (2001). 'Party Control in a Committee-Based Legislature? The Case of the European Parliament'. *Journal of Legislative Studies* 7(4): 63–88.

Wilks, S. and Bartle, I. (2002). 'The Unanticipated Consequences of Creating Independ-ent Competition Agencies'. *West European Politics* 25(1): 148–72.

Williams, S. (1991). 'Sovereignty and Accountability in the European Community', in R. O. Keohane and S. Hoffmann (eds.), *The New European Community. Decisionmaking and Institutional Change.* Boulder: Westview Press.

Wood, G. S. (1998). *The Creation of the American Republic 1776–1787.* Chapel Hill: The University of North Carolina Press.

Zürn, M. (1996). 'Über den Staat und die Demokratie im europäischen Mehrebenensys-tem'. *Politische Vierteljahresschrift* 37(1): 27–55.

—— (1998). *Regieren jenseits des Nationalstaates. Globalisierung und Denationalisierung als Chance.* Frankfurt/Main: Suhrkamp.

—— (2000). 'Democratic Governance Beyond the Nation-State: The EU and Other Inter-national Institutions'. *European Journal of International Relations* 6(2): 183–221.

Index